Communications
in Computer and Information Science 759

Commenced Publication in 2007
Founding and Former Series Editors:
Alfredo Cuzzocrea, Orhun Kara, Dominik Ślęzak, and Xiaokang Yang

Editorial Board

More information about this series at http://www.springer.com/series/7899

Robin Doss · Selwyn Piramuthu
Wei Zhou (Eds.)

Future Network Systems and Security

Third International Conference, FNSS 2017
Gainesville, FL, USA, August 31 – September 2, 2017
Proceedings

 Springer

Editors
Robin Doss
Deakin University
Burwood, VIC
Australia

Selwyn Piramuthu
Department of Information Systems
and Operations Management
University of Florida, Warrington College
of Business
Gainesville, FL
USA

Wei Zhou
Information and Operations Management
   Department
ESCP Europe
Paris
France

ISSN 1865-0929   ISSN 1865-0937 (electronic)
Communications in Computer and Information Science
ISBN 978-3-319-65547-5   ISBN 978-3-319-65548-2 (eBook)
DOI 10.1007/978-3-319-65548-2

Library of Congress Control Number: 2017948180

Printed on acid-free paper

This Springer imprint is published by Springer Nature
The registered company is Springer International Publishing AG
The registered company address is: Gewerbestrasse 11, 6330 Cham, Switzerland

Preface

Welcome to the proceedings of the Future Network Systems and Security Conference 2017 held in Gainesville, Florida, USA!

The network of the future is envisioned as an effective, intelligent, adaptive, active, and high-performance Internet that can enable applications ranging from smart cities to tsunami monitoring. The network of the future will be a network of billions or trillions of entities (devices, machines, things, vehicles) communicating seamlessly with one another and is rapidly gaining global attention from academia, industry, and government. The main aim of the FNSS conference series is to provide a forum that brings together researchers from academia, practitioners from industry, standardization bodies, and government to meet and exchange ideas on recent research and future directions for the evolution of the future Internet. The technical discussions were focused on the technology, communications, systems, and security aspects of relevance to the network of the future.

We received paper submissions by researchers from around the world including Australia, New Zealand, Germany, India, Taiwan, Japan, Sweden, UK, USA, UAE among others. After a rigourous review process 15 full papers were accepted covering a wide range of topics. The overall acceptance rate for the conference was 37% this year ensuring that the accepted papers were of a very high quality. We thank the Technical Program Committee for their hard work in ensuring such an outcome.

August 2017

Robin Doss
Selwyn Piramuthu
Wei Zhou

Organization

FNSS 2017 was held at the University of Florida, Gainesville, from August 31 to September 2, 2017.

Conference Chairs

Robin Doss   Deakin University, Australia
Selwyn Piramuthu   University of Florida, USA
Wei Zhou   ESCP Europe, France

Program Committee

Maythem Abbas	Universiti Teknologi PETRONAS, Malaysia
S. Agrawal	Delhi Technological University (DTU) Formerly Delhi College of Engineering (DCE), India
Rana Khudhair Ahmed	Al-Rafidain University College, Iraq
Adil Al-Yasiri	University of Salford, UK
Abdul Halim Ali	Universiti Kuala Lumpur - International College, Malaysia
Elizabeth Basha	University of the Pacific, USA
Aniruddha Bhattacharjya	Guru Nanak Institute of Technology (GNIT), India
David Boyle	Imperial College London, UK
Doina Bucur	University of Groningen, The Netherlands
Yue Cao	University of Surrey, UK
Arcangelo Castiglione	University of Salerno, Italy
Sammy Chan	City University of Hong Kong, Hong Kong, SAR China
Kesavaraja D.	Dr. Sivanthi Aditanar College of Engineering, India
Eleonora D'Andrea	University of Pisa, Italy
Soumya Kanti Datta	EURECOM, France
Safiullah Faizullah	Hewlett-Packard, USA
Stephan Flake	Redknee Germany OS GmbH, Germany
Felipe Garcia-Sanchez	Universidad Politecnica de Cartagena (UPCT), Spain
Razvan Andrei Gheorghiu	Politehnica University of Bucharest, Romania
Mikael Gidlund	Mid Sweden University, Sweden
Shweta Jain	York College CUNY, USA
Hussain Mohammed Dipu Kabir	Samsung Bangladesh R&D Center, Bangladesh
Mounir Kellil	CEA LIST, France
Piotr Korbel	Lodz University of Technology, Poland
Lambros Lambrinos	Cyprus University of Technology, Cyprus

Contents

Protocol Design and Secure Implementation

Efficient Certificate Verification
for Vehicle-to-Grid Communications

Nico Saputro[1], Samet Tonyali[1], Kemal Akkaya[1], Mumin Cebe[1(✉)],
and Mohamed Mahmoud[2]

[1] Department of Electrical and Computer Engineering,
Florida International University, Miami, FL 33174, USA
{nsapu002,stonyali,kakkaya,mcebe}@fiu.edu
[2] Department of Electrical and Computer Engineering,
Tennessee Tech University, Cookeville, TN 38505, USA
mmahmoud@tntech.edu

Abstract. While public charging stations are typically used for Electric Vehicle (EV) such as charging, home microgrids that may act as private charging stations are also expected to be used for meeting the increased EV charging demands in the future. Such home microgrids can be accessible through their smart meters, which makes advanced metering infrastructure (AMI) a viable alternative for vehicle-to-grid (V2G) communications. However, to ensure secure V2G communications using public-keys, smart meters will need to maintain certificate revocation lists (CRLs) not just for the AMI network but also for large number of EVs that may interact with them. For resource-constrained smart meters, this will increase the storage requirements and introduce additional overhead in terms of delay and CRL maintenance. To eliminate this burden, we propose keeping merely non-revoked certificates that belong to EVs, which are usually driven within the vicinity of that particular microgrid. The motivation comes from the fact that it is inefficient to distribute and store a large CRL that has revocation information about all EVs in the whole system as most of these EVs will never come to the geographic vicinity of that home microgrid. The approach ensures that any status changes of these certificates are communicated to the smart meters. We implemented the proposed approach in a realistic V2G communication scenario by using IEEE 802.11s mesh as the underlying AMI infrastructure using ns-3 simulator. The results confirmed that the proposed approach significantly reduces the certificate verification time and the storage requirements on smart meters.

1 Introduction

Electric Vehicles (EVs) have recently received increasing popularity to reduce carbon dioxide emissions and promote adoption of intermittent renewable energy sources by acting as energy storage systems [1]. Although EVs currently constitute a narrow segment in the market, mass penetration and market dominance are expected in the upcoming years in the US, particularly with reduced

© Springer International Publishing AG 2017
R. Doss et al. (Eds.): FNSS 2017, CCIS 759, pp. 3–18, 2017.
DOI: 10.1007/978-3-319-65548-2_1

production costs, such as for Tesla's new Model 3 which has already globally garnered 400 K pre-orders. Currently, more than 15,000 public charging stations and 42,000 charging outlets have already been deployed in the US [2] for charging EVs. However, due to various constraints such as investment costs and proximity to grid services, public stations may not be able to address the growing charging needs. Such a need is expected to be met by exploiting the existing microgrid users (i.e., homes/campuses that can generate energy via solar or wind) who are willing to sell their excess power to the grid or EV users. In particular home microgrids (often dubbed a nanogrid) are on the rise with the innovations in the current power grid systems [3]. In this way, EV users will have abundant options to charge their vehicles by communicating with the microgrid/nanogrid owners that will act as residential charging stations.

However, the use of microgrids for EV charging requires a communication infrastructure to connect EVs with the microgrids in certain neighborhoods. Besides the option of building a new and completely separate V2G communication infrastructure between microgrids and EVs, utilizing the existing infrastructures can be an option due to reduced costs. Therefore, we advocate use of existing AMI that connects home microgrids to each other and to power grid via wireless communications. Specifically, a smart meter in a home can act as the connection point to communicate with the EVs and utility/third parties. However, one needs to ensure the security of these communications. For instance, once a malicious EV is connected to the Smart Grid infrastructure via AMI, it can perform denial of service attacks or inject false data to the grid.

An integral part of a security solution for V2G is a dedicated public key infrastructure (PKI), which ensures security issues such as confidentiality, authentication, integrity, etc. In our case, this also raises new challenges related to the operation of such a PKI. First of all, there are different energy providers (utility companies) in a country or state. They may all have different PKIs for providing these services to their customers. However, the EVs would travel to different places and thus will need to charge from a station that is served by another utility company. This will necessitate cross-certification among different utility companies.

Second, as there would be a large number of vehicles in a state, the size of the certificate revocation list (CRL), which keeps the revoked certificates, is expected to be significantly large. From the perspective of smart meters, in addition to the management of public key certificates for AMI network, communications with EVs would require adding a new CRL specific to vehicles, which will significantly increase the space requirements for smart meters. Moreover, frequently updating and distributing CRLs to a large number of smart meters is a big burden, while few vehicles may make a connection with that smart meter.

Finally, verifying signatures from fast moving EVs will be a challenge in terms of latency requirements. This is because, the EV must finish message exchanges before leaving the wireless coverage area of the smart meter. As a consequence, if a large portion of this time is spent with certificate verification, then there might not be enough time left to complete message exchanges among two parties successfully. In addition to that, mobile nature of communication makes reliable transmission even more challenging.

Considering these issues, in this paper we tackle the problem of CRL management for V2G communications in multi-provider environments. We first present an architectural model for PKI and secure V2G communications. Then, we propose an efficient mechanism to reduce the storage requirements for CRL management while still providing a reduced communication delay for EV-smart meter message exchanges. Our mechanism is based on the idea of keeping the certificates of EVs of interest in the smart meters rather than following the traditional way of dealing with CRLs.

The idea stems from the fact that EVs in a certain area typically do charging at nearby microgrids. The number of foreign EVs (the EVs that are coming out of town or state) is far less than the number of domestic EVs (the EVs that are coming from the town). Therefore, there is no need to maintain their revoked certificates in the CRLs. Rather, we keep an up-to-date local list of frequently used and *valid* certificates so that EVs in the neighborhood will quickly get verified by checking this *local list* in the smart meter. If a certificate is not in the list, a smart meter can connect to the utility company that has access to up-to-date CRL for every EVs and smart meters. In other words, our proposed approach asks the certificate authority only when a new certificate is presented to a smart meter rather than asking all the time as in the case of traditional approaches [4]. Note that any new revocations for the valid certificates in the local list will be sent to the smart meters by the utility company so that they can be removed.

To assess the performance of the proposed mechanism, we conducted simulations in ns-3 network simulator by implementing an IEEE 802.11s-based wireless mesh network among the smart meters and integrating it with EVs acting as clients. EV-smart meter communication was assumed to be based on Dedicated Short Range Communications (DSRC) [5], which is the current vehicular communication standard for safety applications. The experiments looked at various cases to investigate the gains through using a local valid certificate list. The results indicated that the size of such a list is smaller compared to traditional CRLs and that signature verifications can be achieved with higher success rates in small communication delays compared to Online Certificate Status Protocol (OCSP) [6] which is the current standard used on Internet.

This paper is organized as follows. In the next section, we describe the related work. Section 3 is dedicated to the proposed system model and PKI. In Sect. 4, we explain our proposed approach for certificate revocation in details. Section 5 provides the results of experimentation and Sect. 6 concludes the paper.

2   Related Work

A number of approaches have been proposed to provide secure V2G communications. Some of these studies dealt with certificate issues. For instance, Falk and Fries [7] studied possible attacks stemming from V2G integration and presented the requirements in order to avoid and mitigate from attacks. It is recommended to use short term certificates and OCSP [6] in order to make sure that a certificate is still valid. This requires frequent access to CA servers which may not be feasible. In this regard, another option could be to use OCSP *stapling* [8] where the EVs query the OCSP server at certain intervals and obtain a signed timestamped OCSP response. When any of the EVs attempt to connect to the grid, this response which is directly signed by the certificate authority is included ("stapled") in the certificate. Again, this approach also requires the EVs to connect the certificate authority frequently. Moreover, in order to ensure the signed timestamped OCSP response in the EV's certificate is legitimate, a smart meter must have the public key of the certificate authority who signs the OCSP response. In another approach, Zhang et al. [9] introduced a context-aware authentication scheme for V2G systems based on battery status of the EV. Rather than using a PKI, the EV computes its authentication operators based on an access challenge sent by the local aggregator. However, the authentication of an EV moving from one network to another is presented as an open issue. Our work differs from the aforementioned approaches by considering the case of EV to AMI communication through smart meters and introducing the idea of maintaining valid certificates. In addition, our approach does not require EVs to frequently access their CA.

In addition to security issues for V2G communications, a number of other studies looked at the design of a PKI for this type of communication. For instance, Vaidya et al. [10] proposed a hybrid PKI involving hierarchical and peer-to-peer cross-certification. In the proposed PKI model, intra-domain and inter-domain certification management techniques use Elliptic Curve Qu-Vanstone as implicit certificates since they do not require explicit verification of the certificate authority signature, so they are smaller in size resulting in using the bandwidth efficiently. Later, they discussed the issue of inter-domain PKI trust and proposed another solution based on a peer-to-peer elliptic curve cryptography-based cross-certification mechanism and a self-certified public key technique [11]. In addition, they proposed a certificate path processing technique for the proposed PKI model. Baumeister and Dong [12] suggested the use of Bridged trust model and a compromise of OCSP and CRL model as the ideal models for the V2G system. Finally, Multin and Schmek [13] introduces the project Hubject that enables charging an EV at energy providers other than the one with which the EV has signed a contract. These energy providers should be connected to a clearing house so that the certificates from different providers can be in an interplay for an authenticated communication. In this paper, we utilize a PKI model similar to the Bridge model in [12] and allow participating energy providers to charge EVs in different providers.

3   Vehicle-to-Grid Model

3.1   Model Description

Since our goal is to utilize the existing infrastructure, we consider the available communications options in both vehicular and smart grid for V2G model. Currently, while there is already DSRC standard [5], which is based on IEEE 802.11p, for vehicle-to-vehicle (V2V) communications, there are a variety of options for multi-tier Smart Grid communications networks [14]. Wireless mesh is one of the viable options and widely adopted for smart meter communications by major AMI vendors [15]. Between these two options, we use IEEE 802.11p instead of IEEE 802.11s [16] for the communication between EV and smart meter since our proposed approach requires a reliable and low communication latency in highly mobile environment. IEEE 802.11p was designed for such environments.

Figure 1 represents the considered V2G model for a utility company. A number of residential wireless-enabled smart meters in an area forms an AMI neighborhood area network. This AMI uses a gateway to connect to the utility company through a wide area network. Each smart meter operates as a dual-interface node with the functionality of IEEE 802.11s multi-hop wireless mesh network for AMI application and IEEE 802.11p for communication with an EV.

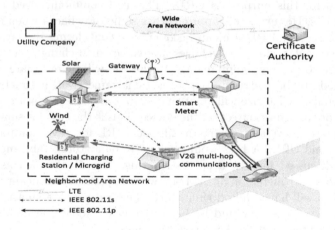

Fig. 1. Vehicle-to-Grid Infrastructure. An EV can communicate with multiple microgrids through smart meters to request some information or to make a charging reservation while the EV is still on the road through V2G multi-hop communications.

The gateway also operates as dual-interface node with the functionality of IEEE 802.11s and Long Term Evolution (LTE). It acts as the IEEE 802.11s root node as well as the portal node to the utility company through LTE network [17,18]. A GPS-enabled On-Board Unit with an IEEE 802.11p interface is available on every EV to support vehicle-to-grid, vehicle-to-vehicle, and vehicle-to-infrastructure communications.

In our scenario, due to the availability of multiple options of residential charging stations in an area, an EV can collect the residential charging station information (e.g., cost, availability, distance, and time required for charging), select the residential charging station, and make a reservation to a residential charging station while the EV is still on the road through the proposed V2G model. Since security is paramount importance for Smart Grid, an EV must first authenticate itself using PKI to the nearest smart meter of the AMI network using IEEE 802.11p before it can use the multi-hop capability of IEEE 802.11s to reach the intended residential charging station(s) for querying or charging reservation. In this way, an EV_i can reduce its traveling time without consuming its battery too much for finding the closest residential charging station that meets its criteria. The considered model also supports out-network/roaming/inter-provider charging where EV_k from a utility company UC_p can use other utility companies' charging stations while the charging usage still be billed to the EV_k account in UC_p through the third party such as a clearing house.

3.2   Problem Motivation and Definition

In our scenario, digital certificates are used to verify the sender's identity in V2G communication. However, it is necessary to identify and remove revoked certificates to prevent misbehavior or attacks. One of the different approaches that are used for this purpose is CRLs. This is a commonly used method in traditional PKIs. However, this approach has some drawbacks when applied to our setting. First, the CRL size can become huge considering the large number of EVs. In particular, since the vehicles are expected to change their identities frequently due to privacy requirements [5], the size will be even larger. Second, the CRL needs to be distributed to every smart meter in a timely manner. However, increased CRL size will create a distribution as well as storage problem if there are not enough resources on the device. This is the case for smart meters. In fact, a smart meter already has a different CRL for AMI communications [19,20]. A second CRL for EVs would definitely be a storage and maintenance burden. As discussed in [21], even distributing a small file such as firmware updates to all smart meters in an AMI network requires a significant amount of time. Yet, EVs will have limited time to communicate with a smart meter due to their mobility. Thus, it would be better to have a locally available CRL on the smart meter to speed up the verification process.

In this paper, we tackle this problem of certificate revocation management for V2G communications. Specifically, our goal is to come up with an efficient mechanism to not only reduce storage requirements but also consider the latency constraints in V2G communications.

4   An Efficient Certificate Verification Scheme

4.1   Motivation and Approach Overview

Our main challenge is to be able to quickly verify the certificate of any EV on the road that is trying to communicate with the smart meter of potential residential charging station for charging information (e.g., the available charging time and duration, charging capacity, etc.) since the contact time for an EV with a smart meter might not be that long due to speed of the EV. Obviously, the traditional solution is to always maintain an up-to-date CRL on the smart meter of residential charging station (i.e., distributed CRL (D-CRL) scheme) so that a quick local search can be conducted on the smart meter. However, this solution would bring a huge overhead on the smart meter in terms of space and communications. The size of this CRL would be very large due to the large number of EVs and this CRL needs to be updated frequently even though the smart meter never uses it. This is particularly a problem when the location is considered. Typically, a certain residential charging station/microgrid will serve the needs of EVs in the neighborhood or town. There will be rarely foreign EVs that would like to charge there (e.g., roaming charging). Thus, for such rare cases, the smart meter needs to maintain the CRL for all vehicles in the state/country which is an overkill.

An alternative solution would be to use OCSP, and each time the smart meter needs to verify a certificate it queries the certificate from CA so that it will not need to deal with huge size CRLs. However, in that case, it requires a communications infrastructure between every smart meter in AMI network and multiple CAs, which is not feasible. Moreover, since security is paramount importance for Smart Grid, enabling every smart meter to have direct access to multiple CAs may introduce a huge amount of new attack venue. Thus, it requires a security handling mechanisms, which eventually cause the verification of the certificate may take a long time and depending on the speed of the EV, the response may not come back on time for completing the scheduling process.

In this paper, as opposed to traditional solutions which follow a CRL-based approach, we follow a different idea to solve this problem and propose keeping valid certificates on the smart meter to speed up the process and favor the local communication requests from EVs. Specifically, whoever makes a connection with a particular smart meter will have its certificate stored on that smart meter in a list after this certificate has been verified by the utility company. This list will then be used for future communications from the same EVs. If a valid certificate is revoked in the future, the utility company should advise the smart meters that store the certificate to remove it from their list. In this way, the CRLs for foreign EVs that would never communicate with that particular smart meter again will not be maintained. The local list of valid certificates will be updated accordingly. Next, we describe the details of our valid certificates management scheme.

4.2   Certificate Verification Based on Verified Certificate List

We introduce two lists for our scheme: (1) Verified Certificate List (VCL) and (2) Location-based Certificate List (LCL). A VCL is maintained in every smart meter to store a customized EV_i certificate, a partial content of the full EV_i certificate that has been verified as a valid certificate by the utility company. The minimum certificate information in the customized EV_i certificate are EV_i

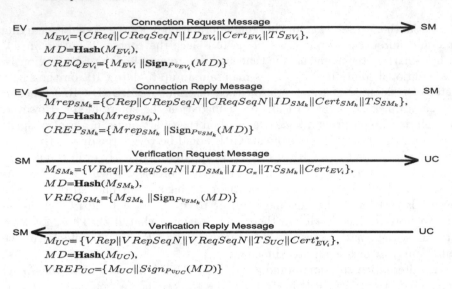

Fig. 2. Message exchanges

identity, EV_i certificate serial number, EV_i public key, certificate authority issuer identity, and expiration date. For each customized certificate in the VCL, a *frequency attribute* is used to indicate how many times this certificate is used in this smart meter within a time interval T. LCL is maintained by the utility company and stores the list of all AMI networks' gateways. Each entry of the LCL consists of the ID of the gateway of an AMI network, the ID of a smart meter that acts as a microgrid under that gateway, and the list of all valid EV certificates (serial number and certificate authority identity) that are currently stored in the VCL of that smart meter. The notation definitions are presented in Table 1.

Table 1. Notations

Acronym	Description
$SM, EV, UC, CA, G, ID, TS, MD$	Smart meter, Electric vehicle, Utility company, Certificate authority, Gateway, Identity, Timestamp, message digest
$CReq$ & $CReqSeqN$	connection request id & sequence number
$CRep$ & $CRepSeqN$	connection reply id & sequence number
$VReq$ & $VReqSeqN$	verification request id & sequence number
$VRep$ & $VRepSeqN$	verification reply id & sequence number
$Cert$ & $Cert^*$	full and customized certificate
Pub & Pub^*	unverified and verified public key
Pv, **Hash**, **Sign**	private key, hash function, digital signature

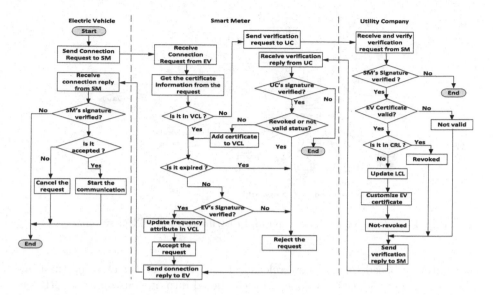

Fig. 3. Certificate verification process

Before an EV_i makes a connection with a microgrid (i.e., smart meter representing it), it collects broadcast messages from the smart meters in the vicinity.
The one with the strongest signal strength (i.e., SM_k) will be chosen. Then, four
messages exchange for EV certificate verification and connection establishment
between the EV_i and the selected SM_k are conducted as depicted in Fig. 2: (1)
a connection request message $CREQ_{EV_i}$ from EV_i to SM_k; (2) a connection
reply message $CREP_{SM_k}$ from SM_k to EV_i; (3) a verification request message
$VREQ_{SM_k}$ from SM_k to UC; and (4) a verification reply message $VREP_{UC}$
from UC to SM_k. Figure 3 shows certificate verification process for EV_i authentication. Note that the public key $Pub^*_{EV_i}$ in $Cert^*_{EV_i}$ that is stored in VCL_k will
be used by the SM_k for the EV_i's digital signature verification since $Cert_{EV_i}$ in
$CREQ_{EV_i}$ has not been verified yet.

4.3   VCL Maintenance Scheme

VCL on each smart meter needs to be maintained periodically to remove
expired certificates, revoked certificates, and temporary-event certificates (e.g.,
certificates from out-of-town EVs). Removing expired certificates is straight
forward based on the expiration date without causing any additional traffic
in the network. Removing revoked and temporary-event certificates however,
introduce additional downlink traffic and periodic uplink traffic respectively as
explained next.

Removing Revoked Certificates. Each time a new CRL update is released
by any participating CAs, the utility company creates a customized CRL for

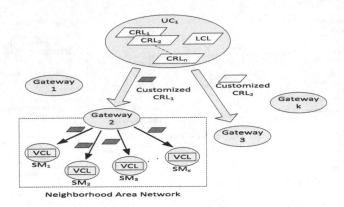

Fig. 4. Customized CRL creation and distribution for VCL maintenance.

each gateway based on this new release. The revoked certificates information from multiple participating CAs can be combined into one customized CRL for each gateway. For each new revoked certificate in the new CRL update, the utility company searches the LCL to identify the gateway(s) of smart meters that keep it as a verified certificate in their VCLs. For each of these gateways, the utility company creates a customized CRL that contains only new revoked certificates for that gateway. Note that not all gateways will receive a customized CRL since this depends on whether there is a new revoked certificate that must be disseminated to that particular gateway. Thus, it can be considered as a randomly occurring event. Figure 4 illustrates this distribution. On receiving a customized CRL, a gateway forwards it to all smart meters in the AMI. Every smart meter will update its VCL based on the received customized CRL.

Removing Temporary-Event Certificates. A Least Frequently Used mechanism is proposed to keep track of the frequency of an EV communication to a smart meter within a time period T (e.g., every month). For each successful connection, the frequency of the corresponding certificate in VCL will be incremented. At the end of each period T, every smart meter will remove certificates from its VCL with a frequency less than a threshold β, where $\beta \geq 1$ and then the frequency attribute of remaining certificates will be reset. Thus, VCL always stores the frequently used certificates in that period only and avoids the previously dominating certificate usage to be carried over to the next period. Even though the Least Frequently Used mechanism can reduce the required storage space for a VCL, coherency issues may arise between VCLs and LCL. Therefore, the removed certificate(s) must be reported to the utility company to update the LCL.

5   Performance Evaluation

5.1   Baselines and Performance Metrics

We compared the performance of the proposed VCL with OCSP and the distributed CRL (D-CRL) that stores the certificates locally at each smart meter using the following metrics: (1) *Storage*, the space required to store the certificate and revocation information at smart meters; (2) *End-to-End Delay*, the delay incurred to verify an EV's certificate, which is the elapsed time between the first connection request sent by the EV and the connection reply the EV received; and (3) *Success Rate*, the ratio of the number of actual connection replies received by EVs to the total number of expected connection replies.

5.2   Experimental Setup

Two experiment scenarios are planned for performance evaluations. In both scenarios, the speeds of 40 mph and 70 mph are used assuming that EVs are in urban or highway environments when they need recharging. In the first scenario, the experiments are conducted in a controlled setup where EVs follow a straight path and start sending a connection request at the same time. 10 smart meters are chosen randomly from each topology representing the microgrids that periodically broadcast service messages to advertise their unit price for charging. A number of VpM (Vehicles per Meter) $\in \{2, 4, 5, 8, 10\}$ are placed at the very edge of the communication range of each of these microgrids. These vehicles broadcast their basic safety related messages periodically to surrounding vehicles. The simulation time is kept shorter (e.g., 20 s) since each EV goes out of the communication range of the associated meter. We assumed 20%, 40% and 60% miss rates where a valid certificate is searched in the VCL and does not exist there. These approaches are depicted as VCL-20%, VCL-40% and VCL-60% in the graphs. In such cases, the search is directed to the utility company.

In Scenario 2, the experiments are run in a more realistic environment using realistic traces that are generated in VanetMobiSim [22] by varying the number of vehicles and their speed. Thus, the amount of time an EV can stay within a smart meter's communication range varies. We assumed that 20% of the EVs need to recharge. The simulation time is 500 s to ensure that all of these EVs receive at least one broadcast service message and send a connection request. The experiment results are collected from 30 random mesh network topologies consisting of 81 nodes for statistical significance.

5.3   Performance Results

Storage Requirements. Obviously, OCSP and D-CRL represent the two extremes of the required space in a smart meter. OCSP does not need any space in the smart meter since everything is stored at the certificate authority. Typically CRL only stores minimum information (e.g., certificate serial numbers) while a smart meter also needs the public key for authentication. Therefore,

Table 2. Storage overhead on smart meters.

Approach	List entry	Certificate	Avg. total
OCSP	0	0	0
VCL	4 bytes	896 bytes	900(KB)
D-CRL	20 bytes	1024 bytes	6.48(MB)

D-CRL stores both CRL and EV's certificates. Thus, the total storage needed for the D-CRL is the CRL size + certificate size. Depending on the number of revoked certificates, the average CRL size for V2V applications can become huge [23] (i.e., order of MBs). Even in case of EVs, there are around 500 K EVs in the US now and a 100 K revoked certificate will require around 6 MB storage space (each revoked certificate holds 68 bytes in CRL). VCL only needs to store the reduced customized EV certificate size (e.g., by omitting the certificate authority's digital signature (128 bytes), the typical 1024 bytes certificates will become 896 bytes). Assuming 1000 entries are kept in VCL, our approach requires around 900 KB when D-CRL is used. A summary of comparison is given in Table 2.

End-to-End Delay. The simulation results for scenario 1 as shown in Fig. 5a and b indicate that speed of the vehicle does not affect the performance of the approaches significantly. The delay performance all approaches for 70 mph almost match the performance when the speeds are 40 mph. In general, since the vehicle density is kept same, 802.11p MAC layer can keep up with the speed.

When looking at different approaches, VCL variants (VCL-20%, VCL-40%, VCL-60%) reduce the delay compared to OCSP. This is because of the network delay of OCSP for accessing the CRL at the certificate authority. In case of VCL, there can be misses which requires the smart meter to communicate with the utility company. This increases the delay slightly in the VCL but still it performs better than OCSP. D-CRL performs the fastest verification at the expense of not only the increased storage but also CRL maintenance that needs to be done from utility companies to smart meters. This is obviously another overhead for the AMI network which does not exist for our approach. VCL minimizes the space requirements with a slight increase in End-to-End delay. However, this slight increase is due to mostly first time contact of smart meters from out of town EVs. For the frequent usage of EVs from the same neighborhoods, this delay will be further reduced.

Figure 5a and b also indicate that as the number of EVs increases the delay increases for D-CRL. This is because the traffic over V2G is impacted from V2V communication. Since every vehicle broadcasts safety messages, this causes congestion on the channel. This observation shows that V2G communication has a communication latency and that verifying signatures from fast moving EVs become even more challenging in terms of latency requirements.

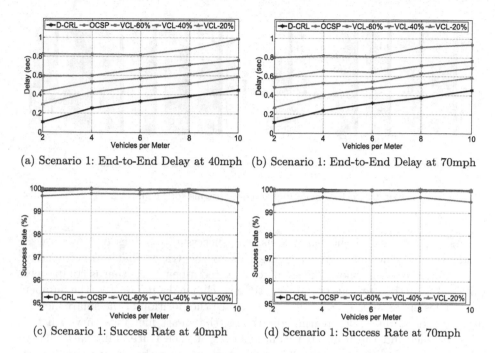

(a) Scenario 1: End-to-End Delay at 40mph   (b) Scenario 1: End-to-End Delay at 70mph

(c) Scenario 1: Success Rate at 40mph   (d) Scenario 1: Success Rate at 70mph

Fig. 5. Performance metric comparisons for Scenario 1.

Success Rate. The success rate values for Scenario 1 are given in Fig. 5c and d, respectively. As in End-to-end delay, there is no significant difference between the speeds in success rate values. The increase in number of vehicles very slightly deteriorates the success rate performance of D-CRL and the VCL variants. The performance of OCSP deteriorates a little bit more compared to the other approaches. This is because it is more probable for OCSP to miss a connection reply since the EV can go out of the smart meter's communication range before the reply arrives. Thus, the EV will need a reattempt.

Figure 6a and b show the results for Scenario 2. The D-CRL approach outperforms the other approaches because it does not require to communicate with the mesh network and this reduces packet losses. The success rate values of our approach are slightly less than D-CRL values due to those EVs whose certificate information is not found in the VCL on the smart meters. This requires to contact the utility company, which consequently decreases the number of connection replies received. The success rate values for our approach decrease when the miss rate increases due to the same reason given in Scenario 1 results. The OCSP approach shows the worst performance as expected because it needs to contact the utility company at each time. Most of the time, the time interval in which the EV stays within a smart meter's communication range is not sufficient to receive a connection reply from the smart meter.

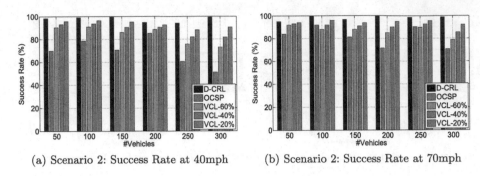

(a) Scenario 2: Success Rate at 40mph   (b) Scenario 2: Success Rate at 70mph

Fig. 6. Performance metric comparisons for Scenario 2.

As can be seen in the bar graphs, the success rate values do not show a tendency and fluctuate. We attribute this to the traces that are completely independent of each other. The simulator created a new trace that is completely different than the previous one at each time we changed a parameter (the number of vehicles or the speed). Since it does not take the position of the smart meters into consideration while creating the traces, the smart meters with which the EVs interact and the round-trip time changes at each trace. This particularly affects the performance of the OCSP approach because the smart meter needs to contact the CA whenever a certificate verification is required.

6   Conclusion

In this paper, we have proposed an efficient certificate verification scheme for EVs-microgrids communications. Our network model uses the AMI networks as the communication network between EVs, smart meters and the utility companies. Using the traditional CRLs is not efficient because the smart meters need to maintain CRLs not just for the AMI network but also for a large number of EVs. These CRLs are long because each EV will use a large number of certificates to preserve privacy for V2V applications. We considered the case of EV to AMI communication through smart meters and introduced the idea of maintaining list of valid certificates. Our scheme maintains an up-to-date list of frequently used valid certificates. This idea is specifically interesting when EVs charge from the same places frequently.

We evaluated the performance of the proposed scheme through an implementation under ns-3 by using IEEE 802.11s, IEEE 802.11p and LTE standards. The results confirmed that the proposed approach significantly reduces the certificate verification time and the storage requirements on smart meters, and that it is highly reliable to be employed in realistic environments.

References

1. Lund, H., Kempton, W.: Integration of renewable energy into the transport and electricity sectors through V2G. Energy Policy **36**(9), 3578–3587 (2008)
2. DoE: Alternative fueling station counts by state, alternative fuels data center. http://www.afdc.energy.gov/fuels/stations_counts.html
3. Hebner, R.: Nanogrids, microgrids, and big data: The future of the power grid. IEEE Spectrum Magazine (2017)
4. Networks, P.A.: Pan-os administrator's guide (2016). https://www.paloaltonet works.com/content/dam/pan/_US/assets/pdf/framemaker/61/pan-os/pan-os/ section_3.pdf
5. Wu, X., Subramanian, S., Guha, R., White, R.G., Li, J., Lu, K.W., Bucceri, A., Zhang, T.: Vehicular communications using DSRC: challenges, enhancements, and evolution. IEEE J. Sel. Areas Commun. **31**(9), 399–408 (2013)
6. Galperin, S., Santesson, S., Myers, M., Malpani, A., Adams, C.: X. 509 internet public key infrastructure online certificate status protocol-OCSP (2013)
7. Falk, R., Fries, S.: Securely connecting electric vehicles to the smart grid. Int. J. Adv. Internet Technol. **6**(1) (2013)
8. Pettersen, Y.: The transport layer security (TLS) multiple certificate status request extension (2013)
9. Zhang, Y., Gjessing, S., Liu, H., Ning, H., Yang, L., Guizani, M.: Securing vehicle-to-grid communications in the smart grid. IEEE Wirel. Commun. **20**(6), 66–73 (2013)
10. Vaidya, B., Makrakis, D., Mouftah, H.T.: Security mechanism for multi-domain vehicle-to-grid infrastructure. In: IEEE Global Telecommunications Conference (GLOBECOM 2011), pp. 1–5 (2011)
11. Vaidya, B., Makrakis, D., Mouftah, H.T.: Multi-domain public key infrastructure for vehicle-to-grid network. In: Military Communications Conference, MILCOM 2015–2015 IEEE, pp. 1572–1577. IEEE (2015)
12. Baumeister, T., Dong, Y.: Towards secure identity management for the smart grid. Secur. Commun. Networks **9**(9), 808–822 (2016). http://dx.doi.org/10.1002/sec.996
13. Mültin, M., Schmeck, H.: Plug-and-charge and e-roaming-capabilities of the ISO/IEC 15118 for the e-mobility scenario. at-Automatisierungstechnik **62**(4), 241–248 (2014)
14. Saputro, N., Akkaya, K., Uludag, S.: A survey of routing protocols for smart grid communications. Comput. Networks **56**(11), 2742–2771 (2012). http://www.sciencedirect.com/science/article/pii/S1389128612001429
15. Neichin, G., Cheng, D.: 2010 U.S. smart grid vendor ecosystem. https://energy.gov/sites/prod/files/oeprod/DocumentsandMedia/2010_U.S._Smart_Grid_Vendor_Ecosystem_Report.pdf
16. IEEE standard for information technology-telecommunications and information exchange between systems-local and metropolitan area networks-specific requirements part 11: Wireless lan medium access control (MAC) and physical layer (PHY) specifications amendment 10: Mesh networking. IEEE Std 802.11s-2011, pp. 1–372, November 2011
17. Koohifar, F., Saputro, N., Guvenc, I., Akkaya, K.: Hybrid Wi-Fi/LTE aggregation architecture for smart meter communications. In: 2015 IEEE International Conference on Smart Grid Communications (SmartGridComm), pp. 575–580, November 2015

18. Saputro, N., Akkaya, K., Tonyali, S.: Addressing network interoperability in hybrid IEEE 802.11s/LTE smart grid communications. In: 2016 IEEE 41st Conference on Local Computer Networks (LCN), pp. 623–626, November 2016
19. Akkaya, K., Rabieh, K., Mahmoud, M., Tonyali, S.: Customized certificate revocation lists for IEEE 802.11s-based smart grid AMI networks. IEEE Trans. Smart Grid **6**(5), 2366–2374 (2015)
20. Rabieh, K., Mahmoud, M., Akkaya, K., Tonyali, S.: Scalable certificate revocation schemes for smart grid AMI networks using bloom filters. IEEE Trans. Dependable Secure Comput. **PP**(99), 1 (2015)
21. Tonyali, S., Akkaya, K., Saputro, N.: An attribute-based reliable multicast-over-broadcast protocol for firmware updates in smart meter networks. In: 2017 IEEE Conference on Computer Communications Workshops (INFOCOM WKSHPS), May 2017
22. Härri, J., Filali, F., Bonnet, C., Fiore, M.: Vanetmobisim: generating realistic mobility patterns for VANETs. In: Proceedings of the 3rd International Workshop on Vehicular Ad Hoc Networks, pp. 96–97. ACM (2006)
23. Khodaei, M.: Secure vehicular communication systems: Design and implementation of a vehicular PKI (VPKI) (2012)

The GENI Test Automation Framework
for New Protocol Development

Erik Golen[(✉)], Sai Varun Prasanth, Shashank Rudroju, and Nirmala Shenoy

Rochester Institute of Technology, Rochester, NY 14623, USA
efgics@rit.edu

Abstract. The National Science Foundation's GENI testbed provides an open infrastructure environment for researchers to develop networking protocols from the ground up. During implementation and testing of a networking protocol, researchers typically begin with small scale topologies to show initial proof of concept before moving on to larger scale topologies. For small scale topologies, it is feasible to manually deploy, compile, and execute protocol code and collect performance metrics. However, when testing with topologies of tens of nodes or larger, the manually intensive task of code deployment, compilation, execution, and metrics collection becomes infeasible. To combat this issue, we present an automation framework for the GENI testbed that requires very little user interaction and utilizes existing GENI APIs and constructs, including the manifest RSPEC file, to perform automated testing of a networking protocol. In this article, we provide the details of the automation framework and its use in the development and evaluation of a new Layer 2.5 protocol, namely the Multi Node Label Routing protocol. The framework can also be used for collection of performance metrics in an automated fashion.

Keywords: Automation framework · Large networks · New protocol development and evaluation

1 Introduction

Recent research trends indicate the popularity of novel techniques to address continuing networking challenges. To evaluate novel techniques several methodologies are available, including analytical models, simulation, and testbeds. Analytical approaches limit testing the techniques in applied environments, while simulations can be very complex if all the environmental conditions are to be taken into account to reflect real life situations. The GENI testbed provides an ideal platform for the development and testing of new protocols. It also allows for evaluation and comparison of such new protocols with existing protocols.

GENI (Global Environment for Network Innovations) is a Lab as a Service (LaaS) that facilitates a distributed system for research and education. As a federated testbed, GENI provides a wide range of heterogeneous devices that abstracts complex and costly physical network creation and provides a virtual infrastructure to explore networks at scale, thus aiding in cutting-edge network research. GENI affords researchers a highly

© Springer International Publishing AG 2017
R. Doss et al. (Eds.): FNSS 2017, CCIS 759, pp. 19–29, 2017.
DOI: 10.1007/978-3-319-65548-2_2

flexible development environment through providing a bare metal image and allows users to install custom software on top of it.

However, to implement, test, and evaluate networking protocols, users are required to develop their own custom tools and scripts. For example, when users request computing resources from GENI, a generic RSPEC file with topology information is first created. There exists no method for pre-determining the host names and port numbers of the computing resources that will be granted to the user until a manifest RSPEC file is generated during topology creation time. This file must be parsed by a user generated script if the user would like to perform common protocol evaluation tasks that require iteration over a collection of network nodes, such as code deployment, code execution, or metrics collection.

To reduce the steepness of the GENI learning curve and to ease the transition of researchers from an analytical or simulation approach, we propose the GENI Test Automation Framework (GTAF) that is based upon a typical workflow for network protocol development and evaluation. In this article, we provide the details of GTAF and how it was used to evaluate a new non-IP based protocol that operates at Layer 2.5 on Ubuntu Linux 14.04.

In Sect. 2 we describe some of the challenges faced in IP based routing, which required the development of a new protocol. This section also provides some operational details on a new Layer 2.5 protocol that can provide routing within an Autonomous System using simple labels. Since it is deployed as a Layer 2.5 protocol, it bypasses IP and its routing impacts. In Sect. 3, we provide the details of the Python based GTAF to enable easy development and testing of the new protocol in large networks. Though we show only a 27-node topology in this work, the automation framework can easily be used in large networks of over 100 nodes. In Sect. 4, we describe how the automation framework was used for the testing and development of the Layer 2.5 protocol. Section 5 provides some initial results and Sect. 6 provides conclusions and future enhancements planned for the automation framework.

2   Development and Evaluation of New Protocols

One major challenge faced by current routing paradigms is scalability. Whether a routing protocol uses link state routing (OSPF) or path vector routing (BGP), as the number of networks increase, routing table sizes increase. In turn, operational complexity increases, resulting in potentially unstable routing. The forwarding information base (FIB) in Internet core routers have exceeded 600 k entries, while the routing Information base (RIB) of core routers has exceeded one million entries [1]. As a result, numerous looping packets and high churn rates are common in the Internet today.

Addressing these routing scalability challenges requires rethinking the fundamentals of current routing techniques [2]. When new approaches are discovered and designed, the next challenge is to craft the new approaches such that they have a deployment or transition path. In this context, it is very important that the solutions be demonstrated for their operation, preferably in testbeds that capture the attributes of a real network and allow for comparison with current solutions. The GENI testbed provides all these unique capabilities.

In this section, we describe this new routing protocol briefly to provide context for how the GENI testbed provided the proper platform to code and demonstrate protocol operations; this is subsequently followed by the description and development of the GENI test automation framework (GTAF) to enable testing the new protocol in large network topologies with up to 100 nodes without the tedium of deploying the code and appropriately configuring each and every node. The GTAF may also be used for collecting performance metrics.

2.1   Multi Node Label Routing (MNLR) Protocol

The MNLR protocol [3] uses commonly existing structures in most networks to derive labels that capture the properties of the structure. These labels also capture the connectivity and relationships existing between sets of routers dedicated for certain operations such as Backbone Routers, Distribution Routers and Access Routers. The relational information in the labels is then used to route and forward packets. To provide an easy and smooth transition path, this protocol was developed as a Layer 2.5 protocol. When not required, MNLR can be turned off and routers would use IP and its routing protocol for routing and forwarding. When required, MNLR can be turned on, and will operate below the IP layer transparently without displacing IP.

MNLR can be deployed in a domain or Autonomous System (AS), as shown in Fig. 1. At the edge of the MNLR domain are IP networks that have not invoked MNLR. When an IP packet has to be delivered between End IP network 1 and End IP network 2 at the source edge MNLR node, the IP packet is encapsulated by MNLR headers (which carry the labels of the source MNLR node and destination MNLR node) and routing operations in the MNLR domain are carried out using only the MNLR label information.

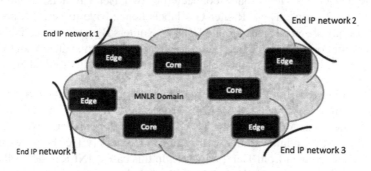

Fig. 1. Implementation of MNLR in IP networks

2.2   Multi Node Label Routing Protocol – Label Significance

Considering a typical AS network construct, MNLR uses a structural abstraction based on router functions, such as backbone (BB) routers, distribution (DB) routers and access

(AC) routers. The BB, DB, and AC router based 3-tier structure is common in many networks. A tiered structure can be noticed among ISPs to define their business relationships, thus in the event MNLR has to be extended for inter-AS routing, the labels can be defined to accordingly capture the tier structure and relationships existing among ISPs. Note, however, that this is out of scope for this article and not further elaborated upon here.

The label notation used in MNLR follows the format TV.UID i.e. Tier-Value.UniqueID. Each value in the label string that makes up a node's UID is separated using ':'. The labels for Tier 1 routers follow the format TV.UID and are denoted as 1.1, 1.2 and 1.3, as seen in Fig. 2.

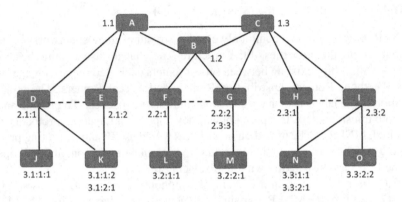

Fig. 2. Label assignment in MNLR protocol

Labels for Tier 2 routers can be allocated administratively, but they have to explicitly show the parent/child relationship to the Tier 1 routers to which they are connected. For example, Router G is a Tier 2 router connected to two Tier 1 routers, B and C, with labels 1.2 and 1.3, respectively. Router G's labels hence have to be 2.2:x and 2.3:y, where x and y have been appended to the UIDs of Routers B and C, respectively. UIDs of Router G (not considering the tier value) are thus 2:x and 3:y, where x and y can be any integer value. In a similar manner, Tier 3 routers are also allocated labels.

Multi Node Label Routing Protocol – Operations and Implementation

One of the configurations required for MNLR operations is the assignment of MNLR labels to all nodes in an MNLR domain. This can be done administratively. The MNLR label format allows for administratively assigning labels to only Tier 1 devices and then enabling auto-assignment from Tier 2 onwards. In this case, MNLR nodes still need to be assigned the tier value of the tier in which they reside.

End IP network addresses and ports may be learned dynamically or configured administratively. There can be multiple end IP networks connected to one edge node. The port information helps in directing the IP packets to the proper end IP network. Edge MNLR nodes populate an IP address to port mapping as shown in Table 1.

Table 1. Local node IP address to port mapping

IP network address	Port
10.10.3.0/24	2
10.10.2.0/24	3
10.10.1.0/24	4

Control Plane Operations

The first MNLR control operation requires the periodic broadcast of 'hello' messages by all MNLR nodes to advertise their MNLR labels to their directly connected neighbors. Receiving MNLR nodes populate a neighbor table. Once MNLR nodes have a label, they can start advertising their labels to their neighbors using 'hello' messages. The advertisements received by other MNLR nodes can be used for two purposes; (1) to check if a neighbor is still connected and (2) to join any other parent node. The reception and absence of the periodic 'hello' messages from neighbor MNLR nodes can inform a parent/child about a missing child/parent.

Table 2 shows the neighbor table at Router G. Port numbers are included in this table, but not shown in Fig. 2.

Table 2. Neighbor table at Router G

MNLR label	Port
1.2	1
1.3	2
3.2:2:1	3
2.2:1	4

End IP Network Address Dissemination

The second MNLR control operation is the end IP network address dissemination to all egress and ingress MNLR nodes. All edge nodes populate a table that maps end IP network addresses to MNLR labels of edge nodes at which they are accessible.

In Fig. 1, the edge MNLR nodes connected to end IP networks should have information about all the end network IP addresses that are connected by the MNLR domain. When an IP packet arrives at an ingress node, the ingress node has to find the label associated with the destination IP address, create the MNLR header with the source node MNLR label and destination node MNLR label, encapsulate the IP packet in the MNLR header, and forward.

Determining the destination node label associated with the destination IP network address requires all edge MNLR nodes to disseminate messages that carry a mapping of their labels to end IP network addresses. The dissemination messages are initiated only by edge nodes and received and stored also only by edge nodes. Core MNLR nodes will forward such advertisements. Let the edge node that has end IP networks as shown in Table 1 have two labels, 2.3:1 and 2.2:1. Another edge node that receives advertisements from this node would populate a table that has a MNLR label to end IP network address table as shown in Table 3.

Table 3. MNLR label to end IP network address mapping

MNLR label	IP network address
2.3:1	10.10.3.0/24
	10.10.2.0/24
	10.10.1.0/24
2.2:1	10.10.3.0/24
	10.10.2.0/24
	10.10.1.0/24

Data Plane Operations

The operations to forward IP packets between end IP networks include encapsulation of incoming IP packets in special MNLR headers at ingress MNLR nodes and de-encapsulating MNLR packets at the egress MNLR nodes to deliver IP packets to the destination IP network. The core nodes forward MNLR encapsulated packets towards egress MNLR nodes using the neighbor table and the forwarding algorithm. Details of the forwarding algorithm are available in [3].

Neighbor Relationships and Packet Forwarding Options

Acloser look at the UIDs of routers reveals the existence of several trees rooted at the backbone routers. The backbone routers themselves may be meshed. Each UID that an MNLR router is assigned provides a path to the root of a tree and vice versa. Due to the fact that a node is allowed multiple labels, a router can reside in multiple tree branches and have multiple paths to reach different backbone routers. The UIDs can be used to identify these multiple paths. A simple decision algorithm will allow a node to decide which path to use while forwarding a packet. Also, nodes in a tier, such as Tier 2 or Tier 3, may be mesh-connected or partial mesh connected, as seen in Fig. 2. In this case, the mesh information, if included in the neighbor table, can be used for forwarding packets.

In Fig. 2, Routers J and K have a common parent in Router D. To forward a packet between Routers J and K, Router D can be used. Looking at the labels of Routers J and K which are 3.1:1:1 and 3:1:1:2, gives the information that they have a common parent at Tier 2, which is 2.1:1. Similar string comparison algorithms and techniques can be used to identify a path to forward packets towards a destination node. Similarly, there is a peering relationship between Routers G and F. Based on the exchange of hello messages by its neighbors Router G records all its neighbors as shown in Table 1. (The ports noted in Table 1 are not shown in Fig. 2). This information can be used to forward packets between Routers L and M.

3   GENI Test Automation Framework

Though GENI provides an infrastructure to assist in new protocol development and testing, adopting the infrastructure to perform these tasks can be a complicated and time-consuming process. However, the new protocol development process can be simplified with the help of a test automation framework. Any protocol during its development phase requires frequent code changes and manually deploying code into a topology for testing, which becomes a time infeasible task as topologies reach as few as six to eight nodes. The primary objective of this GENI Test Automation Framework (GTAF) is to ease the protocol development process in the GENI testbed. It not only helps in expediting this process, but also reduces the chances of hand operated or manual errors. The flowchart with each of the modules used in GTAF is shown in Fig. 3 and are described in the subsequent subsections.

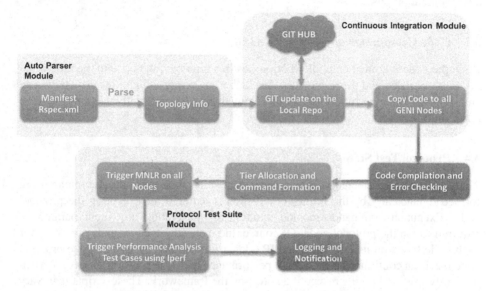

Fig. 3. Flowchart of the GENI test automation framework

3.1 Auto Parser

In order for GENI to allocate resources for a topology, a generic topology is constructed, resulting in an RSPEC file. Once the resources are allocated using one or more aggregates, a manifest RSPEC file is generated that contains all of the hostname and port information specific to the newly available topology. Since GENI does not provide a native parser that allows researchers to iterate over the resources to deploy code or perform other common development tasks, an Auto Parser module was developed with the manifest RSPEC file as input. The Auto Parser extracts all pertinent topology details from the manifest RSPEC, including port numbers, node hostnames, interfaces used, and node connectivity details. Once the parser has completed its operations, the topology information is written into memory and saved locally in the location where the test script was triggered.

3.2 Continuous Integration

Since GENI nodes do not share a common memory space, protocol code has to be individually deployed to every newly spawned node. Software projects, especially large and complex ones, need an infrastructure for continuous integration to a configuration management server to make sure the latest code is tested and verified. GTAF provides a means for continuous integration of code developed by the developers in their local machine to a central repository. The central repository used in this case is GitHub [4]. It should be noted that without loss of generality, other repositories such as Subversion or Perforce could also be substituted into GTAF. The automation framework ensures that the latest code is pulled from the GitHub and copied to all the GENI nodes for development purposes.

3.3   Code Compilation and Error Checking

Once the code is copied onto all GENI nodes in a topology, the code in the individual nodes is compiled and the framework checks for any errors and notifies the user via an email in case of any errors. The user can immediately take corrective actions and then rerun the framework.

3.4   Protocol Test Suite

There are two steps included in a protocol test suite. First, execution commands are formed dynamically by the framework, which is required for executing the protocol code. Execution commands include dynamically generating any input parameters required to run the protocol code. Of course, these execution commands may vary for each node based on its interfaces and IP addresses allocated by GENI. Once protocol code has been confirmed as executing, performance metric generation scripts are automatically executed on the respective nodes by the framework. These scripts may vary in scope from running iPerf [5] to custom metrics collection scripts.

3.5   Logging and Notification

GTAF ensures that all of these processes noted above are executed in their proper sequence. If any of the processes fails during framework runtime, the user is notified with an email including the reason for any failures.

4   Applying GTAF to MNLR

MNLR was proposed for operation in large scale networks. Due to the tedium involved in manually configuring such large testbed networks where different nodes may require different configuration needs, it was decided to develop GTAF. Below are some of the steps involved in MNLR testing and evaluation as applied to GTAF.

1. The test topology shown in Fig. 4, below, was created in the GENI testbed. From this, the manifest RSPEC file is generated once resources were requested.

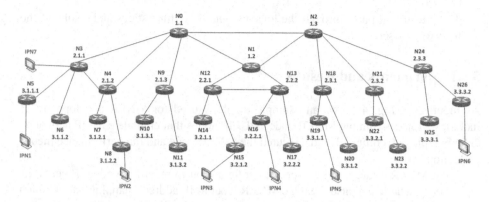

Fig. 4. 27 node topology configured using the automation framework to run MNLR

2. The manifest RSPEC (.xml) file containing the topology information is provided as input to GTAF.

3. The Auto Parser extracts all node information and saves it in a dictionary for later usage. The dictionary uses the node names as a key and their corresponding information as its values. An example is provided below:

   u'node-5': ('pc4.instageni.ku.gpeni.net', '34368', u'interface-8', u'interface-23', u'10.10.5.1', u'10.10.12.2')

   In this example, node-5 is the name of the node, 'pc4.instageni.ku.gpeni.net' is the corresponding hostname, and 34368 is the port number. This node has two interfaces, 8 and 23, whose corresponding interface IP addresses were assigned as 10.10.5.1 and 10.10.12.2.

4. GTAF copies the latest updated MNLR code from its GitHub repository to all the nodes in the topology beginning with 'N' since those are MNLR nodes. 'IP' nodes are IP edge nodes and do not require MNLR code. The Continuous Integration module internally uses SCP (file transfer utility) to take care of the process.

5. The Compilation and Error Checking module compiles the MNLR code on all MNLR nodes and checks for any errors. Simple errors, including stray or duplicate files are handled by the framework. If the system is unable to fix the errors, it emails the user with the appropriate error information.

6. The MNLR protocol requires input command line parameters to execute the code. For example, "./run -T 1.1 -N 1" triggers the code in one of the nodes. In this case, the label is '1.1' and '-N' denotes the type of node, which indicates a core node. An example for an edge node command is/**run -T 2.1.1 -N 0 10.10.13.2 24 eth1.** In this example, **2.1.1** is the label, and the type of the node is **'0'**, which denotes that the node is an edge node, thus requiring two additional parameters - the IP address and the interface. All of these commands are generated and executed by the Protocol Test Suite module with the aid of a user input file containing all label assignments. Future work includes auto label assignment for Tier 2 and below.

7. Once the topology is stable, the Protocol Test Suite module triggers a series of tests executed in sequential order and consolidates the final status of each test that ran.

The parser will parse through the logs and email the final status and results of the tests to the user.

5 Experiments and Results

As mentioned, Fig. 4 shows an example topology used for MNLR development. It includes 27 nodes running MNLR code and 7 IP nodes that emulate edge IP networks. GTAF deployed, compiled, and executed the MNLR code and ran performance metric collection scripts.

Edge MNLR nodes required special configuration to record the edge IP networks and ports in a table and also the edge MNLR label to IP address mapping, all of which was done using GTAF. A similar topology was created with BGP running in all of the nodes using the Quagga Routing Suite version 0.99.21 [6].

The performance metrics collected were churn rate and routing table sizes. Future GTAF performance metrics collection scripts are planned. Churn rate is the percentage of nodes that updated their routing tables in the event of link or node failure. In the topology in Fig. 4, the link between Node 0 and Node 1 was broken and the resultant churn rate was calculated for both protocols. The routing table sizes and churn rate upon the denoted link failure for BGP and MNLR are shown in Table 4.

Table 4. Performance Metrics BGP vs. MNLR

Metric	BGP	MNLR
Routing table size	29	4 (max)
Churn rate	18/27 (67.7%)	4/27 (14.8%)

6 Conclusions and Future Work

The MNLR protocol discussed in this article is to be demonstrated in large networks with more than 100 routers, which is a typical size in an Autonomous System (AS). When such large networks are created in GENI and demonstrated, the initial effort to setup and configure all the nodes can be very time consuming. The GENI Test Automation Framework presented in this article was written in Python and was used for setting up the MNLR topology for a 27 MNLR node topology and collecting performance metrics.

In all, GTAF took approximately 10 min to deploy, compile, and execute MNLR code in the 27 MNLR nodes in the topology and collect data for two performance metrics. If these tasks were done manually, several hours would have been spent and the potential for operator error would have been quite high.

Future work includes evaluating GTAF for larger network sizes as MNLR continues its development. This article provides insights into the use of such automation tools that can be used by GENI users to setup their test topologies faster. GTAF can eventually be used by all GENI users and will be made available upon project completion. In addition, a larger collection of performance metrics collection scripts will be added, including end to end latency in delivering IP packets and calculating the number of lost packets upon link or node failure, among others.

References

1. BGP Analysis Report. http://bgp.potaroo.net/as6447/. Accessed 10 Jan 2015
2. Nozaki, Y., Tuncer, H., Shenoy, N.: A tiered addressing scheme based on floating cloud internetworking model. In: 12th International Conference on Distributed Computing and Networking, IEEE Sponsored ICDCN Conference Bangalore, January 2011
3. Kethe, P., Golen, E.F., Ragila, S., Shenoy, N.: Modularity in routing – a multi-node label routing protocol. In: IEEE International Conference on High Performance Switching and Routing, 14–17 June 2016
4. GitHub. http://www.github.com
5. iPerf – The Ultimate Speed Test Tool for UDP, BGP, and SCTP. http://www.iperf.fr/
6. Quagga Routing Suite. http://www.nongnu.org/quagga

Computational Security and the Economics of Password Hacking

Kanwalinderjit Gagneja[✉] and Luis G. Jaimes

Florida Polytechnic University, Lakeland, FL 33805, USA
{kgagneja,ljaimes}@flpoly.org

Abstract. Internet Security is a growing issue within the modern world. One of the weakest links in computer security is the use and misuse of passwords. As knowledge and technology becomes more widely spread, the methods of hacking passwords become increasingly easier and more accessible. With so much data being protected by passwords, it is important that these passwords are properly protected and secure. In this paper we present numerous methods of hacking passwords, as well as preventative measures that you can take to prevent your passwords from being stolen or misused. Two new algorithms are presented under the category of brute force and dictionary attack and compared with John the Ripper, Cain & Abel, and HashCat algorithms.

Keywords: Passwords · Hacking · Security · Computers · Password cracking

1 Introduction

For many systems and applications, passwords serve as the last or only line of defense for most of us to protect our private information. Despite this, many people don't take care to keep their passwords secure, out of ignorance or neglect [8]. People often disregard the safety of their passwords, believing that simply having a password is keeping their information and identity safe rather than taking proper measures to ensure the security of their passwords. Additionally, many programs and applications also disregard password security. Poor password storage and unreliable security measures allow malicious users to easily obtain other users' passwords or otherwise get into their accounts [9]. There is a new ransomware attack as of May 2017 that is not letting system admins to sleep, as it has affected Microsoft operating system almost worldwide.

2 Different Cracking Methods

There are a few ways to crack a password. Some simple algorithms such as the brute force method which scrolls through every possible combination of characters. This type of attack tends to take the longest and increases exponentially

© Springer International Publishing AG 2017
R. Doss et al. (Eds.): FNSS 2017, CCIS 759, pp. 30–40, 2017.
DOI: 10.1007/978-3-319-65548-2_3

[14]. A slightly more sophisticated attack is the dictionary attack. Many people use simple words as their password, making the password easy to find with a dictionary.

Similar to the dictionary attack is the rainbow table attack. Instead of using words it directly plugs in the hash of the password. In order to protect accounts, passwords are stored in encrypted hashes, that cannot be reversed [18]. Using a rainbow table means there is no longer a need to convert the password into a hash. It is important to note that for any of these to work the correct hashing algorithm must be used. In many spy movies the hero breaks into a secured location in order to find sensitive information. This idea of breaking in to a place may be a bit extreme, but there are still incidents of important information such as passwords being given out to the wrong people [10]. People tend to help others when a person is having a hard time. If someone calls an office and says That he needs the password to get into the system because he is working on an important project tends to work. Although nowadays businesses are training people so that this does not happen, and they do not get into the trap of social engineering.

How to get the passwords? We have chosen two methods: the dictionary attack and the brute force attack. Both of the methods are programmed and tested based on their usefulness. Both of these methods are written in C language.

2.1   Brute Force Attack

It is understood with the literature survey that brute force attack often takes the longest to find a password. It does, however, go through all the possible combinations. Meaning, if the hashing algorithm being used is correct, the password will be found. For this attack to work, all a person needs is the password hash and the hashing algorithm used to find the said hash [13]. The hash can be obtained by sniffing packets by using either WireShark or Kismet or TcpDump etc. Password hashes can also be saved on the local device. There are a number of programs that can be used to find hashes on the system. Brute force attacks are as straight forward as one can get when cracking passwords. However, if it is important to get the password quickly it may not be the best choice. A well-made dictionary can drastically reduce the time needed for an attack [12].

2.2   Dictionary Attack

Dictionary attacks are a common occurrence these days. Most people do not tend to use passwords which differ more than a few characters. This allows a person to collect passwords from other locations and check them against other outlets. An example of this is if Facebook account of a person is hacked. The hacker can then use that password to try and get into the Instagram account of the victim. Another thing to keep in mind is that most people use common words as a password. With these two facts one can create a file which holds a multitude of words to check against a hash.

Dictionaries for these attacks normally have the most commonly used passwords at the top of the list. Even it is important to note that cracking passwords is a time consuming process. Also a weakness of dictionary attacks is that unlike brute force cracking one may not always get the password [15]. This can be remedied slightly by adding in possible capital letters or number. In a sense the program would use the dynamic nature of brute forcing to enhance the dictionary.

3   How the Code Works

For the brute force and dictionary program the sha-512 hashing algorithm was chosen. An open source library was used for the sha-512 algorithm. This program can be outfitted to run with any hashing algorithm with only a few simple changes in the code. The programs were run on Core i5 6200U/2.3 GHz, 64-bit machine with 8 GB RAM, 256 GB SSD TLC, running with Windows 7 operating system. The program allows for either a dictionary attack or a brute force attack to be chosen with command line arguments. The brute force part of the code is a new algorithm that is written. For the dictionary attack again a new algorithm is written to execute on an exhaustive wordlist that is available freely on the World Wide Web.

3.1   Brute Force Program

The program starts by checking that the -b argument is passed in. If it grabs the next argument, that is the string of characters to check against. This can be any number of characters, but should not see any duplicates. Otherwise the program would be checking certain characters twice and slow down the computation.

The last thing the program takes in is the hash of the password that is being cracked. This is then decoded using a simple function, which takes a string. Where '*WreckIt.exe*' is the program name having many different functions, two of them are named: *bruteForce( )* and *dictionary( )*.

Running the code, the interested reader can test the script by running the following commands. For the Brute Force algorithm execute: WreckIt.exe -b abcdefghijklmnopqrstuvwxyz   5baa61e4c9b93f3f0682250b6cf8331b7ee68fd8   - "password".

It then looks at the first two characters, turning them into the corresponding hex value. The reason for this is that the arguments of the program come in as string literals meaning they would give the wrong value when compared against the computed password hash. After the hex decode process, the hash is then printed on the screen to show the correctness and to show that it is working. After all the setup is complete the code jumps into the actual brute force function. The brute force function takes in four variables: the sha1 context used in the sha512 algorithm, the password hash to check against, the character array of elements to loop through, and a pointer to the final password container. The code is shown in Algorithm 1. This function also returns 0 if the password was found and 1 if it wasn't or something went wrong.

Algorithm 1. Brute force code

---

input : SHA1Context *context, uint8_t passHash[SHA1HashSize], char* elements, char *pass
output: 0 if the password was found and 1 if it wasn't or something went wrong

```
begin
    nope ← 1; i ← 0; passSize ← 1; passSize ← 1;
    fin ← 0
    elementSize ← strlen(elements)
    passSizeMulti ← pow(elementSize, passSize) + (elementSize * (passSize − 1));
    round ← 0;
    uint8_t ← hash[SHA1HashSize]
    maxRounds
      ← pow(elementSize, MAX_PASS_SIZE); +(elementSize * (MAX_PASS_SIZE − 1))
    /* Start the clock to see how long the algorithm takes            */
    time ← clock();
    while i ≠ fin do
        /* Make sure we haven't hit the max password length           */
        if round ≤ maxRounds then
            memset(hash, 0x00, SHA1HashSize * sizeof(uint8_t))
            /* Add another space for characters                       */
        end
        if round = passSizeMulti then
            passSize ← passSize + 1
            /* Calculate where the next letter comes in adds the remaining
               possibilities for the previous password characters      */
            assSizeMulti ← pow(elementSize, passSize) + (elementSize * (passSize − 1))
        end
        /* Fill the password array with the next set of characters Note: */
        /* subtract the current position times the power of elementSize   */
        /* to current position this makes sure the 0 position of elements */
        /* string gets called                                            */
        for r = 1 to passSize do
            pass[i] ← elements[(((round − i * pow(elementSize, i))/pow(elementSize, i));
        end
        round ← round + 1
        /* Calculate the hash of the password                         */
        error ← SHA1Reset(context)
        error ← = SHA1Input(context, pass, passSize)
        error ← = SHA1Result(context, hash)
        if compareHash(passHash, hash) then
            /* Recursive call to continue testing combinations        */
            nope ← 0
            fin ← 1
        end
    end
    /* Stop the clock and print the time                             */
    time ← clock() - time
    return nope;
end
```

Initially the variables are setup at the start of the function. A clock is also setup to see how long it takes to setup just before entering the main loop. Once the control steps into the main while loop, a check is there to see if the max amount of rounds has been met. The *maxRound* variable is set to 26^(amount of characters in element string). If the program has not hit that condition, then the check for the increase in password length is run, after the *maxRound* has been checked against the password length is determined.

If the current pass is equal to the next step, the first being calculated in the variable setup, then the password size to check is increased by one and the next step is recalculated. Each step is calculated by taking the number of elements to the power of the password size. It is important to note that the number of elements multiplied by the size of the password minus one must be added to ensure all possibilities are checked for the password. Once this step completes it is time to fill in the password.

To find the next password to check against, a for loop is used to loop through the length of the password. For this algorithm the modulus is used against the number of elements to loop through the list of elements. The mathematics involved is shown in Algorithm 1, but it is important to note however that (round − 1) is used so the zero position of the element array is used.

The last few steps of the code are calling the respective functions in the sha-512 library to hash the password and to return the password if it was found. In this case a sha-512 context is reset to the original values. Using the reset context the password is then loaded in with the input function, and the result is grabbed using the result function. When the brute force is done it prints out how much time it took to find the password and the correct password.

3.2   Comparison with Existing Algorithms

The real question is if this algorithm is good enough to stand up to the competition. For comparison three programs are chosen "John the Ripper", "Cain & Abel", and "Hashcat". These program were chosen because many security geeks suggest that these three programs can generate multiple types of attacks, similar to the program that was created. After testing a few passwords, it was clear which program was better. For the password 'password' it took "John the Ripper" and "Cain & Abel" a little less than a second on its increment setting, "Hashcat" took a bit over a second. On the other hand, our program took a little over half a second as shown in Table 1.

Table 1. Comparison with existing Algorithms

Algorithm	John the Ripper	Cain & Abel	Hashcat	Ours
Time taken to crack password	$\approx 1\,s$	$\approx 1\,s$	$> s$	$> 0.5\,s$

3.3   Dictionary Attack Code

The algorithm for dictionary attack is shown in Algorithm 2. The dictionary attack is a much simpler program when compared to the brute force attack program. Only one difference exists in the arguments for the dictionary attack compared to the brute force. Instead of the elements string being passed in, a path to the password dictionary is taken in. For the matter of opening the dictionary file and then checking the hashed word that is taken in from the file. The following are the instruction on how to run this algorithm. The instructions to run the Algorithm 2, namely the dictionary attack, are as follows: This algorithm takes in only one extra argument: sha256 password hash. Example: WreckIt.exe -d 5baa61e4c9b93f3f0682250b6cf8331b7ee68fd8 - "password"/ Note: This attack looks for the word in the local directory called 'wordlist.txt'.

Algorithm 2. Dictionary attack code

```
input  : SHA1Context *context, uint8_t passHash[SHA1HashSize], char *pass, char
         *path
output: 0 if the password was found and 1 if it wasn't or something went wrong

begin
   FILE *dictionary ← fopen(path, "r")
   uint8hash[SHA1HashSize]
   memset(hash, 0x00, SHA1HashSize*sizeof(uint8))
   nope ← 1; i ← 0; fin ← 0;
   /* Start the clock to see how long the algorithm takes          */
   time ← clock()
   while i ≠ fin do
      memset(pass, 0x00, MAX_PASS_SIZE*sizeof(char))
      if fgets(pass, MAX_PASS_SIZE, dictionary) ≠ NULL then
         length ← strlen(pass)
         pass[length - 1] ← 0x00
         /* Calculate the hash of the password                     */
         SHA1Reset(context)
         SHA1Input(context, pass, strlen(pass))
         SHA1Result(context, hash)
      end
      if compareHash(passHash, hash)) then
         fin ← 1
         nope ← 0
      end
   end
   /* Stop the clock and print the time                            */
   time ← clock() - time
   print time
   return nope;
end
```

This code performed at an almost identical speed to "John the Ripper" and "Cain & Abel", however, faster than "HashCat". The reason that this code executed at the same speed as "John the Ripper" and "Cain & Abel" is because of the way the comparing of hashes is programmed. Therefore, these programs have added to the security world. However, it is important to look at the past algorithms and try new things because security systems grow as attacks get more advanced.

4 Big Hacks in History

In the beginning of the Internet, security was not the focus. The idea of world-wide knowledge overshadowed any thoughts of people using the Internet for harm. This began to change in the years after the Internet started to become more widely used [2,4]. There are multiple key management schemes for secure communication [3,5,6].

However, security breaches still happen. One of the earliest large scale breaches happened to AOL. An employee stole on-line identities and emails of many people and sold them [1]. In 2007 hackers got into a T.J. Maxx WiFi network and stole data from no less than 45.7 million people [7]. This size of an attack is often hard for people to fathom. It hits especially hard when people think that their credit card information should be safe when using them at trust worthy stores.

One of the biggest credit card hacks in the history happened to a payment processing firm called Heartland Payment Systems [11]. It was estimated that 130 million accounts were compromised, and Heartland ended up paying $110 million to Visa, MasterCard, American Express, and other card associations.

5   Preventative Measures

One of the most important reasons to know about the entire aforementioned password hacking techniques is that you can recognize them in order to combat them. Being able to recognize an attempt to steal your passwords allows you to take proper measures to protect your data and prevent the attack from succeeding. If you manage a server or a network, this is even more important because you are responsible for the security of everyone using your server or network.

5.1   Dictionary and Brute Force Attack

Dictionary and brute force attacks are some of the more simple types of hacking passwords, and as such they can normally be deterred just by making strong, difficult to guess passwords.

The dictionary attacks attempt to figure out passwords by guessing many common words and overused passwords. Simply using strange or uncommon passwords is one of the greatest preventative measures you can take to prevent them from being stolen. Avoid predictable passwords like your birthday or the birthday of someone you know, common sequences of letters or numbers like "12345" and "qwerty", words that can be found in a dictionary, or any personal information about you (such as your name, hometown, name of your relative, high school attended, etc.) that can be taken from social media sites.

Another way to prevent these attacks is to use a mix of letters, numbers, and symbols. Randomly capitalizing letters in your password and placing numbers and symbols through out make it nearly impossible to hack using a dictionary attack.

Brute force attacks are even easier to prevent than dictionary attacks. The biggest deterrent to potential brute force attacks is a long password. A password containing seven lowercase letters can be hacked by a brute force attack in two hours, whereas adding just one more letter increases the time it takes to two days. By simply making your password longer than ten characters, you increase the time it takes to brute force your password by orders of centuries.

Because brute force attacks run through every combination of characters possible in your password, the actual content of your password is not as important to its security as with dictionary attacks. Despite this, using a mix of capital and lowercase letters, numbers, and symbols prevents hackers from narrowing down the possible characters they need to try, which delays or deters their attempts to hack it in this fashion. For example, an eight-character password containing only lowercase letters can be hacked by brute force in two days an eight character password containing all possible characters, including numbers and symbols, takes two centuries to hack in this fashion.

For server and network managers, detecting and preventing dictionary and brute force attacks can be made easy with a few security measures. Both of these types of attacks involve rapidly trying different passwords until one succeeds. By only allowing a certain amount of failed attempts before locking the account, you can deter these types of attacks from happening. Additionally, monitoring the login attempts can reveal these types of attacks as sudden spikes in attempted logins within short periods of time.

5.2   Phishing Attacks

The best way to prevent phishing attacks is to learn how to spot them. Never send passwords over e-mail or click on suspicious links. Be wary of fake websites that are meant to resemble a more trusted website. Most importantly, remember that these types of attacks exist, and be cautious every time a company or website requests any of your information via e-mail.

5.3   Keyloggers

The keylogger is very sophisticated method of hacking passwords. The user does not even know that keylogger software is running on their machine. The presence of keylogger on your machine is hard to identify. To prevent having a key logging application installed on your computer, avoid clicking untrustworthy links or downloading suspicious documents or data. For physical keyloggers, keep the ports of your computers/servers secure and prevent unauthorized access to your systems. Unfortunately, once a keylogger is on your computer it becomes very undetectable. Many keylogging applications disguise themselves as useful or otherwise beneficial programs and files. It is far more efficient to prevent this type of hacking before it begins than it is to try and fix it.

5.4   Social Engineering

One of the biggest threats to password security is the repeated use of passwords. By using the same password for a multitude of websites, users allow hackers to gain access to all of their data at once. Hackers will often try to hack a password for a user on a smaller and less secure website and then use that password to gain access to all of the other accounts of the same user on more secure sites.

In addition to reusing the same passwords for many different accounts, users also put their data in danger when they do not change their passwords often. Changing your passwords every few months prevents hackers from having long-term access to your information and makes them go through the effort of hacking your password more than once. For added security, when changing your passwords do not reuse passwords that you have used recently. Keeping your data safe involves keeping the hackers guessing. For companies that have large networks and servers that they must keep track of, social engineering can prove to be very dangerous to their data security. To prevent hacking via social engineering, make sure that only those with proper authentication can access your network/servers. Prevent employees or others from freely giving access to your accounts and data and have proper measures in place for granting and checking authentication. Most importantly, prevent anyone associated with the company from freely sharing their passwords, using easy to hack passwords, or writing their passwords down in accessible locations (particularly on sticky notes).

5.5   Application Security

Many modern programs and applications do not take password security seriously, and as such passwords may be vulnerable through no fault of the user. Applications that allow passwords to be stored for login convenience should keep the stored passwords protected–some applications merely store them as plaintext files in poorly hidden locations on the computers they run on. Username and password combinations should be encrypted with modern encryption algorithms and stored in safe locations on their relevant computers or servers.

6   The Future of Password Hacking

Due to the convenience and security, it is likely that we will continue using passwords in our computer systems. However, as technology becomes more advanced, it is becoming increasingly more important for both users and companies to take password security seriously [17]. Already, many websites and services require passwords to include capital letters and numbers. As technology becomes faster and faster and simple hacking techniques (such as brute force and dictionary attacks) become more widespread and powerful, it is likely that our passwords will become longer and more complex as a countermeasure. Many programs might also force passwords to be changed more often, and they might force new passwords to be completely different from the old ones.

For the hackers themselves, many different methods of stealing passwords are becoming available as technology improves [16]. Improved hacking techniques are being discovered, leading to more powerful hacking techniques such as rainbow attacks. Many technological conveniences, such as browser cookies that store passwords for easy logins, are now being stolen or exploited by hackers who know how to access them.

As passwords are becoming more difficult to maintain and keep secure, programs are being developed to manage password security. Programs such as Password Safe allow for convenient management of passwords whilst still being secure.

7   Conclusions

By researching the different ways passwords can be hacked in depth, this paper prepares users against these types of attacks. On the other hand, computer hackers and malicious users are going to be always around with constantly evolving technology and posing new challenges to security. We all know that there is no silver bullet for 100% security and each user should be given the freedom to choose what they want their passwords to be when it comes to their own security. However, this paper presents the knowledge of how to prevent and counteract these attacks if we ever encounter a situation where we have to manage a network or server, or if we find ourselves being hacked. In this paper we present various methods of hacking passwords that everyone should be careful about. This paper also presents preventative measures that you can take to avoid your passwords from being stolen. Two new algorithms under the categories; brute force and dictionary attack are written and compared with 'John the Ripper', 'Cain & Abel', and 'HashCat' algorithms. In future we plan on comparing it with biometric based authentication schemes.

References

1. Beaver, K.: Hacking for Dummies. Wiley, Somerset (2012). ProQuest elibrary. Accessed 6 Mar 2016
2. Gagneja, K.K.: Secure Communication Scheme for Wireless Sensor Networks to maintain Anonymity. IEEE ICNC, Anaheim (2015)
3. Gagneja, K.K., Nygard, K.: Energy efficient approach with integrated key management scheme for wireless sensor networks. In: ACM MOBIHOC, Bangalore, India, pp. 13–18, 29 July 2013
4. Gagneja, K.K., Nygard, K.: Heuristic clustering with secured routing in heterogeneous sensor networks. In: IEEE SECON, New Orleans, USA, pp. 9–16, 24–26 June 2013
5. Gagneja, K.K., Nygard, K.: Pairwise post deployment key management scheme for heterogeneous sensor networks. In: 13th IEEE WoWMoM 2012, San Francisco, California, USA, pp. 1–2, 25–28 June 2012
6. Gagneja, K.K., Nygard, K.: Key management scheme for routing in clustered heterogeneous sensor networks. In: IEEE NTMS 2012, Security Track, Istanbul, Turkey, pp. 1–5, 7–10 May 2012
7. Gagneja, K.K.: Knowing the ransomware and building defense against it - specific to health care institutes. In: IEEE MobiSecServ, Miami, USA, February 2017
8. Jewell, M.T.J.: Maxx Theft Believed Largest Hack Ever, March 2007 www. nbcnews.com. Accessed 07 March 2016
9. Gagneja, K.K.: Global perspective of security breaches in facebook. In: FECS, Las Vegas, USA, 21–24 July 2014

10. Evanoff, L., Hatch, N., Gagneja, K.K.: Home network security: beginner vs advanced. In: ICWN, Las Vegas, USA, 27–30 July 2015
11. Gagneja, K.K., Nygard, K.: A QoS based heuristics for clustering in two-tier sensor networks. In: IEEE FedCSIS, Wroclaw, Poland, pp. 779–784, 9–12 September 2012
12. McCandless, D.: Ideas, issues, knowledge, data - visualized! (2016). http://www. informationisbeautiful.net/visualizations/worlds-biggest-data-breaches-hacks/. Accessed 07 Mar 2016
13. Pepitone, J.: Massive' credit card data breach involves all major brand, April 2012. http://money.cnn.com/2012/03/30/technology/credit-card-data-breach/ index.htm. Accessed 07 Mar 2016
14. Gagneja, K.K.: Pairwise key distribution scheme for two-tier sensor networks. In: IEEE ICNC, Honolulu, Hawaii, USA, pp. 1081–1086, 3–6 February 2014
15. John, P.: How I'd Hack Your Weak Passwords, December 2010. lifehacker.com. Accessed 6 Mar 2016
16. Arvinderpal, S., Gagneja, K.K.: Incident response through behavioral science: an industrial approach. In: IEEE CSCI, LasVegas, USA, 7–9 December 2015
17. University Alliance. Experts' View of the Future of Passwords. Villanova University (2016). https://www.villanovau.com/resources/iss/experts-view-password-security-future/#.WXAQOoTyvIU. Accessed 6 Mar 2016
18. Davey, W.: Top Ten Password Cracking Techniques, 2 December 2011. http:// www.alphr.com/features/371158/top-ten-password-cracking-techniques. Accessed 6 Mar 2016

Security Protocols and Attack Countermeasures

DNS DDoS Mitigation,
via DNS Timer Design Changes

Todd Booth$^{(\boxtimes)}$ ⓘ and Karl Andersson ⓘ

Division of Computer Science, Luleå University of Technology, 97187 Luleå, Sweden
Research@ToddBooth.Com, Karl.Andersson@Ltu.Se

Abstract. DDoS attacks have been a problem since 2000. In October 2016, there was a major DDoS attack against the service provider Dyn's DNS service, which took the service down. This was one of the largest bandwidth DDoS attack ever documented, with attack bandwidth over 650 Gbps. By taking down just Dyn's DNS service, clients could not obtain the IP addresses, of the organizations hosting their DNS with Dyn, such as Twitter. Our contribution is that we have found a way to mitigate the effect of DDoS attacks against DNS services. We only require some very small algorithm changes, in the DNS protocol. More specifically, we propose to add two additional timers. Even if the end DNS clients don't support these timers, they will receive our new functionality via the DNS resolvers and recursive servers. In summary, our contributions give much more control to the organizations, as to under which specific conditions the DNS cache entries should be aged or used. This allows the organization to (1) much more quickly expire client DNS caches and (2) to mitigate the DDoS DNS attack effects. Our contributions are also helpful to organizations, even if there are no DDoS DNS attack.

Keywords: DDoS bandwidth · DNS protocol · Dyn DNS hosting · Design guidelines · Information Systems

1 Introduction

Our focus is to mitigate Distributed Denial of Service (DDoS) attacks against Domain Name System (DNS) servers. DNS servers are an essential component of ICT based Information Systems. By Information Systems, we are using the category definition of, "Technology View", as defined in [3]. Our case study is concerning a Web (including Web application) service. Web servers are the most popular type of public Internet servers, in "Technology View" based Information Systems. Less common public Internet Information System servers are email and database servers, however even email services are sometimes accessible via Web servers. We have made progress to mitigate these attacks.

1.1 Background

For computer networking, the DNS service is used to translate between symbolic names and IP addresses. The DNS hierarchy levels are shown Fig. 1 [25].

© Springer International Publishing AG 2017
R. Doss et al. (Eds.): FNSS 2017, CCIS 759, pp. 43–55, 2017.
DOI: 10.1007/978-3-319-65548-2_4

Here is a simplified example, showing how DNS works. To access Twitter via a Web browser, you type in the URL, such as https://Twitter.Com. Your browser then makes a request to the operating system to resolve the symbolic name (Twitter.Com) and returns an

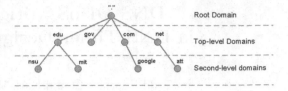

Fig. 1. Summary of DNS hierarchy

IP address. The operating system will already have one or more DNS servers configured (perhaps manually and perhaps automatically via Dynamic Host Control Protocol (DHCP)).

One way or another you should get the relevant IP address. However, if the DNS service is under attack, you might not get an answer at all. The DNS name to IP address resolution process is shown in Fig. 2.

There are many diverse types of network attacks which are intended to decrease the availability of services. One common type is a DDoS attack. DDoS attacks are easy to perform and are difficult to defend against. There are malicious companies who charge a service fee and then perform a DDoS attack, on your behalf. A general DDoS attack strategy, based on a Botnet is shown in Fig. 3.

The term Botnet comes from robot and network. A Botnet is a large group of computers, which are under the command and control of the Botnet owner. For a malicious Botnet, the machines were often exposed to Malware. These

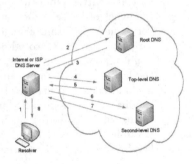

Fig. 2. DNS name to IP address resolution

Botnets are often a collection of thousands (or even hundreds of thousands) of machines. Botnet owners can use the machines to perform a coordinated DDoS attack.

DDoS attacks can render DNS and other online services unavailable [24]. If the attacks are successful against DNS servers, then clients will be unable to obtain the IP address of the intended online service.

1.2 Motivation

Dyn is a DNS hosting provider to thousands of different organizations. For example, Twitter uses Dyn for their DNS hosting. We will refer to Twitter as our case study. Twitter has 313 million monthly active users and one billion unique visits to sites with embedded tweets [20]. There was a successful DDoS attack against Dyn in October 2016, and therefore Twitter became unavailable to many of their customers [1].

Once Dyn's DNS servers were no longer fully
available, no user could contact several Internet
Services, such as Twitter. The problem was that
Twitter's customers tried to perform a symbolic
DNS name to IP address translation, but they
never received a valid answer. For example, when
users asked for the IP address corresponding to
Twitter.com, they did not receive an answer. This
caused Dyn's DNS hosting customers, including Twitter, to become unavailable, even though

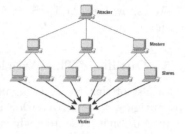

Fig. 3. General DDoS attack

Twitter's Web servers were up and running. If there were adequate easy to
implement DNS DDoS defenses, this Dyn DDoS DNS attack should not have
occurred.

The research community has provided many general DDoS solutions, but
we were unable to find any DNS specific design guidelines and DNS protocol
changes, which would mitigate the DDoS DNS attacks. So, our contribution is
to find minor DNS protocol changes, which can be used to mitigate DNS DDoS
attacks.

1.3   General Related Work

A brief mention of the more general related work follows: In [28], S. Zargar et al.
provides a Taxonomy of DDoS Defenses. In [1], V. Almodia, et al. discuss DDoS
and cyberwarfare. In [29], K. Zeb et al. provides a survey of DDoS attacks and
defenses in cyberspace. In [19], R. Soni et al. provides a summary, concerning
security in the public clouds.

1.4   Contributions

We believe that part of the problem is that many companies do not have the
appropriate security knowledge to defend against some types of DNS DDoS
attacks and we'll discuss our related contribution in this paper.

With our TTL2 contribution, we allow DNS authoritative server administrators to have much control over the actual TTL at the DNS resolvers, recursive
servers, and clients. With our TTL3 contribution, we allow DNS authoritative
server administrators to have much better control over the actual DNS cache
timeout, at the DNS resolvers, recursive DNS servers and clients. Even when
the end client does not support our TTL2/3 timers, we show how the intermediate DNS resolvers and recursive servers can automatically provide enhanced
DNS timer functionality, with no changes to the end client. A summary of our
specific contributions is the following:

1. We propose best practices, which can mitigate some types of DNS DDoS
   attacks
2. Our proposed DNS TTL2 protocol enhancement
3. Our proposed DNS TTL3 protocol enhancement

4. We show how the DNS clients can take advantage of our enhancements with no changes

1.5   Outline of This Article

The rest of this article is organized as follows. In Sect. 2, our design guidelines to mitigate some DNS DDoS attacks is presented. In Sect. 3, our DNS TTL2 contribution is presented, which allows better control of the DNS TTL. In Sect. 4, our DNS TTL3 contribution is presented, which allows better control over DNS caching. In Sect. 5, we cover the related work (which had not been mentioned previously). We wrap it up, with our conclusions and recommended future work, in Sect. 6.

2   Contribution 1 - Design Guidelines

Without making any changes to the DNS protocol, it is quite easy to mitigate some types of DNS DDoS attacks. We're using Dyn and Twitter, as our case study, so let's evaluate the recent Nov. 2016 Dyn attack, that effected Twitter [1]. A summary of the relevant DNS structure for Twitter, follows:

1. DNS root servers
2. DNS TLD servers, including the .Com TLD servers
3. DNS Twitter.Com servers (which were Dyn servers, since Twitter was hosting their DNS at Dyn)

The attack was not against the DNS root or TLD servers, so we can ignore them for the moment. We know the attack was against the Dyn DNS hosting provider, but it affected Twitter. However, was the attack specifically against Twitter. Keep in mind, Dyn hosts DNS for thousands of organizations. Therefore, we should not assume that the attack was specifically against Twitter. Likewise, we should not assume that the attack was specifically against Dyn. The attack could very well have been against just one of Dyn's DNS hosting customers, but not against Twitter.

To simplify the conditions under which our contribution is helpful, let's simplify the case study, as follows: Dyn was hosting DNS for 1,000 organizations. The November attack was against one organization, which was not Twitter. We'll assume that the attacked organization's domain name was, Under-attack.com.

So Dyn's own DNS servers were hosting for Under-attack.com, Twitter.com, and 998 other organizations. When the attack started against Under-attack.com, as a by-product, Dyn's DNS servers were attacked, which meant that they were not 100% available, for their other DNS hosted customers. So, since Twitter was DNS hosted on the same exact Dyn DNS servers, Twitter was also affected.

Our design guideline contributions are that Twitter should have developed a script ahead of time, to deal with this potential vulnerability. The first step is that Twitter should have developed a simple Linux script, which would simply do the following: Make simple DNS requests against all of Twitter's DNS servers, which were hosted at Dyn. The script should measure DNS resolution availability. When the availability dropped below 100%, the following should have been performed: The script should have automatically made a configuration change at the .Com servers, and removed the specific Dyn hosted Twitter DNS servers, which were not at 100% availability. The script should have also immediately enabled DNS hosting at another DNS hosting provider, such as Microsoft, Google, etc. The accounts should have been enabled ahead of time. Under certain conditions, Twitter could have simply moved all DNS hosting to some other provider. With this simple script, Twitter would have only been off-line for a short amount of time for new customers. All the other 998 customers could have run a similar script to greatly mitigate the DNS availability issues for their domains.

If you are considering scripts, we recommend that you check our Google's DNS hosting over HTTPS RESTful JSON API [10]. To learn about OpenDNS's related offering, we refer you to [15] and to [9].

3   Contribution 2 - Anti-DDoS Timer TTL2

Some relevant background on DNS timers is now in order. A summary of the DNS process is found in Fig. 4.

DNS server records include what is called a TTL (time to live). The TTL field is in seconds. Let's assume the TTL for the Twitter's main web page is set for 1 h (3600 s). One might think that after 1 h, clients will try to contact their DNS server, to get a new copy of the DNS record. However, end user DNS clients almost never would contact Twitter's authoritative DNS servers directly (at least far less than 0.01% of the time). As shown in Fig. 4, clients will contact intermediate caches, resolvers, and recursive servers to resolve the symbolic to IP address translation.

We'll provide an example of how the actual TTL does not provide all the control, that we may wish to have (at least not as we might expect), by the end client. We include the logic showing that our TTL2 feature is superior.

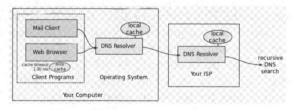

Fig. 4. Summary of DNS process

Time 0, 10:00: Client 1's Web application requests the Twitter.com name to IP address resolution. The answer is not found on the client 1's cache, so the client 1 asks its DNS server, which is ISP 1's recursive DNS server 2, for the answer. DNS server 2 gets the answer from the authoritative server and delivers the answer to client 1, at 10:00:10.

Time 1, 10:01: The server changes its DNS record entry for Twitter.com. The above issues become a big problem, as related to DNS DDoS attacks. I.E., after a DNS DDoS attack, the authoritative server may wish to change their DNS records. However, the authoritative server cannot fully control when all clients will timeout their TTL, due to the above specific DNS design limitation.

Time 2, 10:30: Client 1's Web application requests the Twitter.com resolution again. Client 1 finds the answer in its cache. It should be noted that this is a design limitation of DNS, in its current design.

Time 3, 10:59: Client 2's Web application requests the Twitter.com resolution. The answer is not found on the client 2's cache, and client 2 is using the same ISP recursive DNS server 2. So client 2 asks its DNS server, which is ISP 1's recursive DNS server 2, for the answer. ISP 1's recursive DNS server 2 has the answer cached, due to client 1's previous request. So ISP 1's recursive DNS server 2 provides the cached answer to client 2, at 10:59:10. However, that entry is no longer valid (as of 10:01).

Time 4, 11:58: Client 2's Web application again requests the Twitter.com resolution. The answer is found in client 2's cache (received at 10:59:10). It has only been 59 min since client 2 received the answer, so the cache entry will be used. However, this entry was configured as invalid by the authoritative DNS server at 10:01. This is also the intended design, that clients may lose access (in this case) for up to one hour plus one hour times the number of hops, due to this caching issue. There was one hop, so the current DNS design is that those clients can lose access for up to two hours. The issue is that the DNS zone administrators have no control over this issue, which we will now solve.

As a contribution, we propose some small changes to the DNS protocol, to mitigate this problem. We propose to continue to use the TTL, as is done today. We propose to add a new field, called TTL2. TTL works as today, where the TTL is only based on when the downstream DNS server or client received the TTL. Our proposed TTL2 is a timer, which decreases based on when the very first DNS server received the record, from the authoritative server. So, our TTL2 should be considered as an absolute timer, based on only when the authoritative server sent the record. Let's assume that Twitter sets the TTL timer to 5 min and sets the TTL2 timer to 150% times TTL, or to 7.5 min.

Here is how our proposed downstream DNS sever works, concerning the TTL2 field. Let's suppose the downstream DNS server receives a request, and forwards the DNS record to client 1. As this time, client 1 would receive the DNS record with TTL set to 5 min and TTL2 set to 7.5 min. Let's assume that 4 min later, client 2 asks for the same record. The recursive DNS server would serve this from its cache. However, the DNS server would change the TTL2 from 7.5 to 3.5 (subtract the time that passed, which was four minutes). Client 2 would receive the DNS record with TTL set to 5 min and TTL2 set to 3.5 min. With this TTL2 record, client 2 would know it should perform a new DNS request after just 3.5 min. With our solution, it does not matter how many DNS servers (supporting TTL2) are between the original server and the end clients. The clients can always ask for a new record after TTL2 expires, which is independent of the number of intermediate DNS routers. Even if the authoritative DNS server or a downstream DNS server does not support TTL2, any downstream DNS server could also assign 150% (or whatever they are configured to do by default) to TTL2. Our TTL2 mitigates DNS DDoS attacks by allowing the DNS owner to have much stronger control, as to when the caches expire.

Let's now assume that the client does not support TTL2. As long as any upstream DNS resolver or server supports TTL2, they could properly answer the client, with their adjusted original TTL value.

4   Contribution 3 - Anti-DDoS Timer TTL3

However, there is another major limitation with DNS, concerning DDoS attacks. Let's suppose all of Twitter's customers have a cache DNS entry of Twitter's main site. Then Dyn's DNS service becomes unavailable for a few hours (longer than the TTL or TTL2). Then Dyn can no longer serve DNS records to their clients, since the DDoS attack reduces their availability. Since the client's TTL and TTL2 have expired, they will not use the stale DNS cache record. The client will not use the stale cache and has no access to the DNS service (which is down). Even with stale DNS caches, the clients no longer have access to Twitter.

As another contribution, we propose a slight change to the DNS protocol, to mitigate this specific DDoS problem. So, we propose a new field TTL3 which is also a timer. We call it the DNS service down field, meaning that Twitter can configure how long their DNS might be offline (DDoS attack or not), under which time, the clients and DNS server are specifically instructed to keep using their cache entries.

We'll provide an example of how the actual TTL does not provide all the control, that we may wish to have (at least not as we might expect), by the end client. We include the logic showing that our TTL3 feature is superior.

Time 0, 10:00: Client 1's Web application requests the Twitter.com name to IP address resolution. The answer is not found on the client 1's cache, so the client 1 asks its DNS server, which is ISP 1's recursive DNS server 2, for the answer. DNS server 2 gets the answer from the authoritative server and delivers the answer to client 1, at 10:00:10.

Time 1, 10:01: The server changes its DNS record entry for Twitter.com. The above issues become a big problem, as related to DNS DDoS attacks. I.E., after a DNS DDoS attack, the authoritative server may wish to change their DNS records. However, the authoritative server cannot fully control when all clients will timeout their TTL, due to the above specific DNS design limitation.

Time 2, 10:30: Client 1's Web application requests the Twitter.com resolution again. Client 1 finds the answer in its cache. However, client 1's cache entry has been invalid since 10:01. It should be noted that this is a design limitation of DNS, in its current design.

Time 3, 10:59: Client 2's Web application requests the Twitter.com resolution. The answer is not found on the client 2's cache, and client 2 is using the same ISP recursive DNS server 2. Client 2 asks its DNS server, which is ISP 1's recursive DNS server 2, for the answer. ISP 1's recursive DNS server 2 has the answer cached, due to client 1's previous request. ISP 1's recursive DNS server

2 provides the cached answer to client 2, at 10:59:10. However, that entry is no longer valid (as of 10:01).

Time 4, 11:58: Client 2's Web application again requests the Twitter.com resolution. The answer is found in client 2's cache (received at 10:59:10). It has only been 59 min since client 2 received the answer, so the cache entry will be used. However, this entry was configured as invalid by the authoritative DNS server at 10:01. This is also the intended design, that clients may lose access (in this case) for up to one hour plus one hour times the number of hops, due to this caching issue. There was one hop, so the current DNS design is that those clients can lose access for up to two hours. The issue is that the DNS zone administrators have no control over this issue, which we will now solve.

Well provide an example of how the actual TTL is not obeyed (at least not as we might expect), by the end client

Assume that Twitter wants to allow clients who have accessed their site during the past week, to continue to use their DNS cache for at least one more week. Twitter would then set the TTL3 to two weeks. The reason for two weeks instead of one week is the following. A client might have accessed Twitter's site six days ago. However, Twitter wants them to continue to use their cache for at least one week. If the TTL3 was set to one week, this client would stop using their cache after just one day. Now, after the cache times out, it would look at its TTL3 timer, and would then continue to use its cache entry (for at least one week).

Let's now assume that the client does not support TTL3. As long as any upstream DNS resolver or server supports TTL3, they could properly answer the client, with their stale cache entry. We found that OpenDNS has a similar proprietary solution, which only works on their servers and has other limitations [15].

5   Related Work

Our literature review search initially focused on the more recent DDoS papers, published in 2014 or after. This research topic is well developed. Here are the number of hits, via a few DDoS searches: Via Semantic Scholar, we had 3,352 hits (filtered by just Computer Science). Via Scopus, we had 967 hits (filtered by just Computer Science). Via Web of Science, we had 658 hits (filtered by just Computer Science), which included three sub-categories. We reviewed papers with a higher number of citations, and papers which were more influential. This literature review helped us in this and other papers.

For this article, we then moved back and forth, after reviewing the references and which other papers cited these papers. Some of the more relevant papers follow, with our comments.

5.1   Our Related Work

When we discuss the following works, we will first present the work, as presented by the original authors. When we add our comments, we will precede our viewpoints with the following, **"Our Comments:"**. A few of our own papers, which are related to this article and which we build upon follow:

1. In [4], we (Booth and Andersson) introduced ways to strongly mitigate DDoS reflection attacks. Again, our technique was based on micro-segmentation, and protocol/port firewall rule-sets. The destination IP/protocol/Port was fixed. **Our New Comments:** This previous paper was a general solution, and to address DDoS (in general). However, it did not take into account the specific DNS protocol. In this article, we carefully analyzed the DNS protocol and found better specific mitigations solutions for just DNS DDoS attacks.

2. In [5], we (Booth and Andersson) continue our previous work, but extend the defense to all 3/4/7 network attacks and discuss how to defend against each specific attack. One method is to hide the service behind unique URLs. It is shown how to hide servers behind secret URLs, where a client must be authenticated, to obtain the secret URL. If there is an attack against any URL, we know exactly which client has leaked the information. **Our New Comments:** This article is similar, but focused only on DNS service DDoS attacks. Therefore, we covered numerous specific DNS DDoS attacks and DNS specific protocol change mitigation techniques were provided.

5.2   Other Related Work

We now present other related work to show:

1. How we have accepted previous knowledge
2. How we build upon that knowledge
3. We provide limited comments, concerning the related works

Also, we widened the scope of our literature review to include DDoS related papers, which were not specifically concerning DDoS DNS attacks in order to gain a stronger general theoretical background.

In [21], S. Venkatesan et al., replaced the active public IP addresses on an hourly basis to mitigate the DDoS effect of attacks. In [2], A. Aydeger et al., also performed this moving target strategy, but took advantage of SDN. In [23], H. Want et al., also propose to conceal the address changes from clients, in order to determine which clients are malicious. **Our Comments:** We really like the idea of dynamic change of IP address and these authors have provided great contributions. However, we have two issues against the hourly specific strategy. Since they change the addresses on an hourly basis, either (1) there was no attack and they changed the address too early, or (2) there was an attack earlier, and they waited too long, before changing the address. So, we suggest that the IP address is simply changed only upon attack, and immediately after the attack. SDN simply provides a more efficient solution to a non-SDN solution, which can at times be very helpful. If the reader is interested in SDN, we recommend reviewing [7], Esch, J., to see how SDN can help. Also, in [11], Lim, S. et al. has a lot of specific information as to how SDN can be used to detect and prevent DDoS attacks.

In [27], S. Yu et al. attempt to mitigate DDoS attacks via filtering inline traffic. **Our Comments:** Filtering inline is a good strategy when the DDoS attack bandwidth is low.

In [8], S. Fay et al. tries to mitigate DDoS attacks via scaling up, based on the attack traffic level. **Our Comments:** This is a good strategy to defeat DDoS attacks. However, we must point out that to scale up in the cloud after an attack, often does incur significant charges. These charges can be extremely high, depending on the strength of the attack. So, we recommend that limits are configured, so that the organization is not surprised with a very expensive invoice. To the extent that the limits are reached, then the DDoS attack becomes very successful.

In [11], A. Yaar et al. propose a path identification method, to mitigate DDoS attacks. **Our Comments:** Path identifiers to defeat a DDoS attack are an extremely interesting approach. However, if one can't stop Botnet clients from repeatedly sending massive numbers of requests, requiring traversal via path identifies, we don't see how this will help (however we wish to disclose that we are not yet experts, at DDoS prevention via path identifiers).

In [11], S. Lim et al. propose an SDN solution to defeat DDoS attacks. In [17], R. Sahey et al. also propose DDoS mitigation via SDN. In [14], S. Mousavi et al. propose to use SDN, and to try and prevent inline direct SDN attacks. **Our Comments:** SDN is only a technique for much more efficient and perhaps lower cost networking. Therefore, SDN has the same exact DDoS issues to solve, in general. Having said that, they have done good work at using SDN to mitigate DDoS attacks, in a more efficient way.

In [22], B. Wang et al. propose a DDoS attack mitigation architecture that integrates a highly programmable network monitoring to enable attack detection and a flexible control structure to allow fast and specific attack reaction. **Our Comments:** For the DDoS general case, they have done good work. However, our work was a bit more focused, on DNS DDoS attacks. This allowed us to develop a much simpler strategy, to detect an attack. We simply treat the DNS service as a black box. From the outside, we simply run a script to see if we receive 100% DNS answers to our DNS queries. If not, we assume an attack. Having said that, we could of course, after we detect loss of availability, reuse their contribution to try and determine the type of attack and strength.

In [6], J. Czyz et al. propose how to mitigate reflection DDoS attacks, via the NTP protocol. **Our Comments:** Reflection DDoS attacks are a major issue because they can generate huge bandwidth attacks. To mitigate these problems, organizations can host their DNS services at providers such as Dyn, Microsoft, Google, etc. In security, we call this a transfer of risk. However, as we have shown even Dyn lacked the knowledge or capability to eliminate the vulnerabilities. So, Twitter thought that they transferred the risk to Dyn, however Twitter actually maintained some of the risk.

In [21], S. Venkatesan et al. propose a moving target DDoS defense. **Our Comments:** The idea that after an attack, the services move or change IP addresses is a fantastic contribution. We really hope a lot more researches explore this moving target defense strategy.

In [16], C. Rossow provides a great study, concerning DDoS amplification attacks. **Our Comments:** However, these attacks can be mitigated by simply performing stateless filtering. Having said that, if the bandwidth is too high, the filtering no longer becomes a valid solution.

In [18], M. Shtern et al. have an interesting study, of DDoS, when the attack is low and slow, and how to deal with this special case of attacks.

6 Conclusion

As stated before, as a reminder, we have the following contributions:

1. We propose best practices, which can mitigate the effects of DNS DDoS attacks.
2. Our proposed DNS TTL2 protocol enhancement allows DNS authoritative server administrators to have much control over the actual TTL at the DNS resolvers, recursive servers, and clients.
3. Our proposed DNS TTL3 protocol enhancement allows DNS authoritative server administrators to have much better control over the actual DNS cache timeout, at the DNS resolvers, recursive DNS servers and clients.
4. Even when the end client does not support our TTL2/3 timers, we show how the intermediate DNS resolvers and recursive servers can automatically provide enhanced DNS timer functionality, with no changes to the end client.

We are planning to implement our DNS backup service and recommend others do this, as future work. We are trying to meet other researchers, who wish to work with us to prevent DDoS attacks, using server-less functions [26], such as that Microsoft's [13] and via API gateways, such as from Microsoft [12].

References

1. Almeida, V.A.F., Doneda, D., de Souza Abreu, J.: Cyberwarfare and digital governance. IEEE Internet Comput. **21**(2), 68–71 (2017)
2. Aydeger, A., Saputro, N., Akkaya, K., Rahman, M.: Mitigating crossfire attacks using SDN-based moving target defense. In: 2016 IEEE 41st Conference on Local Computer Networks (LCN), pp. 627–630, November 2016
3. Boell, S.K., Cecez-Kecmanovic, D.: What is an information system? In: 2015 48th Hawaii International Conference on System Sciences, pp. 4959–4968, January 2015
4. Booth, T., Andersson, K.: Network security of internet services: eliminate DDoS reflection amplification attacks. J. Internet Serv. Inform. Secur. (JISIS) **5**(3), 58–79 (2015)
5. Booth, T., Andersson, K.: Network DDoS Layer 3/4/7 mitigation via dynamic web redirection. In: Doss, R., Piramuthu, S., Zhou, W. (eds.) FNSS 2016. CCIS, vol. 670, pp. 111–125. Springer, Cham (2016). doi:10.1007/978-3-319-48021-3_8

6. Czyz, J., Kallitsis, M., Gharaibeh, M., Papadopoulos, C., Bailey, M., Karir, M.: Taming the 800 pound gorilla: the rise and decline of NTP DDoS attacks. In: Internet Measurement Conference (2014)
7. Esch, J.: Software-defined networking: a comprehensive survey (2014)
8. Fayaz, S.K., Tobioka, Y., Sekar, V., Bailey, M.: Bohatei: flexible and elastic DDoS defense. In: USENIX Security Symposium (2015)
9. Google. "API Reference | Cloud DNS Documentation" "Domain Name System". https://cloud.google.com/dns/api/v1/. Accessed 11 April 2017
10. Google. DNS-over-HTTPS | Public DNS. https://developers.google.com/speed/public-dns/docs/dns-over-https. Accessed 24 April 2017
11. Lim, S., Ha, J., Kim, H., Kim, Y., Yang, S.: A SDN-oriented DDoS blocking scheme for botnet-based attacks. In: 2014 Sixth International Conference on Ubiquitous and Future Networks (ICUFN), pp. 63–68, July 2014
12. Microsoft. API Management: Establish API Gateways | Microsoft Azure. https://azure.microsoft.com/en-us/services/api-management/. Accessed 13 April 2017
13. Microsoft. Azure Functions—Serverless Architecture | Microsoft Azure. https://azure.microsoft.com/en-us/services/functions/. Accessed 14 April 2017
14. Mousavi, S.M., St-Hilaire, M.: Early detection of DDoS attacks against SDN controllers. In: 2015 International Conference on Computing, Networking and Communications (ICNC), pp. 77–81 (2015)
15. OpenDNS. OpenDNS Introduces SmartCache - New Feature Enables Web Sites to Load Successfully With OpenDNS, While Offline for the Rest of the Internet. https://www.opendns.com/about/press-releases/opendns-introduces-smartcache-new-feature-enables-web-sites-to-load-successfully-with-opendns-while-offline-for-the-rest-of-the-internet. Accessed 14 April 2017
16. Rossow, C.: Amplification hell: revisiting network protocols for DDoS abuse. In: NDSS (2014)
17. Sahay, R., Blanc, G., Zhang, Z., Debar, H.: Towards autonomic DDoS mitigation using Software Defined Networking. In: SENT 2015: NDSS Workshop on Security of Emerging Networking Technologies, San Diego, CA, United States. Internet Society, February 2015
18. Shtern, M., Sandel, R., Litoiu, M., Bachalo, C., Theodorou, V.: Towards mitigation of low and slow application DDoS attacks. In: 2014 IEEE International Conference on Cloud Engineering, pp. 604–609, March 2014
19. Soni, R., Ambalkar, S., Bansal, P.: Security and privacy in cloud computing. In: 2016 Symposium on Colossal Data Analysis and Networking (CDAN), pp. 1–6, March 2016
20. Twitter. Twitter | About. https://about.twitter.com/company. Accessed 21 April 2017
21. Venkatesan, S., Albanese, M., Amin, K., Jajodia, S., Wright, M.: A moving target defense approach to mitigate DDoS attacks against proxy-based architectures. In: 2016 IEEE Conference on Communications and Network Security (CNS), pp. 198–206, October 2016
22. Wang, B., Zheng, Y., Lou, W., Hou, Y.T.: DDoS attack protection in the era of cloud computing and Software-Defined Networking. Comput. Netw. **81**, 308–319 (2015)
23. Wang, H., Jia, Q., Fleck, D., Powell, W., Li, F., Stavrou, A.: A moving target DDoS defense mechanism. Comput. Commun. **46**, 10–21 (2014)
24. Wikipedia. Denial-of-service attack. https://en.wikipedia.org/w/index.php?title=Denial-of-service_attack&oldid=781501497. Accessed 9 April 2017

25. Wikipedia. Domain Name System. https://en.wikipedia.org/w/index.php?title=Domain_name_system&oldid=779318292. Accessed 27 April 2017
26. Wikipedia. Serverless computing. https://en.wikipedia.org/w/index.php?title=Serverless_computing&oldid=780878012. Accessed 14 April 2017
27. Yu, S., Tian, Y., Guo, S., Wu, D.: Can we beat DDoS attacks in clouds? IEEE Trans. Parallel Distrib. Syst. **25**, 2245–2254 (2014)
28. Zargar, S.T., Joshi, J., Tipper, D.: A survey of defense mechanisms against distributed denial of service (DDoS) flooding attacks. IEEE Commun. Surv. Tutorials **15**(4), 2046–2069 (2013)
29. Zeb, K., Baig, O., Asif, M.K.: DDoS attacks and countermeasures in cyberspace. In: 2015 2nd World Symposium on Web Applications and Networking (WSWAN), pp. 1–6, March 2015

RFID-Based Non-repudiation Protocols for Supply Chains

Selwyn Piramuthu[✉]

Information Systems and Operations Management,
University of Florida, Gainesville, FL 32611-7169, USA
selwyn@ufl.edu

Abstract. RFID-tagged items are highly likely to change ownerships during their lifetime. While there are more than a dozen ownership transfer protocols in extant literature, none of these address the issue of non-repudiation. We purport to fill this gap by proposing non-repudiation protocols with and without a trusted third party that seamlessly also transfer ownership of the tagged item.

1 Introduction

It is not uncommon for an item and its component parts to belong to different owners during its lifetime. For example, the component parts of a car might belong to different suppliers before they are bought and assembled as one complete entity. Once assembled, this car may change ownership from the manufacturer to a distributor and then to a dealership followed by a customer. The car could then belong to several different owners during the remainder of its lifetime. In the digital world, when a message changes hands there are means to verify that it indeed was sent from its origin and received by the intended recipient(s). There are similar set-ups in the physical world whereby the sender (e.g., seller) and receiver (e.g., buyer) have means to certify and acknowledge successful completion of their respective roles. For example, in a supply chain, the sold items are generally (bar code) scanned while the buyer has a means to physically verify the item's delivery. This manual inventory-taking is labor-intensive and in a majority of cases only done at a higher (say, pallet) level. The introduction of item-level RFID tags brings with it an additional set of challenges due in part to the automation of the inventory-taking process. The items are no longer required to be manually scanned to identify their physical presence at a given location and time.

In a supply chain setting, while it is relatively easy to manually verify the physical transfer of a pallet, it is rather difficult to accomplish the same at an item-level granularity. Verification of the presence of individual items in a pallet involves taking apart the packaging (e.g., carton containing 12 boxes of breakfast cereal) and inspecting or (bar code) scanning individual items. This, clearly, is a very inefficient process. RFID tags can improve this through automation of the process of identifying any given entity throughout the supply chain.

R. Doss et al. (Eds.): FNSS 2017, CCIS 759, pp. 56–69, 2017.
DOI: 10.1007/978-3-319-65548-2_5

Recent RFID-tag implementation trends indicate the move toward automating the process of managing inventory. For example, the recent (August 2010) item-level tagging of all Wrangler jeans sold at Wal-Mart stores attest to this trend. When automating tracking and tracing of items in a supply chain, it is critical to ensure that both the physical state of an item (e.g., its physical location) and its electronic state are in sync. When the electronic record states that an item was delivered by A to B at time t, verification of physical reality should confirm the same. I.e., the onus rests primarily on electronic record-keeping as an item physically moves downstream in a supply chain.

When an item moves downstream in a supply chain, it is likely to change ownership. From an RFID perspective, when these tags (or rather the tagged items) change ownership across the supply chain, in addition to needed ownership transfer protocol there is a need to ensure non-repudiation in a secure manner. Unlike electronic message transfer, non-repudiation in the supply chain context adds the additional constraint that the item of interest has to physically change hands during the process with all necessary non-repudiation constraints in place. I.e., the sender (e.g., seller) of an item should receive proof from the receiver (e.g., buyer) upon delivery and reception of this item. When the item is delivered by the sender and received by the receiver, neither of the parties should be able to deny their roles (as sender or seller and receiver or buyer of this item). Zhou and Gollman [19] were the first to consider electronic non-repudiation from a cryptographic perspective. This is an active research area as is evidenced by the large number of extant literature on non-repudiation (e.g., [5,8,9,12–14,16,17,20]). To our knowledge, there is no existing literature that addresses non-repudiation in a combined (i.e., electronic and physical) scenario such as when RFID tags are used to identify items in a supply chain. We fill this gap by presenting non-repudiation protocols with and without a trusted third party that purport to accomplish this when the item of interest is RFID-tagged.

The remainder of this paper is organized as follows: We briefly present and evaluate protocols that have specifically been developed for supply chain applications in Sect. 2. We discuss preliminaries including definitions and notations used in this paper in Sect. 3. We then present the proposed non-repudiation protocols in Sect. 4. We provide a high-level security analysis without formal proof of the proposed protocols in Sect. 5. The last Section concludes the paper with a brief discussion.

2   Related Literature

We consider several protocols that have been proposed over the last few years specifically targeted for supply chain applications. Among the earliest of these protocols is the one by Li and Ding [10], which has been extensively analyzed elsewhere (e.g., [2,7]) and is therefore omitted here. It should be noted that non-repudiation is not considered in any of these protocols.

For each protocol considered in this Section, due to space considerations, we only provide a sketch to facilitate discussion. Each of the protocol sketch is to be read from top to bottom. The interested reader is referred to the original publications for detailed descriptions of these protocols. We identify some vulnerabilities present in these protocols. In some cases, an adversary exploits a vulnerability by sending a null vector to the tag. This is an operational issue and can easily be prevented by the tag explicitly checking for null vectors in its input.

2.1 Protocol of Henseler, Rossberg, and Schaefer (2008)

Henseler et al. ([6]) propose a two-stage protocol for authenticating and accessing RFID data in a supply chain context. The authentication phase is given in Fig. 1 where A3 is $\{ID_R, t_R, r_{R1}, PID, r_T, H(K_{A,T}||PID||r_T)\}_{K_{A,R}}$ and A4 is $\{ID_A, r_{R1}, KA, PID, K_{R,T}, \{ID_R, ID_T, KA, K_{KA,T}, t_A\}_{K_{A,KA}}, r_A, t_{ticket}\}_{K_{A,R}}$. The setup includes an authentication server, several key servers that are responsible for a stochastically predetermined certain number of tags, readers at different nodes in the supply chains, and the RFID tagged objects that pass through the supply chain. The pseudoIDs (PID) are generated using two hash functions and these PID values are designed to repeat after a certain number of iterations. Herein lies a vulnerability. A patient adversary can send the first message (from reader to tag) and copy the tag's response, which has the current PID value. Once an adversary collects a complete set of PID values for a tag, this tag can be tracked by this adversary. A worse attack would be when an active adversary blocks the first message from reader to tag and replaces it (i.e., r_R) with a different nonce. Since the tag computes its session key using r_R sent by the reader, the session key generated by the reader and tag would be different (desynchronization) and the tag won't be authenticated by the reader and the authentication server.

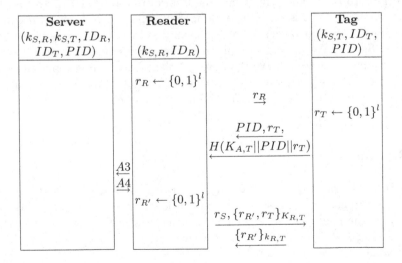

Fig. 1. Authentication protocol of Henseler, Rossberg, and Schaefer (2008)

2.2   Protocol of Cai, Li, Li, and Deng (2009)

Cai et al. ([1]) propose a set of protocols that accomplish reading, switch security mode, and update temporary secret. They consider two modes of security - strong and weak where the latter is used in situations where 'active attacks are impossible' and the former everywhere else. The 'impossibility' of active attacks may not be a reasonable assumption given the ease with which such attacks as well as others including relay attacks can be mounted on RFID tags. They use a tag reading protocol (Fig. 2)for communicating with a tag and security mode switching protocol (Fig. 3) to toggle between the strong and weak security modes.

In *weak* mode, R_T is set to zero in the tag reading protocol (Fig. 3). Moreover, active adversaries are assumed to be absent when in the weak mode. This allows only for the possibility of the presence of a passive adversary who observes the communication between tag and reader. In weak mode, the system is set up such that the tag responds with the same x for a given r_R, which is pre-computed

Reader	Tag
$r_R \leftarrow \{0,1\}^l$	
$\xrightarrow{r_R}$	
	$r_T \leftarrow 0$ if weak mode else choose $r_T \leftarrow \{0,1\}^l$ $x \leftarrow H(r_R\|r_T\|\beta_{ij}$
$\xleftarrow{r_T,x}$	
validate x validate tag	

Fig. 2. Tag reading protocol of Cai et al. (2009)

Reader	Tag
$r_R \leftarrow \{0,1\}^l$ $a \leftarrow \beta_{ij} \oplus r_R$ $b \leftarrow H(switch\|a\|r_R)$	
$\xrightarrow{switch, a, b}$	
	validate b and use switch if b valid
	$r_T \leftarrow f(switch)$ $x \leftarrow H(\beta_{ij}\|r_T\|r_R)$
$\xleftarrow{r_T,x}$	
validate x	

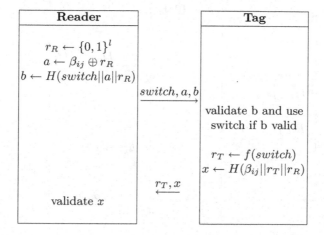

Fig. 3. Security mode switching protocol of Cai et al. (2009)

and stored in the reader's database. Given this, the need for encrypting messages is not clear. I.e., any consistent (say, some constant c) response by the tag to r_R from the reader should suffice since a passive adversary would be able to track/trace the tag in either case.

Moreover, if an adversary is allowed to modify the first message from reader to tag to a desired switch value (Fig. 2), the tag would reply with $x = H(switch||0||\beta_{ij})$. This x value can be used as input in the security mode switching protocol (Fig. 3) as follows: the reader sends (switch, 0, x) to the tag, which would authenticate x and implement the switch. This can be used by the adversary to toggle between weak and strong modes.

2.3 Protocol of Schapranow, Zeier, and Plattner (2010)

Schapranow et al. [15]) propose a mutual authentication protocol that purportedly prevents unauthorized third party access while the RFID-tagged object is in the supply chain. Their setup includes four main types of entities including the RFID tags, readers, distributed middleware, and enterprise middleware (Fig. 4). For purposes of this paper, we omit the enterprise middleware and related communications. We, therefore, consider only the rest of the entities and the essence of the communication among them while ensuring that this does not take away the essence of the vulnerability present in this protocol.

Since the communication between tag and reader is not through a secure channel, an adversary can easily observe the first message from tag to reader (i.e., $h(r_R), ID_{EP}, ID_T$). Now, the adversary has several pieces of information that can be used: (1) the ID_T (the tag identifier), which is sent in plaintext can be used to identify the tag, (2) ID_{EP}, another identifier, which can be used in

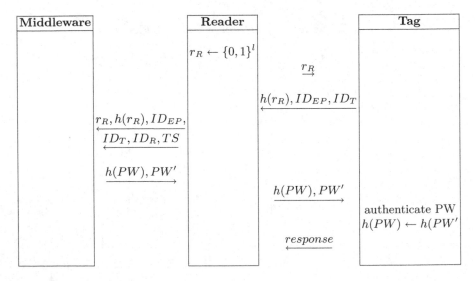

Fig. 4. Authentication protocol of Schapranow, Zeier, and Plattner (2010)

future communication with reader, and (3) repeated replies with the same $h(r_R)$ for a given r_R which can be used to track the tag (in addition to and confirming the information provided by ID_T). In fact, it might also be possible to clone the tag for all practical purposes since the hashing function (i.e., h) is not a secret and the only remaining message from tag to the reader (i.e., the very last message - *response*) seems to not involve any secret information.

3 Preliminaries

3.1 Notation

The following notations are used throughout the remainder of this paper:

O_j	Owner (or, reader) j
o_j	shared key between owner j and TTP
k_i, k_i'	current and next key of tag i
ID_i	Identity of tag i
t_i	shared key between tag i and TTP
r_x	freshly generated nonce by entity x
f_y	encryption function (with key y)
$\text{sig}_p(m)$	digital signature generated by party P on message m
$\text{enc}_p(m)$	public key encryption of m for party P
$\{m\}_k$	symmetric key encryption of m with key k
h	cryptographic hash function
F	Flag indicating message purpose
EOO	Evidence Of Origin
EOR	Evidence Of Receipt

3.2 Formal Definitions

Communication and security model. We summarize the essential concepts needed to define non-repudiation of ownership transfer for RFID systems. The presentation is based on [3]. In short, we require that the behavior of a number of agents executing a protocol is described by a set of traces in which we can identify the events belonging to the same run.

A *protocol* is a map from an n-tuple of distinct *roles* to an n-tuple of *role specifications*. A role specification is a sequence of *events* defining the behavior of an *honest agent* executing the role. An event is the sending or the receiving of a term, the creation of a nonce, a local computation, or the assignment of a term to a variable. The execution of a role specification by an agent is called a *run*.

The terms appearing in a role specification as arguments of an event consist of *variables* and publicly known *constants* to which functions such as concatenation, encryption, and cryptographic hashes can be applied. Actual messages communicated during runs may not contain variables. The variables are substituted during an agent's run by ground terms, i.e., terms built from nonces, publicly known constants and agent names. Substitution occurs implicitly during read events or explicitly through an assignment.

We distinguish between two types of variables. The scope of *local variables* is a run, the scope of global variables is unlimited. In particular, local variables are unassigned at the beginning of a run. The values of *global variables* are maintained across different runs.

An agent's *knowledge* consists of all terms the agent can construct from assigned variables and public constants. In general, these are terms that the agent has received and nonces that the agent has generated.

To analyze the behavior of a system in which a collection of agents executes a set of protocols Π, we consider so-called *traces*. A trace $t = t_0 \ldots t_{n-1}$ is a valid derivation $s_0 \xrightarrow{t_0} s_1 \xrightarrow{t_1} \ldots \xrightarrow{t_{n-1}} s_n$ of *system states* $s_0 \ldots s_n$ and events $t_0 \ldots t_{n-1}$, and $|t| = n$ is its length. A system state is a five-tuple (A, G, SB, RB, I), containing the set of runs A, global variable assignments G, the send and read buffers SB and RB, and the intruder knowledge I.

The set A is used to record active runs. Each run contains an identifier, the name of the executing agent, the list of events that still have to be executed, and the local variable assignments. A run r has been completed successfully in state s if its event list is empty. Otherwise the run is still active or it has terminated unsuccessfully. The current state of the global variable assignments of the agents is stored in G.

We assume communication to be asynchronous. Messages sent by agents are placed in the send buffer SB. Similarly, agents read message from the read buffer RB.

We assume that a standard Dolev-Yao intruder [4] controls the network. The intruder delivers a message by moving it from the send buffer to the read buffer. He eavesdrops on messages by adding them to his knowledge I. The intruder can construct any message from his knowledge and place it in the read buffer. He can block or delay messages by not moving them from the send to the read buffer. Finally, a message can be modified by faking a message and blocking the original one. As usual in Dolev-Yao intruder models, we assume that cryptography is perfect. This means that the intruder cannot reverse hash functions and that he is not able to learn the contents of an encrypted term, unless he knows the decryption key. We assume that there is one agent E which is under full control of the intruder.

Ownership. We define ownership as in [3] which also contains an in-depth discussion on this topic. Ownership of an RFID tag is defined by means of an *ownership test protocol*. The test protocol may merely be a virtual protocol. Any agent able to successfully complete the test protocol is by definition the tag's owner. An agent will need to know an RFID tag's key k_i in order to complete the protocol and thus be considered an owner of the tag. Formally, we define ownership as follows.

Definition 1. *Let Tag_i be an RFID tag agent. Let k_i be the tag's global variable referring to the current key. An agent A is said to own Tag_i in system state s, if and only if the value of k_i in state s is in the knowledge of agent A in state s.*

While an agent's knowledge is the defining notion of ownership, an agent will have its own view on whether it owns a tag or not. This view may not necessarily coincide with the preceding definition of ownership. To distinguish between the two aspects, we say that an agent *holds* a tag if the agent believes it owns the tag.

Definition 2. *Let Tag_i be an RFID tag agent. An honest agent A is said to hold Tag_i in state s if and only if agent A's variable $hold(Tag_i)$ is assigned the constant* true *in state s.*

Using the two views we can now define secure ownership as a consistency condition.

Definition 3. *A set of protocols Π provides secure ownership if and only if in all states whenever an honest agent holds a tag, it owns the tag.*

4 Protocols for Non-repudiation of Ownership Transfer

4.1 Purpose

The non-repudiation protocols are meant to be used for ownership transfer of tagged items in supply chains. This can be considered to be one building block towards preventing counterfeit products and a system for customer verifiable protection against counterfeit products.

Our aim is to reduce the physical exchange to the exchange of digital information and a physical step where both parties hold on to a tag while exchanging digital information. If a dispute occurs, local law enforcement can be used as a physical TTP, an online TTP can be used to resolve the fair exchange of information.

We define ownership of a tag through knowledge of the tag's encryption key. Thus the non-repudiation protocol can be considered to be regarding the exchange of an EOR for a key k. The key k can be the same key that the previous owner knows or a fresh key.

The fairness mechanism is as follows. O_2 needs k in order to be able to interact with the tag and pass on the tag to the next owner. O_1 needs EOR in order to be able to prove that it has passed on the item. (EOR could also be concatenated with digital payment information.)

4.2   Requirements

The following list is adapted from [16].

- *Fairness.* Neither party should have advantage over the other. On completion of the transaction, the previous owner should be able to provide (1) evidence of transferring the item to the new owner and (2) the reception of the item by the new owner.
- *Efficiency.* This refers to the extent of involvement of a TTP. The TTP could be non-existent, off-line, in-line, or on-line. The off-line case refers to the minimal involvement of a TTP which happens only when there is a need for dispute resolution. The on-line case refers to the other extreme where the TTP is present throughout the execution of the non-repudiation protocol. In-line refers to the intermediary case where the TTP mediates communication between the two parties. Clearly, there is a trade-off between efficiency and constant monitoring of the process.
- *Timeliness.* There is a need to realize the completion of a transaction in a finite (and reasonable) amount of time.
- *Policy.* The realization of the non-repudiation service including evidence generation, evidence transfer, evidence verification and storage, dispute resolution, and time duration for each transaction.
- *Verifiability and Transparency of TTP.* The parties involved in a transaction need to have complete trust in the TTP. This trust should be easily verifiable when necessary. The TTP may also need to be transparent during the run of a transaction to protect the privacy of the parties involved as well as to not unnecessarily interfere in existing processes.

We use message sequence chart, such as in Fig. 5, for the description of this protocol. Message sequence chart shows the role names, framed, near the top of the chart. Above the role names, the non-public terms known to the role are shown. Actions, such as nonce generation, computation, verification of terms, and assignments are shown in boxes. Messages to be sent and expected to be received are specified above solid arrows connecting the roles. It is assumed that an agent continues the execution of its run only if it receives a message conforming to its role. Physical actions, such as holding on to an RFID tag or releasing an RFID tag are indicated above dashed arrows. For physical actions, it is assumed that an agent continues the execution of its run only if the physical action succeeds.

For example, in Fig. 5, the role names are O_1, O_2, Tag_i, and TTP. O_1 knows the secret terms o_1 and k_i. The first few arrows in Fig. 5 represent the following execution flow. The protocol is initiated by O_1 who sends EOO to O_2. After reception of that message, O_2 signs EOO and sends it to TTP. The TTP generates the nonce k_i' then replies to O_2. Upon receiving the TTP's answer, O_2 attempts to hold on to the tag Tag_i. If successful, O_2 sends a message to the tag.

4.3   Notation

The following notation is used in the protocol described in Fig. 5.

- A dashed arrow in the message sequence chart below indicates a physical action rather than the sending of messages.
- $ticket = \{k', redundancy\}_{t_i}$
- $EOR = \{O_1, O_2, Tag_i, timestamp\}_{t_i}$

The protocol in Fig. 5 works as follows. The current owner, O_1, starts by sending an Evidence Of Origin (EOO) to the future owner O_2. The future owner verifies the EOO with the TTP and receives a key k' and a ticket which can be used to change the tag's key to k'. The future owner then holds on to the tag (the current owner does not yet release the tag) and sends the ticket to the tag. The tag announces acceptance of the ticket. At this point the tag knows the new key k' and O_1 can request the evidence of receipt (EOR) from the tag and then release the tag.

4.4   Variants

- The previous owner could receive the receipt from the new owner directly instead of through the RFID tag.

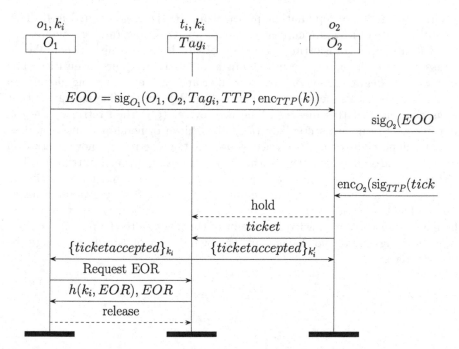

Fig. 5. The proposed non-repudiation protocol without TTP

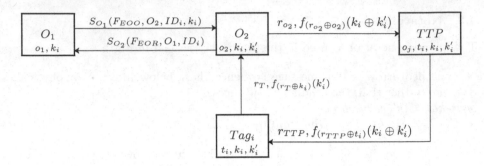

Fig. 6. The proposed non-repudiation protocol with TTP

- The EOR can be optionally registered with the TTP.
- In a more elaborate version, *EOR* could be *($O_1, O_2, Tag_i, timestamp$)*. Then *ticket* would also consist of $\{k_i', redundancy\}_{t_i}$, $\{EOR, redundancy\}_{t_i}$.
- Another version of the protocol could consist in the two parties sending the ticket-acceptance message to the TTP who returns an EOR to O_1 and the key k' to O_2.
- A variant would be that the tag generates a ticket acceptance message which the parties O_1 and O_2 need to collaborate on to obtain the EOR and key k', respectively. This might be interesting for the optimistic TTP scenario.

The proposed non-repudiation protocol for RFID is given in Fig. 6. This protocol is initiated by the current owner of an RFID tag (and, therefore, the tagged item) when transferring ownership of this item to a new owner. We do not assume the presence of secure channels between any pairs of entities. The current owner begins by sending the identifier and the key of the tag along with the destination of this message (i.e., new owner O_2) and the flag indicating that this is the origin of this message. The new owner (O_2) then retrieves the tag identifier (ID_i) and its secret key (k_i). To achieve ownership transfer and to prevent the previous owner from accessing this tag, the new owner generates a new key k_i' and sends a message to the TTP requesting ownership transfer. The TTP then sends the new key along with the previous key in a message that is encrypted by its shared key (with the tag, i.e., t_i) and a freshly generated nonce (r_{TTP}). The tag retrieves the new key and communicates with the new owner. The new owner then acknowledges receipt of the new tag to the previous owner. Upon receiving this acknowledgement, the owners can physically exchange the item of interest.

5   Security Analysis

5.1   Assumptions

We do not assume the presence of secure channels between any pairs of entities. We assume the existence of an online TTP and optimistic law enforcement[1]. The protocols proposed are to be executed during the physical transfer of a tagged item with presence of the two parties (i.e. the current and future owner) involved in the exchange of the item.

5.2   Threats

Non-repudiation of ownership transfer means that O_2 cannot deny having obtained the tag Tag from O_1. The EOR is used by O_1 to show that O_2 has received the tag. Fairness requires that O_1 should not obtain EOR without O_2 obtaining the tag, nor that O_2 obtains the tag without O_1 obtaining the EOR.

The following mischievous actions are possible:

- Stealing. Either party may run away with the tagged item.
  If there is a physical mechanism for both parties to hold on to the tag during the physical exchange, then a fair exchange property in the protocol prevents this threat.
- False promise. A tag may not be attached to the expected item.
  The protocol does not prevent this by itself. A TTP ought to ensure that tags are built into the right items. We additionally have to assume that removing a tag from an item destroys the tag and that no two tags are equal.
- Bait-and-switch. The previous owner may deliver a false item by forwarding communication with a genuine tag which is somewhere else.
  The protocol does not prevent this by itself. Distance-bounding protocols could help, but are considered to be impractical. If a large quantity of RFID tags is transferred, forwarding communication seems to be hard to achieve.
- Ownership sharing. Although the item may have transferred hands, the previous owner may continue to have (RF-)access to the tag whereby the tag can be tracked and traced.
- Simultaneously selling an item to multiple buyers. With access to the (secret) keys, an owner can possibly clone a tag to achieve this. This is an implementational issue, and the presence of multiple copies of a tag can be identified when they are processed by the TTP.

6   Conclusion

As identification of items in supply chains become automated, there is a need for a reliable and trust-worthy non-repudiation mechanism. We considered the use of

---

[1] By optimistic law enforcement we mean that both parties can call upon law enforcement in case they feel cheated.

RFID tags for this purpose since RFID tags are increasingly becoming popular in supply chains at the pallet-level if not yet at the item-level. We developed authentication protocols with and without a trusted third party. Although we do not provide a formal proof for the security of these authentication protocols, we consider some possible attacks and discuss how the proposed protocols are secure under these attack scenarios.

A prime motivation for this paper is to raise awareness for non-repudiation protocols in a supply chain context. We hope that researchers interested in this area are motivated to develop better protocols that are both secure and light-weight.

Acknowledgement. The idea for this paper came from discussions with Saša Radomirović. I gratefully acknowledge Saša's help with discussions on the security of RFID ownership transfer protocols. All error(s) remain my own.

References

1. Cai, S., Li, T., Li, Y., Deng, R.H.: Ensuring dual security modes in RFID-enabled supply chain systems. In: Bao, F., Li, H., Wang, G. (eds.) ISPEC 2009. LNCS, vol. 5451, pp. 372–383. Springer, Heidelberg (2009). doi:10.1007/978-3-642-00843-6_32
2. van Deursen, T., Radomirović, S.: Security of an RFID protocol for supply chains. In: Proceedings of the 1st Workshop on Advances in RFID (AIR 2008), pp. 568–573. IEEE Computer Society, October 2008
3. Deursen, T., Mauw, S., Radomirović, S., Vullers, P.: Secure ownership and ownership transfer in RFID systems. In: Backes, M., Ning, P. (eds.) ESORICS 2009. LNCS, vol. 5789, pp. 637–654. Springer, Heidelberg (2009). doi:10.1007/978-3-642-04444-1_39
4. Danny, D., Yao, A.C.: On the security of public key protocols. IEEE Trans. Inf. Theory **29**(2), 198–208 (1983)
5. Gutscher, A.: Reasoning with uncertain and conflicting opinions in open reputation systems. Electron. Notes Theoret. Comput. Sci. (ENTCS) **244**, 67–79 (2009)
6. Henseler, M., Rossberg, M., Schaefer, G.: Credential management for automatic identification solutions in supply chain management. IEEE Trans. Industr. Inf. **4**(4), 303–314 (2008)
7. Kapoor, G., Zhou, W., Piramuthu, S.: RFID and information security in supply chains. In: Proceedings of the 4th International Conference on Mobile Ad-hoc and Sensor Networks(MSN), pp. 59–62. IEEE Computer Society (2008)
8. Kim, K., Park, S., Baek, J.: Improving fairness and privacy of Zhou-Gollmann's fair non-repudiation protocol. In: Proceedings of ICPP, Workshop on Security (IWSEC), pp. 140–145. IEEE Computer Society (1999)
9. Kremer, S., Raskin, J.-F.: A game-based verification of non-repudiation and fair exchange protocols. In: Larsen, K.G., Nielsen, M. (eds.) CONCUR 2001. LNCS, vol. 2154, pp. 551–565. Springer, Heidelberg (2001). doi:10.1007/3-540-44685-0_37
10. Li, Y., Ding, X.: Protecting RFID communications in supply chains. In: ASIACCS, pp. 234–241 (2007)
11. Li, G., Ogawa, M.: On-the-fly model checking of fair non-repudiation protocols. In: Namjoshi, K.S., Yoneda, T., Higashino, T., Okamura, Y. (eds.) ATVA 2007. LNCS, vol. 4762, pp. 511–522. Springer, Heidelberg (2007). doi:10.1007/978-3-540-75596-8_36

12. Li, L., Zhang, H.-G., Wang, L.-N.: An improved non-repudiation protocol and its security analysis. Wuhan Univ. J. Nat. Sci. **9**(3), 288–292 (2004)
13. Louridas, P.: Some guidelines for non-repudiation protocols. ACM SIGCOMM Comput. Commun. Rev. **30**(5), 29–38 (2000)
14. Markowitch, O., Kremer, S.: An optimistic non-repudiation protocol with transparent trusted third party. In: Davida, G.I., Frankel, Y. (eds.) ISC 2001. LNCS, vol. 2200, pp. 363–378. Springer, Heidelberg (2001). doi:10.1007/3-540-45439-X_25
15. Schapranow, M.-P., Zeier, A., Plattner, H.: A dynamic mutual RFID authentication model preventing unauthorized third party access. In: Proceedings of the 4th International Conference on Network and System Security (2010)
16. Sessler, G.M., West, J.E.: Secure multi-party non-repudiation protocols and applications. In: Sessler, G.M. (ed.) Electrets. TAP, vol. 33, pp. 347–381. Springer, Heidelberg (1980). doi:10.1007/3540173358_15
17. Petropoulos, D., Kotzanikolaou, P.: Some more improvements on a fair non-repudiation protocol. J. Internet Technol. **4**(4), 255–259 (2003)
18. Santiago, J.S., Vigneron, L.: Study for automatically analysing non-repudiation. In: Dans les actes du 1er Colloque sur les Risques et la Scurit d'Internet et des Systmes, CRiSIS, pp. 157–171, Bourges, France, October 2005
19. Zhou, J., Gollmann, D.: A fair non-repudiation protocol. In: Proceedings of the IEEE Symposium on Security and Privacy, pp. 55–61 (1996)
20. Zhou, J., Gollmann, D.: An efficient non-repudiation protocol. In: Proceedings of IEEE Computer Security Foundations Workshop, pp. 126–132 (1997)

Towards Realizing a Distributed Event and Intrusion Detection System

Qian Chen[1]([✉]), Hisham A. Kholidy[2], Sherif Abdelwahed[3], and John Hamilton[4]

[1] Department of Engineering Technology, Savannah State University,
Savannah, GA 31404, USA
chenq@savannahstate.edu
[2] Distributed Analytics and Security Institute, Mississippi State University,
Starkville, MS 39762, USA
hesham@dasi.msstate.edu
[3] Electrical and Computer Engineering Department, Mississippi State University,
Starkville, MS 39762, USA
sherif@ece.msstate.edu
[4] Computer Science and Engineering Department, Mississippi State University,
Starkville, MS 39762, USA
hamilton@cci.msstate.edu

Abstract. Power system blackouts would cause a significant impact on social and economic activities. Therefore, a key underlying requirement for a resilient power system is to detect cyber attacks and provide an appropriate response in nearly real time. However, due to limited computing resource and latency of the current power system Intrusion Detection Systems (IDS), they are not capable to detect cyber attacks for a large-scale system in real time.

In this paper, we designed a Distributed Event and IDS (DEIDS) that provides advance monitoring, incident analysis, and instant attack detection over the entire grid network. The application of the DEIDS will provide an easy and fast way to recognize power system performance trends and the patterns of cyber attacks. To realize such a DEIDS, we used four feature selection methods and applied these methods on selecting the most significant features for a 38GB test dataset. Comparing with previous research work [1,2], we have validated that the DEIDS provides the highest detection accuracy but the lowest overhead by modifying the Particle Swarm optimization fitness function to enhance the NNGE classifier through choosing the best detection attributes.

1 Introduction

Power system blackouts would cause a significant impact on social and economic activities. Electric energy is delivered to consumers from generators through an intricate network of transmission lines, substations, distribution lines, and transformers [3]. A power system disturbance, such as a loss of generator or transmission line due to a natural or human threat can initiate a chain of events that lead to cascading failures. Such cascading failures, if they are not addressed

R. Doss et al. (Eds.): FNSS 2017, CCIS 759, pp. 70–83, 2017.
DOI: 10.1007/978-3-319-65548-2_6

within a certain time frame, would trigger geographically wide spread outage. The biggest blackout in North American history, the 2003 Northeast Blackout, caused at least 11 deaths and six billion dollars financial losses. Such large power outage raised concerns of trees, tools and training that operators require to prevent natural power failures and handle critical events in the power grids [4]. The southwest power outage in 2011 was caused by the loss of a single 500 kilovolt transmission line in Yuma, AZ, which cascaded across the southwest of the U.S., and black out San Diego and parts of Mexico [5].

Critical infrastructures are monitored and controlled by Supervisory Control and Data Acquisition (SCADA) systems. While the SCADA system and its technologies have been deployed to achieve an increasing demand for reliable and resilient energy, they also present a strong dependency on information and communication infrastructures. Therefore, modern power systems are similar to other industrial control systems, which are vulnerable to cyber attacks.

Cyber attackers can exploit the vulnerabilities in control devices, communication protocols, and software to corrupt or alter the system measurement signals and to change operational algorithms and settings of the power systems. The Ukrainian power blackout in 2015 was the first publicity documented power outage attributed to a cyber attack [6]. Attackers used spear phishing to plant BlackEnergy3 malware into the power company's control and management systems, and disconnected the breakers of 30 substations. As a result, workers traveled to the victim substations and manually closed breakers to restore power [7].

Current practices in power systems lack cyber security requirements. The monitoring and controlling practices do not consider the potential cyber borne contingencies to incorporate distributed event and intrusion detection systems (DEIDSs) into power systems to enhance power system operations efficiently and securely. Additionally, to avert cascading failures caused by cyber attacks, the DEIDS must promptly identify the power outage event location, and then isolate the affected substations to ultimately maintain the stability and reliability of the attacked power systems.

This paper first introduces the framework of the DEIDS, and then 38 GB power system datasets including 41 power system scenarios (Multi Class) are analyzed. We categorize the 41 classes into three categories (Triple Class). Data of the Triple Class is labeled as No Event (e.g., power system performs normally), Natural Event (i.e., single line to ground faults) and Attack (i.e., command injection attacks). To characterize and identify normal performance of the power systems, we combine datasets of No Event and Natural Event together and rename them as Normal. Therefore, three datasets, Binary Class (i.e., Normal and Attack), Triple Class (i.e., No Event, Natural Event and Attack) and Multi Class (i.e., 1,2...41) were used to test the detection accuracy of the DEIDS.

To evaluate the impact of all 129 attributes of the test data, we develop heuristics using expert knowledge, brute force, correlation-based, mutual information-based and a modified Particle Swarm Optimization (PSO) feature selections to obtain the optimal attributes for particular scenarios. The NNGE algorithm with PSO feature selection method provides the highest detection rates for classifying the binary, triple and multi-class datasets.

The rest of this paper is organized as follows. Section 2 presents a literature review on detection techniques for identifying power system-specific cyber attacks. Section 3 describes the DEIDS framework. Section 4 presents the detection accuracy of the test datasets by using various feature selection methods and classifiers. Finally, we present our conclusions and future work in Sect. 5.

2   Related Work

The smart grid is a class of technology that is widely used for electricity delivery of the modernized power systems. The smart grid using computer-based remote control and automation [8] relies on Information Technology (IT), which has offered efficient energy but also exposed the power systems to cyber threats. Many researchers have applied various approaches to design Intrusion Detection Systems (IDSs) for identifying cyber attacks.

Rule-based signature techniques are commonly used to detect SCADA-specific cyber attacks. Particularly, this technique is often adopted to detect those cyber attacks that interrupt, fabricate, intercept or modify communication messages between the SCADA devices such as the Human Machine Interface (HMI) and Programmable Logic Controllers (PLC). A behavior rule-based methodology monitoring devices in the smart grid for insider threat detection was proposed in [9]. Results showed that this approach could detect abnormal behaviors in pervasive smart grid applications. However, the number of rules for detecting polymorphic and metamorphic malware can be extremely large. Thus, a more efficient approach must be developed to speedup the detection and enhance accuracy.

The Network-Based IDS (NBIDS) is a type of IDS that monitors network traffic to search for cyber attacks by the attack patterns. NBIDSs are efficient to detect malicious network traffics but cannot detect physical changes in a power system caused by cyber attacks. A synchrophasor specific intrusion detection system using a heterogeneous whitelist and behavior-based approach to detect Reconnaissance, Man-In-The-Middle (MITM) and Denial of Service (DoS) attacks [10]. Zhang et al. [11] developed an intelligent module and deployed it in multiple layers of the smart grid to detect and classify cyber attacks. The design improves system security and supports the optimal communication routing. Researchers proposed anomaly detection techniques, which extract normal behaviors from various communication protocols of Industrial Control Systems (ICSs) to create a full description of the communication pattern [12].

The Specification-Based IDS (SBIDS) monitors system security states and sends the alerts when the system behavior approaching to an unsafe or disallowed state. Bolzoni et al. [13] demonstrated an IDS called Panacea, which integrates anomaly-based with signature-based IDSs using machine learning methodologies. The adoption of Support Vector Machine and RIPPER Rule Learner techniques allows Panacea to classify known and unknown attacks. Manual construction of a state machine to monitor bulk electric transmission system states would be tedious and expensive. A few IDSs developed recently leverage power system theories. Optimal power flow [14] and weighted state estimation [15] methods are used to detect false data injection attacks. However, these methods cannot detect a wide variety of scenarios.

In recent research, a fusion of synchrophasor data along with device and system logs and time synchronization was used to explore the viability of using machine learning methods to detect power system specific cyber attacks [16]. One percent sampled raw heterogeneous data with minimal processing was used to test various data mining algorithms. The test results showed variable classification accuracy across tested algorithms. These experiments were performed without considering the ability of algorithms to handle the sequential nature of heterogeneous data. Some of the algorithms used in the study resulted very high accuracy. However, the false positive rate was high as well. Moreover, these methods did not consider the scalability as they were implemented.

Pan et al. proposed a common path mining approach to create an IDS using heterogeneous data for detecting power system events and cyber attacks [17]. Common path mining uses the State Tracking and Extraction Method (STEM) algorithm to pre-process data and then uses frequent item set mining to extract common paths associated with specific system behaviors [18]. A common path is a temporally ordered list of critical states associated with a specific cyber-attack or power system event type. Common paths can be used as signatures for classification.

The common path mining evaluation shows that observed behaviors matching multiple event common paths are associated with different event types. In this case, observed behaviors are classified as unknown. This method can be used to scale up the power system specific IDS; however, it provides a low accuracy.

Adhikari [1,2,18] presented a Non-Nested Generalized Exemplars (NNGE) approach and a Hoeffding Adaptive Trees (HAT) approach for creating an offline and online Event Intrusion Detection Systems (EIDSs), respectively. STEM is a valid method to process the power system security datasets for the two IDSs. The accuracy of these detection methods is above 90% for both binary and multi-class power system datasets. Although these algorithms showed promising results, their false positive rates are still above 1%.

In the following sections, we will introduce how to improve the detection accuracy of the DEIDSs by selecting the most significant attributes using four feature selection methods. We use the classic supervised learning algorithms (e.g., decision tree, instance-based learning and NNGE) to classify the three datasets (i.e., binary, triple and mutli classes) and compare the detection rates with previous work [18]. The experimental results show that the NNGE algorithm with PSO feature selection method provides the highest detection rates with the lowest overheads.

3   Experimental Design

This section introduces the design to realize the Distributed Event and Intrusion Detection System (DEIDS). We first introduce the DEIDS diagram, and then present the power system attack datasets that are used to validate the functionality of the DEIDS. The dataset contains heterogeneous data that integrates synchrophasor data with system logs. Four feature selection methods are presented for reducing the dimension of the attributes of the attack dataset to enhance the detection speed of the DEIDS. After selecting the most significant attributes, we classify the datasets using machine learning techniques to validate that the reduction of the attribute dimension is a capable approach to enhance the DEIDS detection rate with low overheads.

3.1   Distributed Event and Intrusion Detection Systems

The current IDS or Event and Intrusion Detection System (EIDS) proposed for cyber-physical power system infrastructure is not able to include a global information or infrastructure. This is because cascading failures caused by coordinated attacks require rapid global assessment and mitigation. A key underlying requirement for a resilient system is to detect cyber attacks and provide an appropriate response in nearly real time. Since the volume of cyber and physical attacks to the power grids are speedily increasing, the current EIDS are no longer capable to detect real-time cyber attacks to the large-scale power systems.

Most algorithms used to deploy the EIDS require a data pre-processing step, which takes significant amount of time. Additionally North American power systems that consist of many thousands of nodes, substations, and measuring devices produce extremely big amount of data every day. To detect and classify events of large-scale power systems normally requires very powerful computing resources. Using High Performance Computing (HPC) resources can solve this issue. It enables fast parallel computing but is very costly. In addition, the centralized analysis approach increases latency and time complexity for analyzing power system events. Since the power system operation is deregulated, centralized approach is no longer suitable for local controlling or monitoring. Therefore, we propose a scalable distributed hierarchical EIDS (DEIDS) as shown in Fig. 1.

The DEIDS consists of multiple EIDS over a large network. The DEIDS may communicate with each other or communicate minimally but provide advance monitoring, incident analysis, and instant attack detection over the entire grid network. The DEIDS would manage and create alerts when it detects cyberattacks. It can also provide an easy way to recognize power system performance trends and the patterns of cyber attacks across the power grid.

The DEIDS therefore must be aware of the normal operating behaviors of the protected system to detect actions, which drives the system to a critical state. The DEIDS also must have the ability to detect unknown attacks (or zero day attacks). Specification-Based Intrusion Detection Systems (SBIDSs) technology will be adopted for the DEIDS to model power system behaviors in real time with measurements of physical and cyber events. Meanwhile, the DEIDS uses

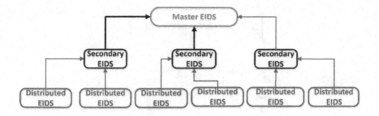

Fig. 1. Hierarchical approach for EIDS scalability and fast autonomic response

signature-based IDS technology to compare the power system security behaviors for identifying known attack signatures.

The advantages of the DEIDS to enhance power system cyber security is significant. For example,

1. the DEIDS will provide a minimum false positive rate by monitoring and detecting cyber attacks for thousands of substations located in a large geographical area as a whole.
2. the early detection feature of the DEIDS will allow operators to take immediate actions to protect power systems from cascading failures caused by cyber attacks or natural faults.
3. the DEIDS is computationally efficient, which is capable to detect anomalies to large-scale power systems in real time.
4. the DEIDS provides better situational awareness and incident and information management.

3.2   Power System Test Dataset

The datasets [19] used to evaluate the feature selection methods consist of synchrophasor measurements from PMUs of four substations. As shown in Fig. 2, in the network diagram, G1 and G2 are power generators. R1 through R4 are Intelligent Electronic Devices (IEDs) that can switch the breakers on or off. These breakers are labeled BR1 through BR4. Line One spans from breaker one (BR1) to breaker two (BR2) and Line Two spans from breaker three (BR3) to breaker four (BR4). Each IED automatically controls one breaker; thus R1 controls BR1, R2 controls BR2 and so on accordingly. The IEDs use a distance protection scheme which trips the breaker on detected faults whether actually valid or faked since they have no internal validation to detect the difference. Operators can also manually issue commands to the IEDs R1 through R4 to trip the breakers BR1 through BR4. The manual override is used when performing maintenance on the lines or other system components.

To enhance the cyber attack detection rate, the security attributes such as relay control panel SNORT logs are included in the test datasets. The size of the heterogeneous data set is approximately 38 Gigabytes and the number of the attributes is 128 (e.g., 29 attributes for a single PMU measurement, and four PMUs generate 116 features along with 12 log attributes), which include nine

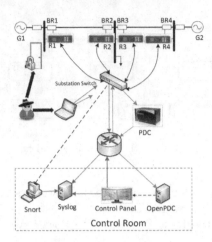

Fig. 2. Power system framework for generating test datasets [19]

power system events and 36 cyber-attacks. Details of the attributes has been introduced in previous work [1,2,19].

Note that the test datasets were generated under 41 scenarios when the power system operated normally (No Event) and distributed by natural faults (Natural Event) and cyber attackers (Attack). Therefore, the 41 scenarios can be combined into three classes. To characterize and identify normal performance of the power systems, the test dataset were combined as No Event and Natural Event classes. Therefore, Sect. 4 validates the DEIDS detection accuracy using Binary Class (i.e., Normal and Attack), Triple Class (No Event, Natural Event and Attack) and Multi Class (i.e., 1,2...41). More details of the datasets can be found in [19].

3.3 Feature Selection Methods

One of the challenges to enhance the DEIDS detection rate while reducing the time complexity is the selection of the most significant attributes. Feature selection methods must be applied to select a subset of features with the best predictive power in the data. The attribute selection process addresses two fundamental problems with high dimensional datasets, and they are

– The irrelevant input features significantly increase computation costs
– The irrelevant input features lead to overfitting and cause overly optimistic classification and detection accuracy.

In addition, the classical supervised machine learning algorithms require to analyze the training data to produce an inferred function. The limited hardware resource (i.e., memory and CPU) prevents the analysis of very large volume of training data. The attribute dimension reduction techniques reduce the size of input datasets for modeling training classifiers. Power system measurements are highly correlated; thus the brute force method, correlation based feature selection (CFS) and mutual information based feature selection methods and the modified PSO method are tested for reducing the dimension of attributes.

Brute Force Feature Selection. Brute force method is chosen to reduce attribute dimension with domain expert knowledge. This method evaluates all possible combinations of the input feature and selects the best subset. The brute force method is computationally very expensive with considerable chances of overfitting. However, domain expert knowledge can guide the process to limit it to the manageable level, which is one of the keys to successfully identify the appropriate attributes for identifying particular event scenarios. A significant attribute for one event may not be significant for different types of event. For transmission line and generator loss, frequency excursion is significant but voltage and current values do not change as much when compared to faulted scenarios. Similarly, measurements of the sensors which are closed to the event locations change significantly than the sensors that are far away.

Correlation-Based Feature Selection. The Correlation-based Feature Selection (CFS) method is based on the hypothesis "A good feature subset is one that contains features highly correlated with the class, yet not correlated with each other." CFS is a filter algorithm using a correlation based heuristics function and ranking subsets of features to select the significant features. The bias of the heuristics function is towards the subsets of features that are highly correlated with certain classes. The irrelevant features are ignored and redundant features are screened out. The CFS subset evaluation heuristics is given as [18],

$$M_s = \frac{kr_{cf}}{\sqrt{k + k(k-1)r_{ff}}} \tag{1}$$

Where M_s is the heuristic merit of feature subset that contains k features, r_{cf} is mean feature-class correlation, and r is the feature-feature inter-correlation. The numerator of the Eq. 1 provides an indication of the ability of a set of feature to predict the class. The denominator provides indication of redundancy among the features [18].

The given power system testing datasets contain the voltage and current of the three phases. To reduce the attribute dimension, by using brute force and CFS methods along with expert knowledge, we calculate the **Power Consumption** of IEDs (R1 through R4) involving 12 attributes (i.e., Voltage Phase Angle and Magnitude and Current Phase Angle and Magnitude) for each IED. Therefore, *48* attributes of the three phase voltage and current features have been reduced to *four* attributes of power utilization.

We also noticed that data of the attributes such as *Frequency and Frequency Delta of Relays, Appearance Impedance Magnitude and Phase Angle* and *Status Flag for Relays* changes insignificantly under all scenarios. Therefore, we eliminated these 20 attributes from the test datasets, and we get a 64 attributes datasets. Furthermore, we use the CFS method to reduce the 64 attributes to 28 features which are shown in Table 1.

Table 1. The most significant 64 VS 28 attributes

64 Features	28 Features
Power1-4 (W)	Power1-4(w)
PA7-9 (VH) *4	R1-PA7,R2-PA7,R3-PA7,R4-PA7
PM7-9 (V) *4	NA
PA10-12 (IH) *4	R1-PA10, R2-PA10,R3-PA10, R4-PA10
PM10-12 (I) *4	R1-PM10, R2-PM10,R3-PM10, R4-PM10
Control Panel Logs1-4	Control Panel Logs1-4
Snort Alerts1-4	Snort Alerts1-4
Relay Logs1-4	Relay Logs1-4

Mutual Information Based Feature Selection. The Mutual Information based Feature Selection (MIFS) method is an optimization algorithm to achieve minimal classification error. It uses the concept of maximal relevance and minimization of redundancy to select the most significant features. The maximum relevance is a feature selection process that selects the features with the highest relevance to target class c. Relevance is expressed in terms of correlation and mutual relevance. Suppose x and y are two random variables. Their mutual information is defined in terms of their probability density functions $p(x)$, $p(y)$, and $p(x, y)$. The mutual information is:

$$I(x; y) = \iint p(x, y) \log \frac{p(x, y)}{p(x)p(y)} \, dx \, dy \tag{2}$$

For maximum relevance, the selected feature x_i will have the largest mutual information $I(x_i, c)$ with the target class c. In the sequential search, features will be arranged in descending order and top m features will be selected. If $e_1, e_2, e_3, e_4, ..., e_n, c$ is a tuple of the heterogeneous dataset with class label 'c', the mutual information $I(E; C)$ is quantitative measure to correctly classify power system events. The measurements can be ranked in descending order and top measurements can be used as input features to the data processing and detection algorithms. Mutual information based method maximizes relevancy while reducing redundancy.

We used Joint Mutual Information (JMI) and Joint Mutual Information Maximisation (JMIM) which are two types of the MIFS method to select attributes from the 64 features. Table 2 shows an example of the number of attributes selected for the binary class using JMI and JMIM methods.

Table 2. The most significant attributes using the MIFS method for binary class

Binary	
JMI	JMIM
Power2-4	Power1-4
R1-PA7, R2-PA7, R3-PA7, R4-PA7	R1-PA7-9, R2-PA7, R2-PA9, R3-PA7, R3-PA9, R4-PA7, R4-PA9
R1-PM7, R2-PM7, R3-PM7	R1-PM7-8, R2-PM7, R4-PM7, R4-PM9
R1-PA10, R1-PA12, R2-PA10, R3-PA10, R3-PA12 R4-PA10-12	R1-PA11-12, R4-PA11
R1-PM10, R2-PM10, R3-PM10, R3-PM12, R4-PM10-12	R4-PM10
NA	Control Panel Logs1
NA	Snort Alerts1-4
NA	Relay Logs1, 3

Table 3. DEIDS classification Rates_Binary class

No. attributes (Feature Selection Method)	Classifier				
	J48	Random Forest	IB1	NNGE	JRip
28 (CFS Expert Knowledge)	93.6971%	96.7781%	**97.201%**	94.6839%	91.2002%
26 (MISF JMI)	92.8111%	96.4358%	**95.7511%**	89.9919%	88.8441%
21 (MISF JMIM)	92.4688%	95.9525%	**95.0665%**	91.5224%	89.2267%
129 (no feature selection)	78.091%	78.4535%	**94.2811%**	65.4249%	90.4551%

Table 4. DEIDS classification Rates_Triple class

No. attributes (Feature Selection Method)	Classifier				
	J48	Random forest	IB1	NNGE	JRip
28 (CFS Expert Knowledge)	93.6971%	96.7781%	**97.2614%**	94.6234%	91.2203%
17 (MISF JMI)	92.8111%	96.4962%	**97.3822%**	92.791%	90.5155%
23 (MISF JMIM)	92.8313%	95.6907%	**94.9255%**	90.3544%	89.8308%
129 (no feature selection)	83.2863%	78.4333%	**94.3818%**	66.4116%	89.8711%

Table 5. DEIDS Classification Rates_Multi Class

No. attributes (Feature Selection Method)	Classifier				
	J48	Random forest	IB1	NNGE	JRip
28 (CFS Expert Knowledge)	84.4543%	90.4148%	**92.1063%**	87.7769%	73.3186%
12 (MISF JMI)	73.7616%	75.8357%	**78.4333%**	74.2046%	61.176%
11 (MISF JMIM)	82.9239%	88.24%	**88.0588%**	80.8901%	68.5461%
129 (no feature selection)	7.2493%	86.9513%	**86.2465%**	23.6609%	73.9428%

Table 6. Comparing classification rates of NNGE-PSO, NNGE and IB1

Approach	Binary CLASS dataset		Triple CLASS dataset		MULTI CLASS dataset	
	No. of features	Detection rate	No. of features	Detection rate	No. of features	Detection rate
NNGE-PSO	17	**98.380%**	19	**98.011%**	22	**94.039%**
NNGE	28	94.6839%	28	94.6234%	28	87.7769%
IB1	28	97.201%	17	97.3822%	28	92.1063%

The modified Particle Swarm Optimization (PSO) Feature Selection.
The modified PSO feature selection method ranking the input features based on their significance is an efficient mechanism to enhance the detection accuracy rate of the DEIDS when using the Non Nested Generalized Exemplars (NNGE) algorithm.

The PSO technique is one of stochastic optimization methods that is based on the swarming strategies in fish schooling and bird flocking [20]. It considers each solution to the problem in a D-dimensional space as a particle flying through the problem space with a certain position and velocity. The PSO method finds the optimal solution in the complex search space through the interaction of particles in the population. Adjusting fewer parameters and escaping from local optima are two main advantages for implementing the PSO method to select significant features. The velocity and position of the ith particle are denoted by the two vectors respectively, $V_i = (v_{i1}, v_{i2}, v_{iD})$ and $X_i = (x_{i1}, x_{i2}, , x_{iD})$. Each particle moves in the search space according to its previous computed best particle position (pbest) and the location of the best particle in the entire population (gbest). The velocity and position of the particles are updated by the following two equations:

$$v_i(t + 1) = w \cdot v_i(t) + c_1 \cdot rand1_t \cdot [pbest_i(t) - x_i(t)] \\ + c_2 \cdot rand2_t \cdot [gbest(t) - x_i(t)] \tag{3}$$

$$x_i(t + 1) = x_i(t) + v_i(t + 1) \tag{4}$$

Where the velocity of the ith particle at iteration t is given by $v_i(t)$ and its position is given by $x_i(t)$ at the same iteration t, w is a weight factor to balance the global and local search function of particles, c_1 and c_2 are two learning factors which control the influence of the social and cognitive components and they are usually set to 2, $rand1$ and $rand2$ are two random numbers within the range of $[0, 1]$, $pbesti(t)$ is the best previous position that corresponds to the best fitness value for ith particle at the iteration t, and $gbest(t)$ is the global best particle by all particles at the iteration t. The fitness value of the particle is evaluated after changing its position to $x_i(t + 1)$. The $gbest$ and $pbest$ are updated according to the current position of the particles. The new particle velocity of each dimension $v_i(t + 1)$ is tied to a maximum velocity V_{max}, which is initialized by the user. We modified the two equations and focus on adapting the PSO to work with the NNGE algorithm through developing a new fitness function $x(t)$. The most significant features are selected for three classes and they are shown in Fig. 3.

Binary Class Dataset			Triple CLASS Dataset			MULTI CLASS		
Order	Feature Name	Fitness Value	Order	Feature Name	Fitness Value	Order	Feature Name	Fitness Value
1	R2-CPA1	9.278	1	R1-VPA1	12.433	1	relay1_log	22.231
2	R3-CPA1	11.186	2	relay1_log	13.243	2	relay3_log	25.256
3	relay1_log	12.599	3	R1-CPM1	16.032	3	R4-VPA2	29.056
4	relay4_log	13.800	4	R2-VPA1	18.832	4	R4-VPM2	33.564
5	relay2_log	17.143	5	relay4_log	18.945	5	R4-VPA3	37.083
6	relay3_log	19.781	6	R2-CPM1	22.042	6	relay4_log	42.456
7	R1-VPA1	20.107	7	R3-VPA1	26.325	7	relay2_log	49.876
8	R4-CPA1	21.034	8	R3-CPA1	29.353	8	snort_log1	51.033
9	snort_log3	28.563	9	R3-CPM1	33.032	9	snort_log2	55.322
10	R1-CPA1	31.059	10	relay2_log	38.231	10	R4-VPM1	59.324
11	R2-VPA1	34.800	11	R4-VPM1	39.029	11	R2-CPA1	62.532
12	R3-VPA1	35.199	12	R4-CPA1	39.732	12	R3-CPA1	64.032
13	R4-CPM1	39.432	13	R4-CPM1	41.324	13	R2-VPA1	68.045
14	R4-Power	40.342	14	R3-Power	47.024	14	R3-VPA1	69.443
15	R3-Power	41.042	15	R2-Power	50.432	15	snort_log3	72.898
16	R3-CPM1	42.984	16	R1-CPA1	53.245	16	R4-CPM1	73.332
17	R2-Power	43.879	17	R4-VPA1	54.342	17	R3-Power	73.532
			18	R2-CPA1	57.032	18	R1-VPA1	75.352
			19	relay3_log	59.411	19	R2-Power	77.543
						20	R2-CPM1	79.453
						21	R4-Power	80.043
						22	R3-CPM1	81.094

Fig. 3. Fitness values of the most significant selected features from the binary, triple, and multi class datasets

4 The IDS Detection Rate Using Classic Machine Learning Technology

We reduced the attribute dimension by using four feature selection methods introduced in Sect. 3. In this section, we use five classic supervised machine learning algorithms such as *J48 tree, random forest and Instance-based learning algorithms (IB1), NNGE and JRip* to test the detection accuracy of Binary, Triple and Multiclass test datasets. As shown in Tables 3, 4 and 5, the 28 features selected using expert knowledge and the CFS method provide the highest accuracy rates. Note that **IB1** is the best algorithm that provides 97.201%, 97.2614% and 92.1063% detection accuracy for classifying Binary, Triple and Multi Class datasets with one of the lowest time complexity among these five algorithms.

We also applied the PSO method to enhance the NNGE classifier. Its detection rate is compared with the classification rates of the NNGE classifier without PSO and the IB1 classifier. As Table 6 shows that the NNGE-PSO classifier is the best among the four feature selection methods and five classic machine learning algorithms to classify the power system-specific cyber attacks.

4.1 Discussion

In this paper, we used four feature selection methods to enhance the detection accuracy of three class datasets. Recent research [1,2] used the same test datasets to validate their EIDS detection rates. Researchers proposed the Hoeffding Adaptive Trees (HAT) algorithm and Non-Nested Generalized Exemplars with State Extraction Method (NNGE+STEM) methods to classify the same datasets. The NNGE+STEM algorithm provides 96% and 93% detection accuracy rates for the Binary and Multi Class datasets, and the HAT algorithm provides 98% and 92% respectively. Comparing with the detection rates shown in previous work, we found that without applying the complex STEM data preprocessing method, the selected 28 features with the simple IB1 algorithm can provide similar classification accuracy. The proposed NNGE+PSO algorithm in this paper provides even better detection rates than NNGE+STEM and HAT classifiers. The experimental results validated that the proposed PSO feature selection method is the most efficient to build a highly accurate DEIDS with a low overhead for our system.

5   Conclusion and Future Work

The current EIDS developed for cyber-physical power system infrastructure is not capable to detect cyber attacks for a large-scale system in real time. Therefore, we designed a DIEDS that consists of multiple EIDSs over a large network. The DEIDS can communicate with each other, provide advance monitoring, incident analysis, and instant attack detection over the entire grid network, which provides an easy way to recognize power system performance trends and the patterns of cyber attacks.

We introduced four feature selection methods (i.e., brute force, CFS, MIFS and PSO) to design the DEIDS. The most significant features were selected by the four feature selection methods and we classify a 38GB dataset by adopting five supervised learning algorithms. Comparing with previous research work, we have proved that NNGE+PSO algorithm is the best for designing a high accuracy rate and low overhead DEIDS.

Acknowledgements. This work was partially supported by the U.S. Department of Homeland Security Science & Technology under contract #HSHQDC-16-C-B0033, and by the Office of Naval Research (ONR) grant N0014-14-1-0168.

References

1. Adhikari, U., Morris, T.: Applying hoeffding adaptive trees for real-time cyber-power event and intrusion classification. IEEE Trans. Smart Grid **99**, 1–1 (2017)
2. Adhikari, U., Morris, T.H., Pan, S.: Applying non-nested generalized exemplars classification for cyber-power event and intrusion detection. IEEE Trans. Smart Grid **PP**(99), 1–1 (2016)
3. U. D. of Engery, Chapter 3: Enabling modernization of the electric power system, Quadrennial Technology Review 2015 Transmission and Distribution Components (2015)
4. Minkel, J.: The 2003 northeast blackout-five years later. Scientific American, April 2008. https://www.scientificamerican.com/article/2003-blackout-five-years-later/
5. F.E.R. Commission, Arizona-southern california outages on September 8, 2011 causes and recommendations (2012)
6. F.I.I. Report, Cyber attacks on the ukrainian grid: What you should know. https://www.fireeye.com/content/dam/fireeye-www/global/en/solutions/pdfs/fe-cyber-attacks-ukrainian-grid.pdf

7. Bacet, J.A.B.: Inside the cunning, unprecedented hack of ukraines power grid, March 2016. https://www.wired.com/2016/03/inside-cunning-unprecedented-hack-ukraines-power-grid/
8. Department of Energy, Smart grid. https://energy.gov/oe/services/technology-development/smart-grid
9. Bao, H., Lu, R., Li, B., Deng, R.: BLITHE: behavior rule-based insider threat detection for smart grid. IEEE Internet Things J. **3**(2), 190–205 (2016)
10. Yang, Y., McLaughlin, K., Sezer, S., Littler, T., Pranggono, B., Brogan, P., Wang, H.F.: Intrusion detection system for network security in synchrophasor systems. In: IET International Conference on Information and Communications Technologies (IETICT 2013), pp. 246–252, April 2013
11. Zhang, Y., Wang, L., Sun, W., Green II, R.C., Alam, M.: Distributed intrusion detection system in a multi-layer network architecture of smart grids. IEEE Trans. Smart Grid **2**, 796–808 (2011)
12. Hadeli, H., Schierholz, R., Braendle, M., Tuduce, C.: Leveraging determinism in industrial control systems for advanced anomaly detection and reliable security configuration. In: 2009 IEEE Conference on Emerging Technologies Factory Automation, pp. 1–8, September 2009
13. Bolzoni, D., Etalle, S., Hartel, P.H.: Panacea: automating attack classification for anomaly-based network intrusion detection systems. In: Kirda, E., Jha, S., Balzarotti, D. (eds.) RAID 2009. LNCS, vol. 5758, pp. 1–20. Springer, Heidelberg (2009). doi:10.1007/978-3-642-04342-0_1
14. Valenzuela, J., Wang, J., Bissinger, N.: Real-time intrusion detection in power system operations. IEEE Trans. Power Syst. **28**, 1052–1062 (2013)
15. Morteza Talebi, J.W., Qu, Z.: Secure power systems against malicious cyber-physical data attacks: Protection and identification. World Academy of Science, World Academy of Science, vol. 6 (2012)
16. Hink, R.C.B., Beaver, J.M., Buckner, M.A., Morris, T., Adhikari, U., Pan, S.: Machine learning for power system disturbance and cyber-attack discrimination. In: 2014 7th International Symposium on Resilient Control Systems (ISRCS), pp. 1–8, August 2014
17. Pan, S.: Cybersecurity testing and intrusion detection for cyber-physical power systems. Ph.D. thesis, Mississippi State University (2014)
18. Adhikari, U.: Event and intrusion detection systems for cyber-physical power systems. Ph.D. thesis, Mississippi State University (2015)
19. Industrial control system (ics) cyber attack datasets. http://www.ece.uah.edu/~thm0009/icsdatasets/PowerSystem_Dataset_README.pdf
20. Wang, H., Sun, H., Li, C., Rahnamayan, S., Shyang Pan, J.: Diversity enhanced particle swarm optimization with neighborhood search. Inform. Sci. **223**, 119–135 (2013)

Adjusting Matryoshka Protocol to Address the Scalability Issue in IoT Environment

Gaith Al$^{(\boxtimes)}$, Robin Doss, and Morshed Chowdhury

School of Information Technology, Deakin University, Geelong, Australia
galiyev@deakin.edu.au

Abstract. The security and privacy issues in large scale deployments of RFID/IOT systems is of critical concern to researchers and industry alike. However scalability is often a forgotten aspect of protocol design and is not well addressed. In this paper, we propose an extension to an existing RFID protocol to address the scalability issues required in an IoT context. We also present a review of work by other researchers in this context.

Keywords: Scalability · IoT · RFID · Matryoshka

1 Introduction

Scalability is one of the major issues that faces RFID technology as it is finding widespread deployment especially in the Supply chain, internet of things and other industries. "Internet of things" refers to the network of electronic devices, sensors and RFID components connected together that enables those devices to collect and exchange data between each other. Some novel approaches deal with the increasing amount of tags especially when implementing this technology in IoT which have been proposed by researchers as we will see later in the literature review section. In the following section we will use a method which was used before to address the same issues mentioned above but in different areas. Since using RFID technology in other industries such as supply chain systems has increased the use of grouping protocols, We suggest an implementation for the "Matryoshka" protocol [1] in IoT environment by grouping many RFID tags together and extending that to other devices and components as well. In addition we discuss the increased security and privacy concerns in a scalable system, that can be caused by the increasing numbers of RFID tags.

2 Literature Review

To understand the problems previously discussed by the researchers in the field of IoT, we noticed a huge amount of concern regarding the scalability issue, yet we will first pass by some studies that gave some understanding about IoT in general such as [2] when the authors discuss Trust management 'TM' in IoT, and

© Springer International Publishing AG 2017
R. Doss et al. (Eds.): FNSS 2017, CCIS 759, pp. 84–94, 2017.
DOI: 10.1007/978-3-319-65548-2_7

addressed some of the issues facing the IoT systems which contains three layers "physical layer, network layer and application layer". Also, in [3] the authors described IoT as a distributed system of physical objects that require the seamless integration of hardware (e.g., sensors, actuators, electronics) and network communications used to exchange information. In [4] the authors proposed a protocol that address the scalability requirements in IoT as a large number of requests, results in packet-loss through collision when configuring each IoT device based on the traditional registration protocols. Molnar and Wagner [5] proposed a tree-based tag identification technique to address the scalability issue. The protocols proposed by [6,7] were vulnerable to various attacks and showed weakness in scalability and customizability according to [8]. In [9] the researchers presented a protocol for group-based technique to increase scalability, as tags are divided into groups of equal size that share a secret key. But later in [8] authors proposed a novel identification technique based on a hybrid "group-based approach and collaborative approach" and security check handoff 'SCH' for RFID systems with mobility to ensure a secure and scalable deployment for RFID systems in IoT by using an incorporated malware detection technique. That will offer better security, scalability and customizability according to the authors.

Katina Michael [10] highlighted the pros and cons in managing multi tags in RFID supply chain while [8] classified the protocols which deal with scalability, into: delegation technique such as [7], tree based approach such as [5], group based approach such as [11] and collaborative approach such as [12]. The approach proposed by [8] show that there is a tremendous increase in computational complexity when the number of tags increases. The proposed protocol has four system components works at the Application Level Event "ALE" layer of EPC global Architecture Framework, authors also test their protocol against other existing protocols and they suggest it offers better security and customizable than existing protocols. They conclude that their protocol has parameters to limit the read number of a tag which helps to control the tag read. Overall, this is a security protocol that has the potential to ensure secure and scalable business operation in SCM, ERP system, counterfeit branding, and other similar processes. In [13] the author pointed 8 problems and topic areas which required more research: a. massive scaling: trillions of things and smart devices being deployed to name and authenticate.etc., b. Architecture and dependencies: the need adequate architecture that permits easy connectivity, control, communication, and useful applications. c. Creating knowledge and big data, d. Robustness: many IoT application will be based on a deployed sensing, actuation and communication platform which require these devices to know their locations and to have synchronized clocks., e. Openness: which require the sensor based systems to be open systems rather than closed system as we can see now in cars, airplanes etc. f. security g. Privacy h. human in loop. When it comes to grouping the RFID tags together Ari Juels lately presented a similar idea based on Yoking- Proofs for RFID Tags [14]. The Aim of this Idea was to enable a pair of RFID tags to generate a proof that is readable simultaneously by a reader [14]. Later Leonid Bolotnyy and Gabriel Robins In their paper "Generalized

Yoking— Proofs for a Group of RFID Tags" [15] gave a brief examples on where this is useful, mentioning legal requirement in pharmaceutical distribution were one RFID tag is embed in a container for the medication while another is embedded in an accompanying leaflet.

Since our "adjusted Martroshka protocol" will also be using the supply chain environment specially during reading the pallets or tagged items. We will have some brief literature study about the use of RFID in supply chain Management. The use of RFID technology in supply chain was also a topic of interest for the researchers such as [10]. In this paper the authors presents the pros and cons of using radio-frequency identification in supply chain management or SCM. It states and explain some of the pros of the use of RFID system in SCM such as $Non - Line - of - Sight$, Technology including, Automatic $Non - Line - of - Sight$ Scanning, Labor Reduction, Asset Tracking and Returnable Items Improved Inventory Management, Ability to Withstand Harsh Environments, and Cost Savings. Also they address some of the cons of the RFID use in SCM such as: Deployment Issues, Manufacturing Sector Concerns, Lack of Standards, Privacy Concerns, and Interference and Reading Considerations. The authors elaborate on each term used here. While in [16] the authors proposed a software frame work to integrate Both RFID and WSNs into SCM systems by establishing a communication channel between EPCIS for RFIDs and mediation layer, (MDI) for WSNs while the RFID focus on Identification of the objects the WSN will monitor the control of the supply chain environment, they address the problems associated with this approach of integration such as disjoint network between RFID and WSNs, and their different objectives and capabilities for each industry. They describe the EPCIS as a special web service interacting with the whole RFID system and work as a gateway between any requester of tag information and database. Also they explain a use case which describes their approach yet they did not mention the security and privacy issue in such framework, which we strongly recommend it. Since the RFID tags are used widely in the warehouses some authors such as [17] developed an energy efficient tag searching protocol in Multiple reader RFID system namely ESiM. For the tags powered by built-in batteries to reduce not only the time but the energy efficiency as well. Yet all the above studies did not produce a practical solution for the problem of RFID scalability in IoT environment, specially it will be a real topic of concern in the near future due to the tremendous increase in RFID tags, micro sensors and other components.

3   Applying a New Approch to the IoT Environment

3.1   A Brief Summary of Matryoshka and the Issues Designed to Address in SCM

We should first explain what is the Matrysohka protocol which was presented by Al et al. in [1]. The Matryoshka protocol is a new approach which uses a pyramid structure in dealing with a large number of RFID tags by grouping them together in one single tag called the Master tag in order to use this tag instead of hundreds or thousands or maybe millions of tags when dealing with an environment that uses such a large number of them. The protocol does not require the reader to read each one of those tags as long as they were similar or packed in a place with no physical disruption [1]. This method will reduce the tag reads to almost minimum depending on the number of Master tags reads which is 1 in each case. Since the master tag number is limited, this will minimize the following possible problems that might occur due to the increased reads.

- RFID Reader Collision: happens when two or more readers signal overlaps. This problem causes the tag to fail to respond the same time, many systems use anti-collision protocols to avoid this problem.
- RFID Tag Collision: this problem occurs when using many tags in a small area.
- Interference and reading possible issues
- Software and equipments upgrade and maintenance
- Privacy and security concerns

We determine that the Matryoshka protocol was designed to provide a new secure method in scalability and managing RFID tags in "SCM" which supposed to provide more accuracy and more reliability in tags security and management. This method was also designed to decrease the problems, threats and errors associated with tag readings in RFID systems, such as disruption, tag collision, tag counterfeiting threats etc. The decrease of tag readings can also be very important for privacy and security and can be adapted for IoT environment as shown below.

As for the Matryoshka protocol the structure has three layers of tags or devices as follow

Level 1 components: The tags ID and components in level 1, will be named as $LS(TID)$. The database then will generate a random numeric value for each $LS(TID)$ called $LS(TID)'$ this valued will be stored in a table called LS table see Table 1 below.

Table 1. The LS table

TID	Random generated number (K)	LS (TID)'
$LS(TID)_i$	k_i	k_i
$LS(TID)_{i+1}$	k_{i+1}	k_{i+1}
$LS(TID)_{i+2}$	k_{i+2}	k_{i+2}
$LS(TID)_{i+n}$	k_{i+n}	k_{i+n}

The DB then will determine the tag or device ID TID for each Level 2 tags "$LSM(TID)$" by adding the values of $LS(TID)'_{i+1}$ assigned in LS tables together,

$$LSM(TID)' = \sum_{b=1}^{n} LS(TID)'_b \tag{1}$$

The readers will assign a new tag ID for level 2 tags from formula 1 above. Then all the tags for Level 1 will be muted. Level 2 components all the tags IDs as well as other device IDs or components, will be allocated at a table in database named LSM table. The Reader will Write the original $LSM(TID)$ values in column 1 and use formula 1 to generate new values for $LSM(TID)'$ and then write those values at column 2 from the LSM table as shown in Table 2 below:

Table 2. The LSM table

TID	$LSM(TID)'$
$LSM(TID)_i$	$LSM(TID)'_i$
$LSM(TID) + i + 1$	$LSM(TID)'_{i+1}$
$LSM(TID)_{i+2}$	$LSM(TID)'_{i+2}$
$LSM(TID)_{i+n}$	$LSM(TID)'_{i+n}$

The generated numeric $LSM(TID)'$ value will replace the $LSM(TID)$ in the data base. The data base will determine the $LM(TID)$ of Level 3 by XORing the values of $LSM(TID)'_{i+1}$ as shown in formula 2 where n is the number of components and tags, while $i = 1$ (Table 3).

Table 3. Protocol notations

Notations	
LS	Slave tag level
LSM	Slave-Master tag level
LM	Master tag level
A	Source
B	Destination
n	Number of tags or components
W	Variable
TID	Tag ID
S	Shared secret
K	Random number

The reader then will replace the actual $LM(TID)$ with the value of the master components $LM(TID)$ which supposed to be on top of the pyramid structure. Then mute level 2 components.

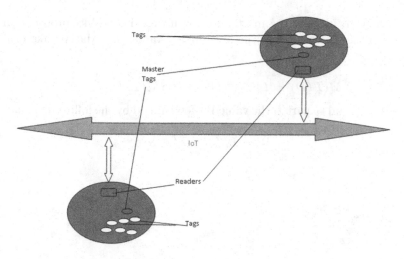

Fig. 1. Communications between two RFID readers via IoT using the Matryoshka Protocol

While in level 3 the tags and other devices will also be named as master components since they are located on the top of the pyramid structure of the Matryoshka protocol. The components and tags here will represent all the tags and components located underneath it which will allow the reader to communicate with one instead of many since the other tags and components in level 1 and 2 are muted.

Later we can reverse the operations above to retrieve the RFID tags into their original values in order to communicate with them individually. This will help the stock flow to de-group the tags again at any time. The main element in this procedure is to follow the value of the master tags and allocate them in the LSM or LS tables in order to determine which master tag is allocated in which table.

3.2 Applying and Adjusting the Protocol to IoT Environment

As we mentioned above, in the next few years we expect to have a huge number of RFID tags or other components in every home, government department,store, retailer shop etc., attached to devices, objects, animals or even humans. Having said that we expect the RFID readers to increase dramatically as a result of this tremendous increase in RFID use. The devices will need to communicate with each other or with other devices using the internet and this can be possible but might hit the obstacle of scalability which will cause a lot of confusion, noisiness, collisions and security threats as mentioned above in "A".

We adjust the protocol in order to allow it to fit our approach in handling the scalability issue in the IoT environment. This will be made by adding a shared secret key S XORed by $LM(TID)'$ in W as we can see the formulas below, which will enable the other parts of networks in IoT to retrieve the values of $LM(TID)'$.

This can help to identify the master tag by using Matryoshka protocol on the other side of the network. Since the Master tags value from Matryoshka protocol determined by:

$$LM(TID)' = LSM(TID)'_i \oplus LSM(TID)'_{i+1} \oplus n \qquad (2)$$

Part A will send to part B the value W determined by the following equations:

$$W = LM(TID)' \oplus S \qquad (3)$$

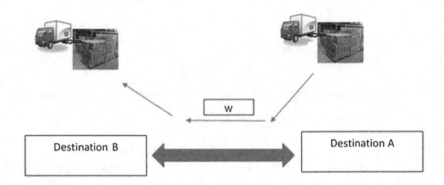

Fig. 2. Transferring the Master tag (TID) from destination A to destination B

Now let's assume that a two retailer shop uses Matryoshka protocol to manage a huge number of goods and objects which uses RFID tags to prevent scalability, see Fig. 1. And lets assume that both readers wanted to communicate with each other "assuming that each reader has its own Database", for some reason, such as ownership transfer, stock availability, census or authentication verification see Fig. 2. Here the whole process will be much easier when using only the Master tag ID or $LM(TID)'$ and transfer W to the other end. The both ends must adapt the same protocol as well as store the same data base, in order to be able to communicate. And also to be able to retrieve the original tag ID's. Otherwise the system has to request it from the other end while transferring or processing. The same concept can be applied on other devices which create the components of the IoT such as sensors, other items embedded with electronics, softwares, etc., by adding a code or a reference or a unique number for each component or device and store this number in LS and LSM tables. Those items cans also work just as the RFIDS tags as long as all of these items or devices will use the same method and share the same secret key S. Also it can be used for electronic devices that are in a geographical near position and managed by one entity such as home items, home electronics and smart devices which are all connected to one router, as well as the RFID systems. Using other devices other than RFID systems will have different measurements that we have to take into consideration, this we will address in the future work as it needs more detailed graphs and protocols security analysis which would need further elaboration. Yet the scenario which we provided here will be more than sufficient and secure in transferring the master tag ID to other networks connected to the IoT or through the internet. As the main idea of embedding more devices in one device will reduce the scalability to the minimum as the protocol suggested.

$$LM(TID)' = W \oplus S \tag{4}$$

3.3 Algorithms

In this section we will adjust the algorithms which we used in "Matryoshka protocol" as follow: The reader (R) will read all the tags in LS level then read the $LSM(TID)_i$.

Algorithm 1. Begin Algorithm 1 at reader in destination A

1: Read $LS(TID)_i$
2: Send "Mute" to $LS(TID)_i$
3: Read $LSM(TID)_i$
4: Send "Mute" to $LSM(TID)_i$
5: Read $LM(TID)$
6: Call DB1
7: Send W, to destination B

Algorithm 2. Begin DB1

1: Create LS table
2: Write $LS(TID)_i$ to LS table Column 1
3: Generate Random number (K) for LS table
4: Write $(K)_i$ to Column 2
5: $LS(TID)'_i = (K)_i$
6: Find $LSM(TID)'_i$ from Eq. 1
7: Repeat step 1 n times
8: Create LSM table
9: Write $LSM(TID)_i$ to LSM table column
10: Write $LSM(TID)'_i$ to LSM table column 2
11: Determin $LM(TID)'$ from Eq. 2
12: Get S
13: Determine W from Eq. 3

To retrieve the tags ID's to their original values in the destination B, we will apply the following algorithms after receiving the tagged goods in Pallet at destination B. Then the reader will read the LM tag, LSM and LS tags and compare it with the values from the equations above.

Algorithm 3. Begin Algorithm 3 reader at destination B

1: Read W
2: Call DB2
3: send response to destination A

Algorithm 4. Begin DB2

1: Get S
2: Read W
3: Determine $LM'(TID)$ from Eq. 4
4: Read $LM(TID)$ from Pallet
5: **if** $LM(TID) = (LM(TID)')$ **then**
6:     Un-Mute $LSM(TID)_i$
7:     Read $LSM(TID)_i$
8:     Determine $LSM(TID)_i'$ from Eq. 2 and from the reader B
9:     **if** $LSM(TID)_i = (LSM(TID)_i')$ **then**
10:        Un-Mute $LS(TID)_i$
11:        Read $LS(TID)_i$
12:        Determine $LS(TID)_i'$ from LS table
13:        **if** $LS(TID)_i = LS(TID)_i'$ **then**
14:            Correct $LS(TID)_i$
15:        **else**
16:            wrong value of LS
17:        **end if**
18:     **else**
19:        wrong value of LSM
20:     **end if**
21: **else**
22:     wrong value of LM
23: **end if**

4   Future Work

Scalability and security were always the concern of researchers in dealing with a huge number of RFID tags in different environments such as supply chain or IoT. We applied an existing method with some adjustment in dealing with a huge number of RFID tags as one entity to reduce collisions and reduce security risks that accompany the reading process for the RFID tags. We will be conducting more studies in the future for the same protocol. Furthermore, we will address the issue of scalability and security in IoT taking into consideration some other methods used in the past such as [18,19], then we will try to implement these methods in the IoT environment to obtain better results in solving those problems. Also we will be making more studies on how to connect other devices other than RFID tags by using the "Matryoshka" approach, these studies will be detailed and will have more security analysis in order to provide a secure communication that takes privacy and security into consideration and prevent counterfeiting and theft for the items during the process.

References

1. Al., G., Doss, R., Chowdhury, M., Ray, B.: Secure RFID protocol to manage and prevent tag counterfeiting with Matryoshka concept. In: Doss, R., Piramuthu, S., Zhou, W. (eds.) FNSS 2016. CCIS, vol. 670, pp. 126–141. Springer, Cham (2016). doi:10.1007/978-3-319-48021-3_9
2. Yan, Z., Zhang, P., Vasilakos, A.V.: A survey on trust management for internet of things. J. Network Comput. Appl. **42**, 120–134 (2014)
3. Fernández-Caramés, T.M., Fraga-Lamas, P., Suárez-Albela, M., Castedo, L.: Reverse engineering and security evaluation of commercial tags for RFID-based IoT applications. Sensors **17**(1), 28 (2016)
4. Ashraf, Q.M., Habaebi, M.H., Sinniah, G.R., Chebil, J.: Broadcast based registration technique for heterogenous nodes in the IoT. In: International Conference on Control, Engineering, and Information Technology (CEIT 2014), Sousse (2014)
5. Molnar, D., Wagner, D.: Privacy and security in library RFID: issues, practices, and architectures. In: Proceedings of the 11th ACM Conference on Computer and Communications Security, pp. 210–219. ACM (2004)
6. Biplob, R., Chowdhury, M.U., Pham, T.: Mutual authentication with malware protection for a RFID system. In: ITS 2010: Proceedings of the Annual International Conference on Information Technology Security, pp. 24–29. Global Science & Technology Forum (GSTF) (2010)
7. Song, B., Mitchell, C.J.: Scalable RFID security protocols supporting tag ownership transfer. Comput. Commun. **34**(4), 556–566 (2011)
8. Ray, B.R., Abawajy, J., Chowdhury, M.: Scalable RFID security framework and protocol supporting internet of things. Comput. Networks **67**, 89–103 (2014)
9. Avoine, G., Buttyant, L., Holczer, T., Vajda, I.: Group-based private authentication. In: IEEE International Symposium on a World of Wireless, Mobile and Multimedia Networks, WoWMoM 2007, pp. 1–6. IEEE (2007)
10. Michael, K., McCathie, L.: The pros and cons of RFID in supply chain management. In: International Conference on Mobile Business (ICMB 2005), pp. 623–629. IEEE (2005)
11. Fouladgar, S., Afifi, H.: Scalable privacy protecting scheme through distributed RFID tag identification. In: Proceedings of the workshop on Applications of private and anonymous communications, p. 3. ACM (2008)
12. Solanas, A., Domingo-Ferrer, J., Martínez-Ballesté, A., Daza, V.: A distributed architecture for scalable private RFID tag identification. Comput. Networks **51**(9), 2268–2279 (2007)
13. Stankovic, J.A.: Research directions for the internet of things. IEEE Internet Things J. **1**(1), 3–9 (2014)
14. Juels, A.: "Yoking-proofs" for RFID tags. In: Proceedings of the Second IEEE Annual Conference on Pervasive Computing and Communications Workshops, pp. 138–143. IEEE (2004)
15. Bolotnyy, L., Robins, G.: Generalized "Yoking-Proofs" for a group of RFID tags. In: 2006 Third Annual International Conference on Mobile and Ubiquitous Systems: Networking & Services, pp. 1–4. IEEE (2006)
16. Gomez, L., Laurent, M., El Moustaine, E.: Risk assessment along supply chain: a RFID and wireless sensor network integration approach. Sens. Transducers **14**(2), 269 (2012)

17. Zhang, S., Liu, X., Wang, J., Cao, J., Min, G.: Energy-efficient active tag searching in large scale RFID systems. Inf. Sci. **317**, 143–156 (2015)
18. Al, G., Ray, B., Chowdhury, M.: RFID tag ownership transfer protocol for a closed loop system. In: 2014 IIAI 3rd International Conference on Advanced Applied Informatics (IIAIAAI), pp. 575–579, August 2014
19. Al, G., Ray, B., Chowdhury, M.: Multiple scenarios for a tag ownership transfer protocol for a closed loop system. IJNDC **3**(2), 128–136 (2015)

Big Data and Future Applications

Is High Performance Computing (HPC) Ready to Handle Big Data?

Biplob R. Ray[1]([✉]), Morshed Chowdhury[2], and Usman Atif[2]

[1] Centre for Intelligent Systems (CIS), School of Engineering and Technology,
Central Queensland University, Cairns, Australia
b.ray@cqu.edu.au
[2] School of Information Technology, Deakin University, Melbourne, Australia

Abstract. In recent years big data has emerged as a universal term and its management has become a crucial research topic. The phrase 'big data' refers to data sets so large and complex that the processing of them requires collaborative High Performance Computing (HPC). How to effectively allocate resources is one of the prime challenges in HPC. This leads us to the question: are the existing HPC resource allocation techniques effective enough to support future big data challenges? In this context, we have investigated the effectiveness of HPC resource allocation using the Google cluster dataset and a number of data mining tools to determine the correlational coefficient between resource allocation, resource usages and priority. Our analysis initially focused on correlation between resource allocation and resource uses. The finding shows that a high volume of resources that are allocated by the system for a job are not being used by that same job. To investigate further, we analyzed the correlation between resource allocation, resource usages and priority. Our clustering, classification and prediction techniques identified that the allocation and uses of resources are very loosely correlated with priority of the jobs. This research shows that our current HPC scheduling needs improvement in order to accommodate the big data challenge efficiently.

Keywords: Big data · HPC · Data mining · QoS · Correlation

1 Introduction

The High Performance Computing (HPC) system uses distributed computing paradigm to tie together the power of large number of distributed resources across networks. Scalability, reliability, information sharing, and information exchange are the main objectives to achieve by implementing an efficient distributed computing [1]. The resource request mechanism is considered one of the central themes that determines the amount of resource allocated by a HPC system for the job. The resource commitment efficiency of HPC systems determine the number of jobs that can be handled by a HPC system at a time [2, 3]. The relationship between the priority of the job and resource allocation enforces resource management based on QoS (Quality of Service). This helps HPC to

© Springer International Publishing AG 2017
R. Doss et al. (Eds.): FNSS 2017, CCIS 759, pp. 97–112, 2017.
DOI: 10.1007/978-3-319-65548-2_8

provide deterministic services according to Service Level Agreement (SLA) within HPC, between HPC providers and users [2, 3].

The computing and processing power of HPC is aggregated through a data centre, which is an array of cluster networks. The overall performance of the cluster computing system depends on the features of the system [4, 5]. Different cluster computing features have different levels of contribution for efficient resource management, which has been investigated extensively in the literature. In clusters networks, using the resources effectively is one of the prime challenges. For example, due to underutilization and improper provisioning of resources, the HPC will have high costs and increased time complexity [6, 7]. Therefore, accurate prediction of CPU and memory usage prior to committing the resources will reduce the resource management complexity. This can significantly reduce the workload on the clusters and also reduce the overall cost involved to perform the specific task. Moreover, resource allocation and uses need to adhere to the job priority to ensure that high priority jobs have more resources than low priority [8, 9].

Virtual existence of all the things (objects and human) around us is rapidly increasing as a result of the quantity of data being collected and processed in the digital world, and this has emerged as the universal term "big data". It is a collection of data sets so large and complex that traditional data processing applications are inadequate to perform computation on them efficiently [23]. Therefore, there is a growing need to investigate the efficiency of current HPC resource provisioning to handle big data [2]. A volume of research has been conducted within different resource allocation contexts to identify if the tasks are given enough resources and whether the tasks are managed efficiently. However, there has been very little work done to identify the correlation between two or more features such as resource allocation, resource uses and priority. The correlation between resource allocation, resource usage and priority in the current HPC domain will let us understand the current resource provisioning status and improvement direction to accommodate big data.

The aim of this research is to identify the correlations between different parameters affecting workload of clustered networks. We will use Google Cluster Dataset (GCD) [20] and a number of data mining tools to determine the efficiency of resource provisioning for big data handling. Our research will investigate resource provisioning in three main contexts: resource (in terms of CPU, memory and disk space usage) allocation, resources usage, and priority of the jobs. We aim to find out:

- The degree of resource wastage or management overhead caused by over committing of resources by the HPC to a job.
- Do the resource provisions follow the task priority?

The rest of the paper is organized as follows. In Sect. 2, we detail the Google cluster dataset and the data structure used in this research. In Sect. 3, we present related work that is followed by brief detail of data mining tools and techniques used in this analysis in Sect. 4. In Sect. 5, we present detail discussion on our experiment result. Followed by detail analysis on our experiments output is Sect. 6. Finally, the conclusion is presented in Sect. 7.

2   Data Set

In this section, we detail the Google cluster dataset in Subsect. 2.1 that is followed by a detail data structure workflow used in this research in Subsect. 2.2.

2.1   Google Cluster Data Set

In Google's data center, the clusters are made up of machines connected with a high-bandwidth [11]. Google clusters are a set of machines connected together in racks, connected by a high bandwidth network [15]. A set of machines may be called cells, which have the same cluster management system that allocates work to the machines. Work arrives in the cell in the form of a job which has further tasks, each of which is comprised of resource requirement used towards the scheduling, and run on one or more cores as illustrated in Fig. 1. Each of the tasks represents a Linux program [15]. The tasks that are using more than their allocated resources may be throttled in the case of CPU and killed in the case of memory [15]. The scheduler may over-commit resources on a machine if there are free resources when the usage is lower than the request. As a result, there may be not enough resources to meet the runtime requests, in which case one or more low priority tasks may be killed [15].

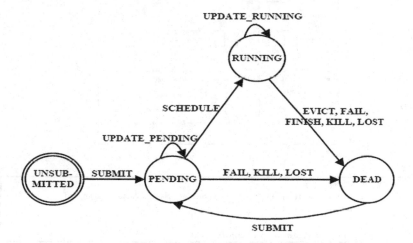

Fig. 1. State transition for job tasks

According to Google, approximately 70 out of 449855 jobs (for example, job number 6377830001) have no task event records. We believe that this is legitimate in a majority of cases: typically because the job is started but its tasks are disabled for its entire duration [20].

2.2 Data Structure Workflow Used in This Research

In our research we are investigating the correlation between resource allocation, resource usage and priority; this requires us to use the task event and the task usage tables of the Google dataset [20].

The task event table has the detail of resource allocation (the same as resource request) that consists of maximum CPU, memory and disk space requested by a task. The allocated amount of resources (CPU, memory and disk space) by the HPC system for a task is the same as the requested amount. The table also has a field name priority, a small integer that is mapped into a sorted set of values, with 0 as the lowest priority (least important) [15] and 11 as the highest priority (most important). Tasks with larger priority numbers should get preference for resources over tasks with smaller priority numbers.

The usage table consists of many fields but we are concerned with the CPU usage, memory usage and disk space usage of each job task. Additionally, the table contains the assigned memory field which holds the requested memory by the job task. It is not necessary that all of these allocated resources would be used [15]; this creates free resources to be allocated to other job tasks. The data workflow used in this research is illustrated in Fig. 2.

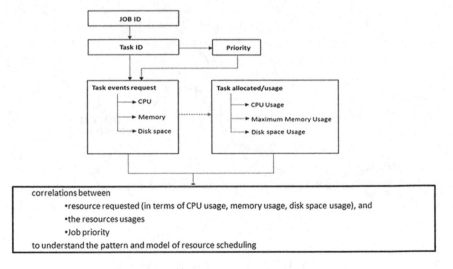

Fig. 2. Workflow used for analysis

As shown in Fig. 2, we have used CPU, memory and disk space fields from tables (task event request and task uses). We have also used the job priority given in the task event table and populated the task uses table with priority on the basis of their job ID and task ID similarity. We will use this information to determine resource allocation and resource management efficiency of Google HPC by identifying correlation factors of resource requested, resource usage and job priority. This will give us an idea about almost all HPC, as Google clusters is one of the best performing clusters in the world [20].

3   Literature Review

A lot of work has been done on Google's trace data to better understand the working efficiency of Google clusters. We have extensively reviewed the existing work on Google trace analysis [10–14, 22, 23].

Sheng et al. [10] published the pioneering article on Google trace analysis that investigated resource utilization in the Google trace with relation to the pareto principle [10]. They have used the mass-count disparity evaluation to present the distribution of the task/events per application [10]. Mass-count is a metric made up of mass and count distribution. Count refers to the cumulative distributed function, whereas mass weights each item to determine the probability that a unit of mass belongs to an item. Let $\int (t)$. be the probability density function, the values in mass-count disparity evaluation is calculated based on the formula presented in Eqs. (1) and (2).

$$F_c(x) = P_r(X < x) \tag{1}$$

$$F_m(x) = \frac{\int_0^x t \cdot \int (t)\, dt}{\int_0^\infty t \cdot \int (t)\, dt} \tag{2}$$

By comparing the curves the paper [10] has determined that the pareto principle was being followed. It was conceived that 86.7% of the jobs belong to only 13.3% of the applications. Furthermore, the distribution of CPU workload and memory workload per application was also studied. It was concluded that only 1.5% of the application contributed to 98.5% CPU and 1.8% of the applications contributed to 98.2%, which means that the majority of the applications contributed to low CPU and Memory usage [10]. The k-means algorithm was used to observe the workload based application clustering. Different numbers of clusters were used, to evaluate if the pareto principle was being followed in each case [10]. It was concluded that most of the applications were located near the origin point (0, 0) which means that the majority of the applications in Google utilize low CPU and Memory [10].

Liu et al. [11] have examined the daily machine events and identified that 40.52% of the jobs are killed at least once [11]. The paper [11] has concluded that "The overall throughput is determined by the jobs with a few tasks rather than a few jobs with many tasks". Although the nature of the jobs is not disclosed in the dataset, it is believed that jobs with a smaller number of tasks are easier to schedule [11]. Further, the paper investigates the CPU usage with relevance to the CPU cycles spent on tasks that complete normally, failed and killed. For this the data used was a day's worth [11]. The results showed that 60% of the CPU cycles are used for tasks that are killed out of which 50% of the kills occurred to jobs which were latency insensitive or low priority tasks. The CPU cycles are considered as wasted and only 10 to 15% of the CPU cycles are towards the tasks that complete normally [11]. This implies that there are opportunities to improve the scheduling process in the Google trace dataset.

Xiao et al. have [22] investigated the link between resource allocation and job execution. They have identified that the job submission or mitigation to a workstation depends on the availability of CPU and memory resources at that time [22]. Some jobs that are allocated a large amount of memory tend to increase the queuing delay for the rest of the jobs which may only require normal allocation [22]. This tends to slow down the execution of each individual job, which results in a decrease in the system throughput. This phenomenon can be called job blocking, where the big jobs block the execution pace of small jobs or lesser priority jobs. It is clear that no job would be accepted if the workstation had no ideal memory. It has been observed that during blocking the CPU and the memory are not being fully utilized. The workstations reaching their CPU threshold may still have ideal memory space and job slots available [22]. Schemes such as the memory reservation (where workstations with large memory allocation space are dedicated to jobs with large memory requirement) is used to minimize the ideal memory [22]. However, existing studies show that even load sharing schemes that dynamically schedule and assign are also not able to fully utilize the available resources.

Sheng et al. [12] have compared some of the renowned grid computers to the Google cluster cloud, claiming that the job utilization in Google cluster is much lower compared to the grid computers. The reason being that the Google jobs are more of interactive and real time as compared to scientific batch jobs [12]. The paper concluded that the host load on some of the grid computers such as the AverGrid and HARCNET was more stable during relatively long hours, whereas Google clusters load changed frequently. This indicates that the majority of the tasks in Google clusters are smaller than that of Grids [12]; owing to which predicting Google's host load is difficult. As the Google clusters have not been tested with scientific batch jobs it is likely to show a better job utilization in comparison to Grid computers.

Mishra et al. [13] have considered the resources (CPU and RAM) and the duration of the tasks in their work. In this work [13], small classes were constructed consisting of tasks with similar resource usage. It also considered the average usage and the duration of that particular task [13]. In this work, if the tasks have compatible magnitude they belong to the same workload. The challenges faced were that the task within a workload should have very in resource demand. They used the simple k-means algorithm to avoid bias task classes [13]. However, the different qualitative coordinates were done manually. The result of this analysis shows that relatively more tasks had short duration. Most resources were being consumed by fewer tasks with longer duration. The work done in this paper is based on categorizing the jobs tasks according to their usage in terms of the duration and can aid in improving the scheduling within the Google clusters [13].

Charles et al. [14] analyzed the Google dataset using clustering algorithm and concluded that there were large numbers of task resubmission in the Google clusters (these are cases when a job fails and is restarted after the failure). Many of the 14 Kilobytes and 10 Megabytes (M) jobs were failed where 10 M jobs had a three time crash loop. There were 4.5 M evictions recorded in the trace [14], and the rate of eviction is related to priority tasks. Almost all of these evictions, according to the paper, occurred within half a second of start of another task with the same or higher priority. This signifies that these job evictions are made to free resources [14]. There is evidence that the scheduler evicted before the resource came into conflict and after around 30% of evictions resources requested by the evicted tasks appeared to remain free. This suggests that either the evictions were unnecessary or made to handle the spikes of usage in the clusters. Regarding the resource usage and request, the paper suggests that if the scheduler can predict the actual usage more accurately, tasks can be packed more tightly without degrading performance [14]. The Google trace has a high frequency of repeated submissions. This provides a natural opportunity for predictions, and the scheduler can use this to its advantage and allocate the job exactly the resources that it requires [14]. The paper suggests that longer-running jobs have relatively stable resource utilization [14]; this can be used to help adapt the resource scheduler.

With the quantity of data being collected rapidly increasing, a special approach to the resource allocation is required. It has been proved with certain assumptions that reduction in the resource wastage is directly related to cost minimization [23]. In [23] Hassan et al. used algorithms such as the First Come First Served (FCFS), single-resource-Min-Min heuristic (CPU), multi-resource-Min-Min heuristic with proposed metric, and Min-Min heuristic with tuning parameters to minimize this problem [23]. This research proved that the proposed Min-Min heuristic can help to save up to 20% of the cost and also showed that the resource utilization of the CPU, RAM and Local disk were much higher using this algorithm [23]. The paper provides significant evidence that resource provision in HPC is one of the major drawbacks that will be costly and slow the big data analysis process [23].

As seen in the literature review, there is very little existing work focused on correlation of two or more factors that might help us better understand the performance level of current HPC and QoS performance levels. This triggers the need to investigate the correlation between relevant resource provisioning parameters and its role in prioritizing of the jobs. In our research, we are investigating the relationship between resource allocation, resource uses and a task's priority to identify the degree of efficiency of HPC on resource provisioning and QoS to support big data.

4   Data Mining Tools and Techniques Used

This section detail data mining tools used in this study. For our analysis, we have selected linear Regression, simple k-means and decision tree algorithms [21]. We selected linear regression and decision tree algorithms for data classification. Simple k-means and decision tree algorithms are used for data set clustering. Moreover, linear regression and decision tree algorithms are used for prediction based on given training data set. This paper used Weka 3.6 software in Windows platform to run selected algorithms [16]. Each data mining algorithms are briefly detailed below.

4.1 Linear Regression

This is a statistical technique that is widely used to classify data. Its main intent is to approximate a functional relationship between two or more variables of interest by a mathematical model. It finds the relationship between two variables using formula shown in Eq. (3) [17].

$$y = a + bx \qquad (3)$$

Here x and y are variables, 'b' is the slope of regression line and 'a' is the interception point of the regression line [17]. The output of this technique consists of finding the line of best fit, which is called the regression line [17]. In our research we have used the linear regression to find the resource allocation line that is the best fit for a task on the basis of its task uses.

4.2 Simple k-Means

The simple k-means is a clustering algorithm. It is a technique of grouping or classifying the data into k groups using Eq. (4) where k being the user specified number of clusters. The groupings of the objects are made by minimizing the sum of squared distances between the items and the corresponding centroid [18]. The algorithm first randomly selects the k number of objects, where k is the user defined number of clusters; these objects represent a cluster mean or the centre. The remaining objects are assigned to the cluster they are most similar to, based on their distance from the object and the mean of the cluster [18]. A new mean is computed for each cluster after every data instance, refining the clusters with the next iteration. Let term $\left\| x_i^j - c_j \right\|^2$ provide the distance between an entity point and the cluster's centroid, simple k-means uses Eq. (4) to group data.

$$\sum_{j=1}^{k} \sum_{i=1}^{n} \left\| x_i^j - c_j \right\|^2 \qquad (4)$$

4.3 Decision Tree

The decision trees algorithm is considered to be a powerful and popular tool which can be used for classification and prediction. A decision trees is a hybrid algorithm and incorporates different methods for creating a tree; it supports multiple analytic tasks, which includes regression, classification, and association [19]. A decision tree provides unique capabilities and substitutes for traditional statistical forms of analysis, which includes linear regression and a variety of data mining tools and techniques such as neural networks [19].

5 Experiment Result

In this section, we present our experiment results that are the outcome of our analysis using data mining tools detailed in Sect. 4 on the Google Cluster Dataset (GCD) illustrated in Fig. 2. These analyses performed to find answers of the research questions detailed in Sect. 1. We detail our results in two categories. In Subsect. 5.1, we discuss results of data analysis that address correlation between resource allocation and resource uses for jobs in GCD. This is followed by data analysis results that will answer correlation of priority with resource provisioning in Subsect. 5.2.

5.1 Correlation Between Resource Request and Resource Uses

In order to find a correlation between resource requested and resource used, the resource usage table was used as a training set in the linear regression algorithm. For each of the resources (CPU, RAM, Local disk), a supplied test set was provided in the form of the resource request table. The linear regression predicted the actual resource usages out of resource requested. In Tables 1, 2 and 3, we illustrated the output of linear regression for each resource (CPU, RAM and Local disk). The linear regression also calculated correlation coefficient between predicted usages of one resource with rest of the requested resources.

Table 1. Linear regression predicts CPU usage

Predicted CPU usage	Requested RAM	Requested local disk
0.0082	0.2961	7.174
Correlation coefficient: 0.4743		

Table 2. Linear regression predicts RAM usage

Predicted RAM usage	Requested CPU	Requested local disk
0.042	0.2279	7.174
Correlation coefficient: 0.6076		

Table 3. Linear regression predicts local disk usage

Predicted Local Disk usage	Requested CPU	Requested RAM
0.0002	0.2279	0.2961
Correlation coefficient: 0.4697		

The data in Tables 1, 2 and 3 shows that none of the requested resources are fully utilized by the job.

We plot this result in Fig. 3 to illustrate that almost 50% of requested resources by jobs are wasted or reallocated. Most of the requested resources are wasted or reallocated for local disk. A total of 53% of requested resources were wasted or reallocated. The graph also shows that the best possible local disk space resource request should not exceed 50%.

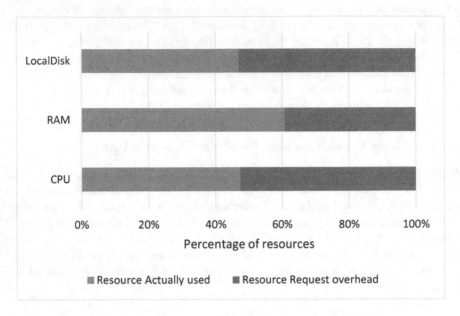

Fig. 3. Resource request overhead based on linear regression's prediction

We further analysed the Google trace dataset using the simple k-means algorithm. We used task event table as the training set data and the task usage was provided as the test dataset in simple k-means. The number of the cluster (k) was initially chosen to be high but was decreased to five as higher number of clusters make cluster values lot closer to each other. Choosing a cluster value of five provided evenly distributed cluster centroids. This experiment provided us with an overview as to how many of the jobs are requesting higher resources than their actual usage.

As shown in Tables 4 and 5, different numbers of clusters have different centroids and the number of instances under them.

Table 4. Simple k-means clustering

Attributes	Priorities	0	1	2	3	4
Full data set	449855	104923	107722	190787	16969	29454
CPU	0.0441	0.0744	0.0182	0.0217	0.2248	0.0719
RAM	0.0361	0.0429	0.01	0.0294	0.0911	0.1184
Local Disk	0.0003	0.0002	0.0001	0.0004	0.0004	0.0013

In Table 4, we present resource usages under each cluster for each resource. The simple k-means also provided percentage of total resources allocated and used in each cluster as presented in Table 5. The results from Tables 4 and 5 are plotted in Fig. 4 to better illustrate our findings. The graph in Fig. 4 shows the cluster numbers in the x-axis and the percentage of the tasks that lie within these clusters. The blue line signifies percentage of resource allocation and the red line signifies percentage of resource usage.

Table 5. Resource allocation and uses of each clusters based on simple k-means

Clusters	Resource allocation	Resource uses
0	23%	10%
1	24%	77%
2	42%	11%
3	4%	2%
4	7%	1%

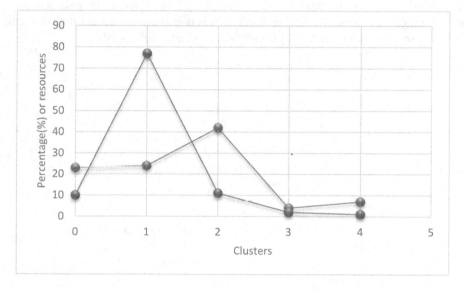

Fig. 4. Comparative graphical illustration between resource allocation and uses clusters (Color figure online)

The result showed that 42% of resources allocated to cluster 2, whereas only 11% of resources used in cluster 2. The results also show that 77% of the resource usage belong to cluster 1, whereas only 24% of resources were under cluster 1 from the task allocation table. This shows that there are still improvements that can be made in the Google clusters to minimize this gap between the requested and used resource according to the job tasks.

5.2   Correlation Between Task Request, Uses and Priority of the Job

To find out the role of priority in resource allocation and usages, we have used simple k-means and the decision tree algorithm to test the Google trace dataset. Google has twelve priorities that are based on the jobs, which mean that all the tasks in a particular job would have the same priority. The Google document states that larger priority numbers get preferences over the smaller priorities. The lower priorities are latency-insensitive and require little charging, whereas the higher priority tasks are latency-sensitive and require regular charging [15]. It would be interesting to see if the priority also plays a role when it comes to the resource request and usage. We used task event and task usage table that were populated with jobs priority. We used the task event table as a training set to train the Simple k-means algorithm. The cluster size k was set to be 12, as the number of priorities that the Google trace dataset had in total were 12 [15].

The results obtained from simple k-means are plotted on a graph as illustrated in Fig. 5. The graph in Fig. 5 has cluster numbers on its x-axis and a percentage of resources on the y-axis. It shows the average resource allocation and usage against the Priority. From Fig. 5, we can say neither the resource usages nor the resource allocation follow jobs priority. This tells us that GCD does not strictly follow priority to make resource provisioning. In priority 11 and 1, resource uses is one of the lowest but both of them have different importance based on Google's interpretation of priority.

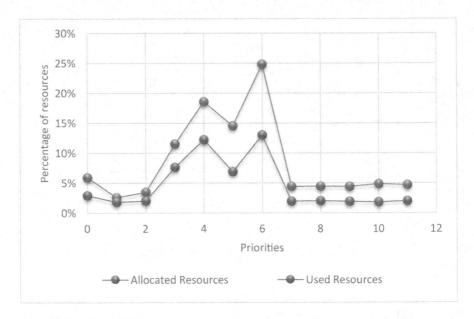

Fig. 5. Correlation between priority, resource allocated and uses using simple k-means

To evaluate the dataset further, we used a decision tree to find out the relationship between priority and resource provisioning. In this simulation, the base class was set as priority. The decision tree algorithm was run on the task event table to check if the resource request had any relationship with the priority when the resource was being requested. The decision tree builds a tree categorizing each record into a group. In our case we have chosen priority as the base class, hence the records would be categorized according to priority. The decision tree observes the records. We plotted the experiment result from the decision tree in Fig. 6, where the x-axis denotes the priority and the Y-axis denotes the percentage of resources for a task.

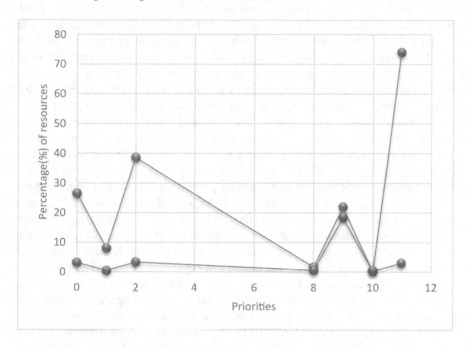

Fig. 6. Decision tree analysis between priority, resources allocation and uses

The graph has used original resource allocation and a predicted resource usages based on decision tree classification and prediction algorithm. The graph in Fig. 6 shows the difference between the percentage of the resource allocated and used against the priority. As we can see from the graph, task allocation and usages did not follow priority.

6   Analysis on Our Experiment Result

Analysis of GCD using three data mining tools of Weka shows that the resource allocation in the Google cluster is not fair. The system's resource request is lot higher compared to resource usage. As a result a lot of resources are being re-allocated to other jobs in GCD. Resource provisioning of the system did not follow priority to address QoS as our analysis failed to find a clear pattern for the same.

Our initial analysis of Google cluster data using linear regression algorithm tells us that a large amount of resources require fewer resources. This suggests that the resource provisioning needs improvement. Furthermore, the results showed that the usage for each job task was lower than its request. A predicted CPU, RAM and Local disk request were generated according to the resource usage table as presented in Tables 1, 2 and 3. The results showed us how much of the resources should have been requested and how much were actually requested for the job tasks. Hence, this could help minimize the resource allocation complexity in the Google clusters.

Additionally, the use of simple k-means algorithm helped us to compare the requested and the usage of the resources. This provided us with the result as to what percentage of job tasks resource request lay in a certain centroid, comparing them to the usage of resources and percentage of the job tasks that lay in that same centroid. Based on our findings, we can conclude that a large percentage of job tasks requested high resources but actually used fewer resources. This shows that resource request should be minimized in order to decrease the allocation complexity in the Google clusters.

While finding a pattern between the resources and priority using simple k-means, our results show that resource provisioning does not follow any pattern to address priority. When considering the decision tree result, we can see that there is no relationship between the priority and the resource request but there is some pattern when it comes to the resource usage: the lower priority job tasks had a lower resource usage.

The effect of allocation not being fair results in high re-allocation of resources increasing scheduling complexity within the Google clusters. If there are large amounts of free resources, the scheduler would over commit resources to the tasks already running [15]. If this happens, the high priority tasks that come in afterwards would have no free resources to be allocated to them, resulting in low priority tasks being killed [11].

These experiment results and analysis on the GCD shows that the complexity within the Google cluster in relation to resource allocation need to be improved to support big data provisioning. The complexity come from the fact that resource request does not follow job's priority and resource actually use by the job. The system needs to provision higher resources to high priority tasks to decrease resource management complexity. This will also improve systems overall capability and boost performance of our current HPC to support big data.

7   Conclusion

We are moving into the new state of data computation where HPC needs to maximize its performance to address computation of large volumes of heterogeneously formatted and complex data computation and mining. The Google cluster is one of the largest and highest performing HPC in the world. In this paper we have investigated the Google cluster data to identify the level of efficiency that our existing HPC offer in their current state. We also further investigated areas of improvement to boost their performance, capability and reduce resource management complexity.

We have used three data mining tools: linear regression, simple k-means and decision tree from Weka to analyse GCD. Analyses on linear Regression results of GDC showed that the usage for each job task was lower than its request. A predicted CPU, RAM and Local disk request were generated according to the resource usage table. The results showed us how much of the resources should have been requested and how much were actually requested for the job tasks. Better allocation mechanisms could help minimize the resource allocation complexity in the Google clusters. Additionally, the use of the simple k-means algorithm helped us to compare the requested resources, resource usage and jobs priority. Our analysis of these experiment results concluded that a large percentage of job tasks required fewer resources than they requested. This shows that resource request should be minimized in order to decrease the allocation complexity in the Google clusters. The simple k-means with priority shows us that there is not much of a relationship between the resource request and the priority. When considering the Decision Tree, we can see that there is no relationship between the priority and the resource request, but there is some pattern when it comes to the resource usage: the lower priority job tasks had a lower resource usage.

Therefore, this result shows that the complexity within the Google cluster in relation to the allocation of resources could be improved further by the effective use of priority to handle the big data challenge.

References

1. Amir, Y., Awerbuch, B., Barak, A., Borgstrom, R., Keren, A.: An opportunity cost approach for job assignment in a scalable computing cluster. IEEE Trans. Parallel Distrib. Syst. **11**(7), 760–768 (2000)
2. Kokkinos, P., Varvarigos, E.: A framework for providing hard delay guarantees and user fairness in grid computing. Future Gener. Comput. Syst. **25**(6), 674–686 (2009)
3. Pinel, F., Pecero, J., Khan, S., Bouvry, P.: A review on task performance prediction in multi-core based systems. In: 11th IEEE International Conference on Computer and Information Technology (CIT), pp. 615–620, September 2011
4. Mostafa, S.M., Rida, S.Z., Hamad, S.H.: Finding time quantum of round robin CPU scheduling algorithm in general computing systems using integer programming. Int. J. Res. Rev. Appl. Sci. (IJRRAS) **5**(1), 64–71 (2010)
5. Dong, F., Akl, S.G.: Scheduling algorithms for grid computing: state of art and open problems. Queens University. Technical report. http://research.cs.queensu.ca/home/akl/techreports/GridComputing.pdf. Accessed 15 Aug 2016
6. Valentini, G.L., Khan, S.U., Bouvry, P.: Energy-Efficient Resource Utilization in Cloud Computing. Wiley, Hoboken (2013)
7. Stankovic, J., Ramamritham, K.: Scheduling algorithm and operating system support for real-time systems. Proc. IEEE **82**(1), 55–67 (2002)
8. Berstein, P.: http://research.microsoft.com/en-us/people/philbe/chapter3.pdf. Accessed 16 Aug 2015
9. Wieder, P., Waldrich, O., Ziegler, W.: Advanced techniques for scheduling, reservation and access management for remote laboratories and instruments. In: 2nd IEEE International Conference on e-Science and Grid, p. 128, December 2006
10. Di, S., Kondo, D., Cappello, F.: Characterizing cloud applications on a Google data center. In: 42nd International Conference on Parallel Processing (ICPP), October 2013
11. Liu, Z., Cho, S.: Characterizing machines and workloads on a Google cluster. In: 8th International Workshop on Scheduling and Resource Management, September 2012
12. Di, S., Kondo, D., Cirne, W.: Characterization and comparison of cloud versus Grid workloads. In: International Conference on Cluster Computing (IEEE CLUSTER), pp. 230–238, September 2012
13. Mishra, A.K., Hellerstein, J.L., Cirne, W., Das, C.R.: Towards characterizing cloud backend workloads: insights from Google compute clusters. SIGMETRICS Perform. Eval. Rev. **37**, 34–41 (2010)

14. Reiss, C., Tumanov, A., Ganger, G.R., Katz, R.H., Kozuch, M.A.: Heterogeneity and dynamicity of clouds at scale, San Jose, CA, USA, October 2012
15. Reiss, C., Wilkes, J., Hellerstein, J.L.: Google cluster-usage traces: format + schema. Google Inc., Mountain View, CA, USA, Technical report (2011)
16. N.A., Weka from The University of Waikato. http://weka.wikispaces.com/ZeroR. Accessed 10 Oct 2015
17. Lane, D.M.: Introduction to Linear Regression. http://onlinestatbook.com/2/regression/intro.html. Accessed 11 Oct 2016
18. Sharma (Sachdeva), R., Alam, M.A., Rani, A.: K-means clustering in spartial data mining using weka interface. In: International Conference on Advances in Communication and Computing Technologies (2012)
19. Microsoft Developer Network. http://msdn.microsoft.com/en-us/library/cc645868.aspx. Accessed 10 Oct 2016
20. Wilkes, J., Reiss, C.: Googleclusterdata (2011). https://code.google.com/p/googleclusterdata/wiki/ClusterData2011_1. Accessed 20 Aug 2016
21. Wilkes, J.: September 2014. https://code.google.com/p/googleclusterdata/wiki/Bibliography. Accessed 15 Sep 2016
22. Xiao, L., Chen, S., Zhang, X.: Adaptive memory allocations in clusters to handle unexpectedly large data-intensive jobs. IEEE Trans. Parallel Distrib. Syst. 15, 577–592 (2004)
23. Hassan, M.M., Song, B., Hossain, M.S., Alamri, A.: QoS-aware resource provisioning for big data processing in cloud computing environment. In: International Conference on Computational Science and Computational Intelligence (2014)

Transportation at the Confluence of Engineering and Big Data: Design of Automated Motorway Lane-Changing Systems

Michael Lawry[✉], Asfahaan Mirza, Yidi Wendy Wang, and David Sundaram

Department of Information Systems and Operations Management, University of Auckland, Auckland, New Zealand
{mlaw405,ywan916}@aucklanduni.ac.nz,
{a.mirza,d.sundaram}@auckland.ac.nz

Abstract. Transportation is an aspect of life that touches every one of us. With rapid advances in technology and lifestyles, modern civilization is witnessing an ever-increasing need for improvements in transportation efficiency and effectiveness to keep pace with modern demands and steadily increasing populations.

This paper explores the wider problem landscape and then targets a specific subset of these issues by presenting a vision for how existing technologies could be uniquely combined to create safe, intelligent, and fully-automated lane-changing infrastructure to fully maximize the efficiency of key motorway sections and bottlenecks.

Keywords: Transportation infrastructure · Smart cities · Smart traffic · Decision support · Big data

1 Introduction

Transportation is a fundamental part of life that impacts all of us. While there are many more modes of transport today compared to recent history - such as multiple modes of flight - this research will focus on what has remained one of the most important areas of modern transportation – land vehicle transport through road networks. Even with this limitation of scope, improving the efficiency of road transportation is still a hugely complicated problem, with a plethora of contributing problems and possible solutions that could be investigated.

This paper focusses on presenting a theoretical model for how modern technology, which is already available, could be uniquely combined to create automated motorway lane-changing infrastructure utilizing the under-employed field of information systems and big data. Some consideration and context will be paid, however, to further problems and solutions that could be addressed to give the reader a holistic understanding of the problem landscape and where our particular approach, and its contributing value, fits in.

We have grounded our theoretical exploration in the case of Auckland, New Zealand, and in particular, our construct's applicability to a preeminent landmark and bottleneck of the city – the Auckland Harbor Bridge. We will also be consequently grounding our research on the transportation context within Auckland, New Zealand – and in particular,

© Springer International Publishing AG 2017
R. Doss et al. (Eds.): FNSS 2017, CCIS 759, pp. 113–125, 2017.
DOI: 10.1007/978-3-319-65548-2_9

we will pay heed to the organization Auckland Transport, the primary overarching transportation operator in the city, and New Zealand Transport Agency (NZTA) – the government entity responsible for nation-wide transport initiatives. Auckland Transport is owned by Auckland City Council and provides all of the bus, train, and ferry public transportation needs of the city. NZTA is the national government department tasked with transportation initiatives across the whole country – especially road maintenance and major new infrastructure development. This context will help demonstrate how our solution would work and the value it could bring in one particular circumstance – although the benefits would be transferable to a multitude of other contexts.

1.1 Motivation: Problems and Issues

Auckland has a population of about 1 495 000 – constituting about 32% of the entire population of New Zealand [1]. Auckland is acknowledged by its own citizens, however, to have major traffic problems and faces increasing traffic congestion issues [2]. From a high-level perspective, Auckland's congestion problems come down to two key factors – excess demand and under-capacity. Both of these factors lead to immediate net effects on worsening congestion levels.

Excess demand can be a result of poor urban planning, like having one central Central Business District (CBD) location with major geographical bottlenecks surrounding it; increasing immigration, population and population density levels; greater car availability, and per capita ownership rates; lifestyle choices, such as reluctance to use alternative forms of transport; and natural geological features. Auckland, in particular, faces many challenges that result from a solitary, hard-to-access CBD location. This CBD area is almost the exclusive home for all of Auckland's high-rise accommodation and office blocks, as well as a far higher concentration of job opportunities due to its popularity with large multi-national companies. Resultingly, as with many other examples of major cities across the globe, this has lead to disproportionate demand to access the CBD area during peak commuting times; placing an unmanageable burden on key infrastructural elements – in our case, the Auckland Harbor Bridge.

Under-capacity is, at a high level, the result of either an insufficient amount of resources or an inefficient use of existing resources. The kinds of resources of interest to us in our situation are things like roads and motorways, intersections and roundabouts, traffic lights, on-ramps, off-ramps and overpasses and various other infrastructure devices left unnamed – the most import one being, of course, the roads themselves. All of these infrastructure devices can be under-resourced and inefficiently utilised – leading to insufficient overall transportation network efficiency and finally greater congestion. These relationships are shown in Fig. 1, with the path of our particular research area within its wider context displayed in red.

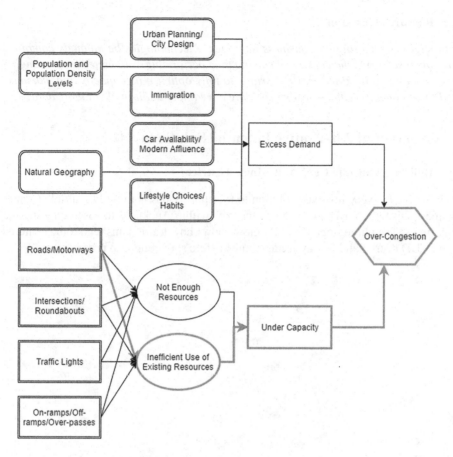

Fig. 1. Research context and scope

In this paper, we address the problem of under-capacity resulting from an inefficient use of resources. We have chosen to address this aspect of the overall congestion problem because we deem it wiser to solve inefficiencies in capacity before seeing initiatives to increase the building of new infrastructure. This area is also more aligned with our skill-set and technology knowledge and therefore more practical for us to address. We opt to leave the demand-side issues unaddressed at this point as, while such measures can indeed reduce congestion problem, such decisions - such as whether to reduce immigration levels or not – tend to have far higher human consequences, and we believe that such adverse situations should never be necessary if supply-side issues are adequately addressed.

We also address one of the most critical aspects of transportation infrastructure to achieve the maximum impact possible – and hence our area of investigation is how roads and motorways might be made more efficient in order to reduce transport capacity issues - and thereby reduce ensuing congestion problems.

1.2 Research Question

How might engineering and business intelligence technologies be uniquely combined to create a safe and efficient way of making, and performing, automated lane-changing decisions on the Auckland Harbor Bridge to fully optimise its capacity and maximise total throughput of vehicles while providing a wealth of additional valuable data?

2   Overview of Alternative Potential Solutions

2.1   Building Multiple Central Business Districts

An effective but very involved solution to transport issues is to build multiple Central Business Districts (CBDs) or business centres within Auckland to ease congestion at peak times. The photograph (Fig. 2) below shows how traffic jams tend to be centered in the CBD district and its key feeder-routes before spreading into urban areas.

Black = Congested   Red = Heavy   Yellow = Moderate   Green = Free Flowing

Fig. 2. Auckland traffic map [3]

The urban areas close to the CBD also have the worst traffic congestion as a result. The underlying cause behind this is that most people come to work in the CBD, and many big schools are also in or around the CBD. As a result, the behaviour pattern of most Aucklanders is to frequently travel to the same CBD location - a problem compounded by the fact that these key demand drivers also involve similar demand spikes temporally rather than uniform increases the transport system could possibly handle. Accordingly, a powerful long-term answer for traffic congestion would be to develop multiple business centres away from the CBD that will result in a more even distribution of transportation system use – rather than one primary bottleneck being utilized in a single location.

However, a key limitation of this solution is that it is arguable that Auckland has too small a population to have multiple CBDs, as every CBD location would have to have a population with a sufficiently large critical mass. There would also be major challenges in incentivising businesses to shift to new locations, creating all of the additional supporting infrastructure necessary for greater population densities in alternative locations, and the problem of sunk costs in the existing CBD.

2.2 Improve Public Transportation

One prominent potential solution to Auckland's congestion issues, on a shorter time horizon, is to improve the public transportation system - including buses, trains and ferries. At the moment, there are two ways to travel between the CBD and the Northshore - by road, over the Harbor bridge, or by water [4]. By road, people can choose to either take a bus or drive a private car. From Fig. 2, we can see that there is major congestion on HW1 and in and around the Harbor bridge.

One way to directly ease this congestion would be through greater utilisation of the water as a transport medium. There is currently only one main ferry pier at the CBD which connects to 6 wharfs on the Northshore. Four out of six of these wharfs on the North Shore have timetables where the rate of ferry departures is every 30 min-60 min depending on the time of day, and whether it is during a peak period or not. Only ferry travel to Devonport Wharf has a more frequent timetable, where departures are every 15 min-30 min in frequency due to heavy demand [5]. This is still arguably still not frequent enough during peak times. Because of the infrequency of ferry departures, many people choose to take the bus which offers more routes and less waiting time – a choice which still contributes to heavier congestion in road traffic. Therefore, by improving the frequency of ferry departures throughout the day, more people can be incentivised to switch to this method of travel and road congestion can be decreased. There is also potential to build a greater number of wharfs and ferry connection points to increase the convenience of using this mode of transport for a greater variety of people.

2.3 Toll the Harbor Bridge

As many people have suggested, one of the most efficient ways of reducing traffic congestion is to change people's behaviour by adding a toll for crossing the Auckland Harbor Bridge. A small toll for each vehicle would bring a reasonable income to the city council in which to invest in further transportation infrastructure maintenance or re-design. There can be different standards of tolling according to the size and weight of vehicles according to their social costs. Partnerships with other organisations such as New Zealand Automobile Association (AA) or Auckland Transport (AT) are also possible; allowing tolls to be paid in different time periods or charged differently according to customer membership, etc.

On the other hand, the toll would not apply to public transportation, which would further increase its utilisation and help contribute to overall reductions in pollution and congestion levels. The primary concern with this method of intervention is public receptivity, but it is still a valuable tool to have available. In fact, New Zealand Transport

Agency (NZTA) already has tolling systems in other parts of the county which have met with a lot of success in improving journey times [6].

2.4 Reversible Lane Control System

The very first reversible lane control system was established in late 1970 in Canada [7]. In March 2010, the city of Calgary Canada completed the implementation of an automatic lane control system organised by the "Transportation Optimization" department of its Transportation Planning Business Unit [8]. The Reversible Lane Control System operates by switching LED lights on each lane to adjust lanes according to morning or afternoon peak times. Traffic in one direction will be shown a green arrow above a lane to indicate that they can use it, while traffic in the opposite direction will be shown a red cross to ensure they do not also use the lane. These electronic signs can then be easily reversed to efficiently re-allocate a lane for use by the other traffic flow when necessary.

This system has already shown a lot of success in its implementation in Canada and serves as a source of inspiration for our own artefact. However, we feel that the safety measures in this system could be improved, as there are no barriers physically protecting drivers and flows of traffic, and it relies on people obeying the traffic signals without error. This may be a useful system in low speed areas in Canada, but there are many other situations – such as our case study, the Auckland Harbor Bridge, where this system would be too dangerous.

3 Artefact Description and Development

Building on previous knowledge in the field of intelligent transportation infrastructure, particularly the reversible lane control systems used in Canada and road tolling technology, we set out to construct an artefact that would use a unique combination of engineering and information systems technologies to provide the safest and most efficient automatic motorway lane changing system possible. Our idea, in its broadest overview, takes its inspiration from automatic bollard technology. This allows barrier structures to be raised and retracted into the ground, which, when combined with advanced information capture, business intelligence, and analytics technologies, can facilitate safe automated lane changing.

The current lane changing process using machinery and labour, as shown in Fig. 3, would essentially be left unchanged in our artefact but would replace machinery and labour with automated decision making and barrier reconfiguration. Below, we detail exactly how our artefact would function, and go into depth with the various technology choices that could be implemented at each step along with our own recommendations.

Fig. 3. Current lane-changing process on the Auckland Harbor Bridge

We first present a process model as illustrated in Fig. 4 and then a detailed explanation of it. We pay more attention to the areas of the process model that are most important and unique in our construct and glide more quickly over those that are more intuitive and simplistic to understand. For the sake of brevity, we also assume a certain level of business intelligence and technology knowledge but recommend that the reader uses our sources as further reading should a more granular analysis be desired.

The resting state of our system is to continuously be monitoring real-time traffic speeds and frequencies, and assessing whether current lane configurations are appropriate to the current traffic conditions. Activation of subsequent lane-changing tasks are only initiated when the system detects a change in traffic conditions that is sufficiently great to warrant a lane-change. Regardless of whether any lane-changing operations are taking place or not, additional data such as licence plate information, car make, model and occupancy numbers are recorded. Such enormous volumes of data, requiring capture and analysis with such high velocities, will almost certainly require advanced big data techniques, but stands to provide immense value to a range of external public and private stakeholders. When lane-changing operations are triggered, multiple steps and technologies are required to ensure safety as they are efficiently carried out.

We believe that all of the key technological building blocks required for such a solution exist in the world today. Automatic bollards demonstrate how easy it would be for sections of retractable barriers to be hidden beneath the ground ready to be used. Instead of requiring a slow and inefficient barrier machine, with no real-time analytics capabilities, to move barrier blocks one by one, it is easily feasible for retractable barriers concealed beneath the road to first close off a lane, and then 'move' the barrier sections from one lane to another by retracting the barrier section in the 'old' location and raising the hidden barrier section in the 'new' location.

We believe that all of the key technological building blocks required for such a solution exist in the world today. Automatic bollards demonstrate how easy it would be for sections of retractable barriers to be hidden beneath the ground ready to be used. Instead of requiring a slow and inefficient barrier machine, with no real-time analytics capabilities, to move barrier blocks one by one, it is easily feasible for retractable barriers concealed beneath the road to first close off a lane, and then 'move' the barrier sections

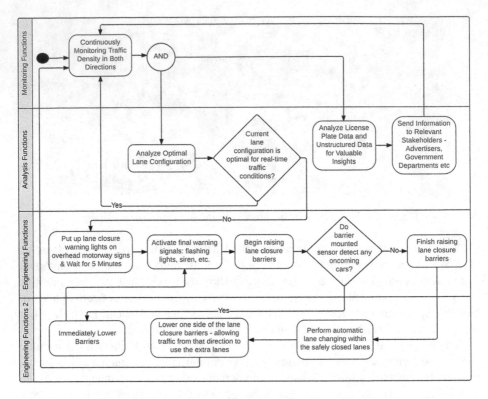

Fig. 4. Real-time automated motorway lane-changing process

from one lane to another by retracting the barrier section in the 'old' location and raising the hidden barrier section in the 'new' location.

Aside from this key observation, we believe that there are multitudinous options for the information capture and IT infrastructure technologies that would be required. Monitoring traffic frequencies and speeds can be achieved using video vehicle detection [9, 10], pneumatic road tubing [9, 11], piezo-electric sensors [9, 12], inductive loops [9, 13–15], magnetic sensors [9, 16], acoustic detectors [9, 17], passive-infrared sensors [9, 18, 19], and Doppler and radar microwave technology [9]. Overall, camera technology may prove to be the most versatile, as it allows for a greater range of information capture, such as determining vehicle occupancy levels, and also allows for the simple addition of future road-tolling capabilities if needed.

Analysis methods for determining optimal lane allocations would normally be motivated by an objective of maximum throughput – which is achieved by simply matching the ratio of traffic density in each direction with the ratio of lanes allocated to each direction as closely as possible. Statistical forecasting methods and time-series analysis can be used to predict required lane changes ahead of time to high degrees of accuracy – allowing the constant real-time analysis to make only minor enhancements where necessary. Statistical analysis of the variability in real-time traffic flows also allows for tolerance levels to be set so that a lane changing operation is only triggered when traffic conditions have been judged to have materially changed – rather than with every transient change that is simply a result of natural variability. Setting the tolerance level too high would lead to inefficiencies arising from a lack of responsiveness to authentic traffic changes. Setting it too low, on the other hand, would entail inefficiencies arising from making large numbers of superfluous changes that were only in response to ephemeral events. With statistical techniques, responses to real-time data collection can be honed to perfection, and, when potentially combined with machine-learning algorithms, minor adjustments to these statistical analyses can be carried out autonomously. For instance, intelligent programming would also allow city officials to make rare interventions if necessary – allowing traffic flow in one direction to be eased at the expense of the other in order to allow for the smooth journey of a very important international delegation.

The three Vs of big data - volume, velocity, and variety - apply to our proposed solution's analytic landscape, and big data techniques would be hugely beneficial. Traditional business intelligence revolves around RDBMS systems that are well suited to structured data, such as licence plate numbers, [20] but may still potentially struggle under very high demands of volume and velocity. Massively distributed parallel processing technologies, taken from the field of big data, such as Hadoop/Map Reduce could be immensely useful in giving our system the analytic power necessary to process huge real-time datasets in problems of real-world scale. NoSQL databases, which do not strictly adhere to the traditional RDBMS principles of atomicity, consistency, isolation and durability, could also provide worthwhile trade-offs in the form of faster processing speeds at sufficient, but not optimal, levels of accuracy [21]. Column-based or in-memory databases could be used where the accuracy of RDMBS systems is still imperative, but performance enhancements are necessary for practicability [20]. In reality, a combination of these systems and technologies may best suit differing requirements for accuracy, processing speed, and the level of structure in the data.

Safety is one of the biggest concerns with any solution as radical as the one we are proposing, and there are a number of key elements of our system that we see as key to alleviating these concerns:

1. Our automated system should follow the existing manual processes as far as possible. By mirroring the proven steps we are all familiar and comfortable with, our system will introduce as few opportunities for increased risks as possible – it is only the mechanical operations that require change, not the processes themselves.
2. As is current practice, it is crucial that any lane in question is first safely closed before the subsequent shifting of barriers takes place. Our system will use a series of electronic signs and final warning lights to warn motorists of impending lane changes, as is already standard practice.
3. Sensors are necessary to detect any vehicles that are not obeying road signs so that collisions can be avoided even if a small percentage of drivers are not alert or non-compliant to the abundant warning. Overhead sensors and barrier mounted sensors can both be used to detect vehicles that are in the path of a barrier that has partially begun to rise in order to block a lane. In such a circumstance, the barrier will have time to immediately lower back into the ground to avoid the collision and re-initiate its sequence of warning motorists with flashing lights and then rising again. Once the lanes are fully closed the risk to motorists will be no greater than under current

scenarios. Emergency sensors can effectively mitigate the risk of accidents arising from dare-devil motorists during the closure sequence, however.

4. Infrastructure should be reinforced against emergencies and power outages. Backup batteries, generators and power supplies are an important part of the infrastructure design, and lane changes will never be permitted to be performed when back-up power supplies decline to an unsafe level. Failsafe systems should also be incorporated such that if a power-outage does occur, lane-closing barriers will remain in place rather than retract into the ground. This ensures that if a lane-changing operation has blocked off a lane, but not fully completed moving the rest of the lane barriers, the lanes will not re-open before the operation is complete and allow a crash to happen. This may lead to higher congestion compared to if the operation completed, but will prevent critical accidents.

5. With growing world-wide concerns around hacking groups, including both skilled private groups and government-backed cyber warfare, cyber security is also a key issue. In light of this, we would see it as prudent to ensure the system is entirely air-gapped and has no wireless or internet capabilities whatsoever. Instead, the servers controlling the system would have to be located in a highly secure room of fairly close physical proximity. While this means that occasional manual overrides to the system could not be performed remotely, these occasions should be few and far between, and physically travelling to the server room to perform these rare operations is a small sacrifice to make to ensure system security. Furthermore, we have envisioned our system design as running autonomously with highly advanced algorithms and statistical methods intended to eliminate human decision making or intervention. We hence anticipate that there will be little to no need for intervention in the first place. A very secure, but cheap option for monitoring system status remotely would be to simply have high quality, real-time CCTV footage of key computer screens and electronic dashboards sent remotely in real-time. In such a way, remotely hacking into the monitoring system in no way allows a compromise of the core IT infrastructure itself. Responses to alerts would still require physical intervention, but the ability to detect problems early with remote monitoring, while still maintaining absolute security, is a big advantage. Of course, security always involves a trade-off with convenience, and if real-time information sharing and remote access were highly valued in one particular context, the stakeholders involved could always allow for this if they are prepared to accept the weakened security posture.

Overall, we believe that each step of our proposed solution, and every challenge it faces, can be feasibly solved with a novel combination of existing technologies. The solution itself has the potential to yield a combination of efficiency and safety that is unattainable with current systems and would provide an additional piece of the puzzle in attaining overall transportation improvements in real-world cities.

4   Conclusion

We have proposed and analysed the feasibility of a new method for automatically performing optimal lane-changing operations on motorways using a combination of engineering and information systems technologies, as well as its wider context and the problem landscape. Our system comprises advanced camera and auxiliary detection systems that constantly monitor traffic flow densities in both directions of a stretch of motorway. These detection devices feed vehicle speed and density information, along with many other types of data, to processing engines that analyse whether it is optimal to perform a lane-changing operation or not according to various algorithms that can occasionally be modified based on the operator's objectives. These commands are then sent to the mechanical parts of our system where warning signals are given, barriers are raised and lowered, and the lane changing operation takes place in an automated, sequential and safe fashion. While the system is performing these functions, it also gathers a lot of data unrelated to changing a lane. This information includes such things as the makes and models of cars that pass by, user habits like speeds and directions travelled and many other more detailed attributes of each vehicle that can be ascertained through its licence plate information. All of this structured and unstructured data is then also analysed by a combination of traditional and big data related business intelligence technologies and made accessible to various stakeholders, such as car companies or the government, under different conditions.

The key contributions of our paper are: a futuristic vision of IT-enabled infrastructure which we hope will inspire others to work in a field we believe holds immense potential but is currently under-emphasised in the literature, and a skeleton framework for a feasible automated lane-changing system that has the potential to greatly improve the efficiency of key sections of motorway in a safe manner using existing technologies.

The solution itself, other than helping alleviate bottlenecks, improve transit times, and reduce the need for expensive construction of additional lanes, also stands to reduce the ongoing costs of labour and carry out a large amount of extraneous data collection and analysis. This data collection and analysis can then provide government bodies with higher quality and more timely information on travel-related trends to develop further strategies for strategic transportation improvements, as well as potentially bringing in a revenue stream from private entities that also stand to benefit from the data. The solution also allows for existing camera systems to be effortlessly converted into a mechanism by which to charge a toll – allowing economic incentives to quickly be used to influence congestion levels should the road still reach capacity under optimal efficiency. Law enforcement agencies could also receive significant aid in catching fleeing offenders if they were given access to automatically be notified of when select licence plate numbers are detected. As with information related products, however, we expect the full list of benefits to grow as more and more ways in which the data can be applied to new situations are discovered.

Key questions that limit the immediate viability of our plan are the cost and difficulty of implementing such a system – and whether these would be judged to outweigh their immediate potential benefits. While we would love to do a more rigorous analysis of the potential costs and benefits of our system in a future paper, for the moment, we hypothesize that that the system could be cost-efficiently produced in the long-run given it only requires the novel use of existing technologies. In the short-run, however, the innovation entailed in our solution would require sizable amounts of research and development funds to test prototypes and establish processes and methods to implement the technologies synergistically. The relatively high start-up costs make it unlikely that the pioneer of such an endeavour would undertake it simply to fix their own congestion problems. It is much more likely that the first mover in the market will be an entity that sees wider potential for the technology and is willing to meet large initial investments in order to commercialise their experience gained and implement the solution for others as well as for themselves.

The other key limitation is receptivity concerns with the general public; whether they would feel safe with algorithms and sensors taking control rather than a human agent. While we believe it is possible to create the solution with a level of safety that is just as high, if not higher, than current methods – public faith is an entirely different matter from reality. We certainly recognise this to be a significant limitation surrounding our solution, and would certainly never ignore the human implications of such a topic in order to blindly focus on the technology. While we have not been able to address this limitation with any amount of rigor in this particular paper, we would assume significant levels of distrust and resistance among the general public to such a solution at the current point in time. We would also assume that digital natives would be more accustomed to and trusting of ceding control to algorithms, however, and that resistance will gradually dwindle with the emergence of new generations as well as the ever-increasing proliferation of such technologies in our lives. This is another key topic we seek to address in future research.

In this paper we have presented and justified some ideas that we hope will one day shape our transportation systems, but more than that – that an increased interest will be sparked around the confluence of IT and advanced transportation infrastructure, and that many more researchers will continue to take this exciting field forward.

References

1. Statistics New Zealand, 'Subnational population estimates'. http://nzdotstat.stats.govt.nz/wbos/Index.aspx?DataSetCode=TABLECODE7541. Accessed 22 Jun 2017
2. Auckland traffic worsens – "it's just bad all the time'', New Zealand Herald, 10 June 2015
3. Live traffic congestion. https://at.govt.nz/driving-parking/live-traffic-congestion/. Accessed 15 Jun 2017
4. Auckland Transport: Ways to get around Auckland. Auckland Transport. https://at.govt.nz/driving-parking/ways-to-get-around-auckland/. Accessed 18 Jun 2017
5. 'Timetables + Fares', Fullers Ferries. https://www.fullers.co.nz/timetables-plus-fares/. Accessed 30 Sept 2016
6. Toll Roads: NZ Transport Agency. https://www.nzta.govt.nz/roads-and-rail/toll-roads/. Accessed 30 Sept 2016
7. Reversible Lane Control Systems. ISL Engineering and Lane services, Calgary, Special Projects (2011)
8. Delanoy, C., Gaede, T., Wong, Y.: The City of Calgary's reversible lane control systems.pdf. In: presented at the Annual Conference of the Transportation Association of Canada, Edmonton, Alberta (2011)
9. Skszek, S.L.: State of the Art Report on Non-Traditional Traffic Counting Methods. Arizona Department of Transportation, 503, October 2001

10. Mithun, N.C., Howlader, T., Rahman, S.M.M.: Video-based tracking of vehicles using multiple time-spatial images. Expert Syst. Appl. **62**, 17–31 (2016)
11. McGowen, P., Sanderson, M.: Accuracy of pneumatic road tube counters. In: Proceedings of the 2011 Western District Annual Meeting, Anchorage, AK, USA, vol. 1013, p. 2 (2011)
12. Li, Z.-X., Yang, X.-M., Li, Z.: Application of cement-based piezoelectric sensors for monitoring traffic flows. J. Transp. Eng. **132**(7), 565–573 (2006)
13. Oh, S., Ritchie, S., Oh, C.: Real-time traffic measurement from single loop inductive signatures. Transp. Res. Rec. J. Transp. Res. Board **1804**, 98–106 (2002)
14. Ali, S.S.M., George, B., Vanajakshi, L., Venkatraman, J.: A multiple inductive loop vehicle detection system for heterogeneous and lane-less traffic. IEEE Trans. Instrum. Meas. **61**(5), 1353–1360 (2012)
15. Charles, H., Shiquan, P.: Automatic vehicle classification system with range sensors. Pergamon J. Ltd, 231–247 (2001)
16. Cheung, S., Coleri, S., Dundar, B., Ganesh, S., Tan, C.-W., Varaiya, P.: Traffic measurement and vehicle classification with single magnetic sensor. Transp. Res. Rec. J. Transp. Res. Board **1917**, 173–181 (2005)
17. Martin, P.T., Feng, Y., Wang, X.: Detector technology evaluation, Citeseer (2003)
18. Ahmed, S.A., Hussain, T.M., Saadawi, T.N.: Active and passive infrared sensors for vehicular traffic control. In: 1994 IEEE 44th Vehicular Technology Conference, pp. 1393–1397 (1994)
19. Hussain, T.M., Baig, A.M., Saadawi, T.N., Ahmed, S.A.: Infrared pyroelectric sensor for detection of vehicular traffic using digital signal processing techniques. IEEE Trans. Veh. Technol. **44**(3), 683–689 (1995)
20. Chen, H., Chiang, R.H., Storey, V.C.: Business intelligence and analytics: from big data to big impact. MIS Q. **36**(4), 1165–1188 (2012)
21. Leavitt, N.: Will NoSQL databases live up to their promise? Computer **43**(2), 12–14 (2010)

Efficient Transportation - Does the Future Lie in Vehicle Technologies or in Transportation Systems?

Michael Lawry[✉], Asfahaan Mirza, Yidi Wendy Wang, and David Sundaram

Department of Information Systems and Operations Management, University of Auckland, Auckland, New Zealand
{mlaw405,ywan916}@aucklanduni.ac.nz
{a.mirza,d.sundaram}@auckland.ac.nz

Abstract. Transportation is one of the most fundamental aspects of modern society; a key enabler of the many other ways modern man has developed. This paper assesses the issue of transportation from both a high-level and more detailed perspective to provide a holistic picture of the current landscape for potential transportation efficiency improvement – along both congestion-related and environmental sustainability dimensions.

First, we present a literature review of a broad range of transportation-related issues and categorize them into a framework distinguishing the unique roles of vehicle technologies, transportation system design, and what we term 'fusion' technologies – focusing on the emergent fields of connected vehicles and autonomous driving.

We conclude that traditional focus on vehicle technologies and transportation systems - while still holding value along the environmental sustainability dimension - are reaching a plateau of effectiveness in addressing the congestion issues of tomorrow. We believe that more disruptive changes are necessary in the form of greater adoption and integration of information systems and data capture and analysis. We validate our conclusions with in-depth discussion around each of the key technologies surrounding all three lines of enquiry of our framework and focus on demonstrating the immense benefits, as well as key challenges, that emergent fusion technologies hold; urging that a greater emphasis be redirected towards these areas by the research community.

Keywords: Transportation infrastructure · Traffic models · Vehicle technology · Transportation systems · Smart cities · Smart traffic · Decision support

1 Introduction

Transportation is undoubtedly one of the primary examples of human technological advance that springs to mind when pondering human development. From the earliest beginnings of time, man has sought more efficient ways to journey from one place to another, and the passage of advancement in transportation has spanned almost every age and technology mankind has experienced – from taming animals, and then the seas, to soaring through the skies and beyond into space itself. Mechanical engineering, engines, and machines have not ceased to develop in power, speed, and efficiency – driving

© Springer International Publishing AG 2017
R. Doss et al. (Eds.): FNSS 2017, CCIS 759, pp. 126–138, 2017.
DOI: 10.1007/978-3-319-65548-2_10

forward the frontier of what is possible in transportation. However, this impressive increase in transportation efficacy has seen an equally large increase in the demand for travel and the expectations of ease and speed at which transportation should operate. It is only natural that demand should constantly expand to fill new possibilities as they are created, but this has meant that vast improvements in vehicle capabilities have not led to the great oversupply of transportation needs that one might have expected in the shoes of the average person only a matter of generations ago. As it stands, we are still constantly pressed to improve transportation efficiency further. However, in addressing this challenge, one must quickly appreciate that its overall remediation is a far bigger and more complex system than the mere improvement in the modes of transportation alone. With the far greater mobility of people and use of modern transportation methods, complex rule systems have been necessitated in order to regulate and control the flow of traffic and to maintain safety as well as efficiency.

1.1 Efficient Transportation

Overall transportation efficiency depends on both the abilities of vehicles to transport their passengers and the efficiency and design of the underlying system and processes that govern how these vehicles may operate. While there have undoubtedly been some impressive protocols developed for governing transportation along land, sea and air, it is the progress in engineering that one first thinks of when considering human advance in transportation – not the efficiency of traffic flow and resource utilization. It could be argued that we are coming to a time now where, in many places and situations in the world, advancement in the mechanics of vehicles is no longer yielding commensurate benefits in shorter journey times and transportation efficiency - although benefits in other areas, such as energy efficiency and environmental sustainability continue to be realized. This is not to diminish the value such improvements in vehicles are having on the world, indeed the environmental benefits alone are of great importance in our day.

For the purposes of this paper, a definition of transportation efficiency that considers both congestion and travel time efficiency, as well as environmental sustainability is assumed. Furthermore, although a wide and fascinating field, this paper will limit its scope to the area of perhaps greatest immediate importance – road network efficiency in urban areas. With the importance of continual improvement in transportation efficiency clear, and the diminishing value of traditional approaches, it is time greater attention was paid to how advances in other fields – namely computing and data analysis – can be applied to the task of improving transportation efficiency.

1.2 Conceptual Framework/Methodology

We conducted an exploratory analysis of the different categories of transportation technologies in the literature to help build our conceptual framework as shown in Fig. 1. The primary database used in the exploratory phase was Google Scholar as it is perhaps the best general purpose database and has a wide scope.

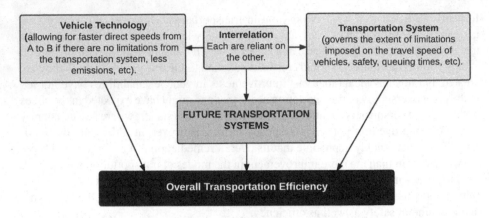

Fig. 1. Conceptual framework

Our overall objective is the improvement of transportation efficiency, an objective that is influenced by two key factors – vehicle technology and the dynamics of the transportation system itself. Overall transportation efficiency is primarily concerned with the speed and efficiency with which vehicles can physically travel from one point to another in the system, but it also includes other important considerations like the environmental impact and emissions produced by vehicles and the safety of vehicle users within the system. Vehicle technology is a factor primarily concerned with the speed and movement capabilities, safety, and emission rates of the vehicles themselves. Advances in vehicle technology, both within the same vehicle class and the development of new classes of vehicles, such as aeroplanes, has led to improvements in transportation speed and efficiency over the years.

The second main influencer of overall transportation efficacy is the efficiency of the transportation system in place. This encompasses the infrastructure necessary for the vehicles to operate and the efficiency of the rule systems governing the safe flow of vehicles. These two factors are mutually dependent upon each other, as a vehicle of even the highest caliber is of no use without the infrastructure with which to use it, and the best infrastructure in the world is of no purpose without vehicles using it. Each of these also have direct effects on overall transportation efficiency.

Vehicle Technology impacts overall efficiency by governing the maximum speed of a journey, given no impediments, while the Transportation System dynamics govern the actual limit that is experienced in real life due to the ability of the system to manage safety concerns and flow control. One of the most interesting relationships in the transportation world that we are beginning to see in the modern era is an entirely new type of phenomenon, which we will coin as Fusion Transportation Systems. These Fusion type technologies include elements of both vehicle technologies and infrastructure technologies that are linked together and can often communicate both ways. Fusion transportation technologies are creating their own unique effect on transportation efficiency through the unique synergy of the existing two main parameters. The relationships in our conceptual model are quite apparent when one looks into the literature, but our model helps summarize the overall influences in the transportation landscape in a concise way.

2 Vehicle Technologies

2.1 Electric Vehicle Technology

Two key modern technology trends were extracted from the literature relating to the construct of vehicle technology: electric vehicles and fuel cell technology. Electric vehicles, although thought of as a cutting-edge, modern technology, have, in fact, been around since the early 1900s and enjoyed a strong market presence and popularity up until around 1918 [1]. However, with the current technology of the time, electric vehicles were slower and more expensive than their internal combustion engine counterparts and died out by 1933 [1]. Chan's paper [1] provides a fascinating perspective, as it predicted that the limitations that doomed early electric vehicles to failure in the past would soon be surmountable and electric vehicles would have the potential to make a resurgence [1]. As predicted, this is indeed the reality we are stepping into: where electric vehicles - and the advantages they bring to transportation efficiency - are becoming a present day reality and already have a toe-hold in the market. Electric vehicle technology has huge potential to create disruption in transportation efficiencies – especially in the areas of environmental impact. Like many, Chan sees the essential challenge facing electric vehicle technology as being whether it becomes commercially viable on a large scale [1]. For this to take place, electric vehicles will have to both overcome technical challenges that stand in the way of satisfying consumer demands and do so at prices that allow electric vehicles to penetrate the mass market – rather than remaining a luxury good. Electric vehicles will have to provide the range, performance, comfort, safety, and simplicity of operation that is foremost in the average consumer's mind when contemplating the new technology [1].

Aside from purely electric options, there are also a number of hybrid-electric technologies that may present opportunities to reap the benefits of a partial departure from reliance on petroleum-based fuels, while also retaining some of the benefits that make such a departure difficult. This class of technology utilizes dual power sources – both electric and petroleum-based – to try and enjoy the best benefits of each of them. Different hybrid models exist for how these power sources are combined, however. The two primary classes of hybrid technologies are Plug-In-Hybrid-Electric-Vehicles (PHEV) and Extended-Rage-Electric-Vehicles (E-REV) [2]. Plug-in-hybrid-electric-vehicles utilize both an electric and petrol motor attached to the drive train of the vehicle so that either system can directly power the car's propulsion – either independently or jointly [2].

These cars can operate in one of two modes, initial EV mode or blended mode [2]. Initial EV mode, standing for initial electric-vehicle mode, means that the functionalities and movement of the car will be powered by its on-board battery – operating as a fully electric vehicle until the battery reserves are depleted [2]. Once the battery is exhausted of power, the internal combustion engine seamlessly starts up to provide a continuous driving experience [2]. In a blended mode, the hybrid car will simultaneously use both power sources – using the direct electric motor and battery power during driving conditions where combustion engines would be inefficient, and allowing the combustion engine to take most of the load when it is at its most efficient [2].

Typically, electric power will be used to start the car and also in stop-start and congested conditions, as these require proportionately more fuel per kilometre with combustion engines but not with electric ones. Internal combustion engines are particularly inefficient in these scenarios because they burn fuel even if no propulsion power is being generated - unlike a battery which is only depleted when used [3]. This problem is a key contributor to the fact that combustion engines are only 10–15% efficient at converting the energy contained in the petrol through combustion into motion [3]. The combustion engine will then take over when speed or acceleration is necessary, where it can provide a lot more power and save a large amount of loss of charge to the battery [2]. In real-world conditions, it is very uncommon for PHEV's to ever run purely on electricity, however, even in initial EV mode, as the combustion engine will still be engaged whenever the battery and electric motor are unable to provide the acceleration or power that the driver is demanding [2]. This means that PHEV hybrid vehicles never quite reach the ideological ideals of fully electric vehicles, but they are still undoubtedly more fuel efficient and less polluting than their full-combustion counterparts – with an increase in energy conversion efficiency from the 10–15% of complete combustion engines to the 30–40% of hybrids [3].

Extended-range-electric-vehicles (E-REX), on the other hand, only have one mode of operation. They have larger battery capacities than PHEV's, and the drive train of the car is only directly powered by an electric engine – although they also have an on-board petrol generator to use petrol to recharge the car's battery whenever it gets critically low [2]. These types of hybrids are able to operate at peak performance of speed and acceleration off battery power alone – and their performance levels match those of combustion engines, just like fully electric vehicles [2]. They also have the benefit, however, of having an extended maximum range thanks to the back-up petrol generator - a mitigation of what is often seen as the number one limiting factor of fully electric vehicles [4]. An E-REX vehicle operates in essentially the same fashion as a PHEV in initial EV mode, except that battery energy is sufficient for even the most strenuous driving conditions and is exclusively used until exhausted; at which point use of the back-up petrol generator becomes necessary [2].

In any case, electric vehicle technology, in all its various classes, has been shown by patent data to be advancing – and with a pattern of being open to partnerships with competitors and companies outside of the automobile industry which is quite unique to see [5]. This kind of collaboration can only be positive for driving the technology forward - and coupled with strategic advances in areas such as battery technology, which has been breaking through to new performance levels [6] - we are likely to see even more potential benefits from this technology in the near future.

2.2 Fuel Cell Vehicle Technology

Fuel cell technology is another vehicle technology which has the potential to revolutionize the environmental impact and efficiency of transportation. The first fuel cell was invented by Sir William Robert Grove in 1839 [7]. A fuel cell converts the energy contained in a fuel into electricity using an electromechanical reaction rather than combustion, as required in a traditional engine [7]. Current research and limited real-world experiments are focussed on using hydrogen as the fuel of choice. For this to be possible, a number or processes would have to take place in the hydrogen supply chain.

Firstly, hydrogen would be extracted from water through a process called electrolysis which uses electricity to split water up into its constituent parts of hydrogen and oxygen; allowing the hydrogen to be extracted and collected [8]. The tapped hydrogen then needs to be stored and transported to where it will be used; contained in very strong tanks in either gaseous or liquefied form [8]. The hydrogen would then be fuelled straight into an appropriately designed car at hydrogen stations similar to our current petrol ones. The actual conversion of hydrogen to usable energy within a hydrogen fuel cell car is highly efficient – typically with between 40–85% efficiency – which is significantly higher than in internal combustion engines [7]. The technology is considered promising by some for its high efficiency, low environmental impact, and flexibility. It is also currently still a very immature technology, as well as being very expensive and lacking the same maximum distance capabilities of traditional engines, however [7]. Still, others see the production and transportation processes necessary for hydrogen technology, and especially its safety concerns, as superseding any potential benefits it may have.

The first time that hydrogen fuel cells were used commercially was NASA's Apollo space missions in the 1930s [7], however, we have not yet seen the technology hit the mass market significantly and this example is arguably an entirely different scenario to the nationwide hydrogen distribution networks that would be necessary for applying the technology to the transportation industry.

3   Transportation Systems

We focussed on two key variables when investigating the impact of our Transportation Systems construct on overall transportation efficiency – the ability of various technologies to efficiently control vehicle flow, and also their safety concerns. Of the various extant ideas surrounding transportation system improvement, the two key technologies in the literature that we see as impactful on real-life situations are cutting edge intersection designs and reversible lane systems. The focusses of our analysis into intersection design is the concept of continuous flow intersections (CFI). This type of intersection design has the potential to improve critical bottleneck intersections that cannot be further enhanced by signal parameter adjustment alone [9]. This is a critical concept to explore because many intersections that are over-burdened and gridlocked are already at, or near, their theoretical maximum efficiency from signal changing [9]. Hence, many other ideas in the literature, such as signal timing optimization, are not adequate to fully address real-world problems, while this revolutionary reconceptualization on intersection design does hold significant potential.

The aim of continuous flow intersections is to eliminate the need of having separate traffic light phases for traffic that is turning at an intersection across a lane – and hence the path of other traffic. In the United Kingdom, for example, left-hand turns are free flowing as they do not cross a lane while our right-hand turns require their own dedicated traffic light phases. However, a lot of the literature around continuous flow intersections comes from a US context, where this is reversed, and it is their left-hand turns that are the problematic ones. We will hence, follow the context of the predominant literature and use a US perspective in our analysis.

The first CFI intersection was seen in Mexico, but it quickly gained popularity in the United States as well, which had three already by April 2006 [10]. In a traditional intersection, left turning traffic would arrive at the intersection directly and then have to wait for its own dedicated traffic signal before it could safely pass through. Right turning traffic would be free to turn using the signal for straight through traffic, however, as it does not involve crossing the path of any other vehicles. A continuous flow intersection, though, eliminates the need for a dedicated left-turn traffic signal with two clever phases. First, traffic approaching the intersection on each of its legs that intend to turn left will be stopped earlier at an initial set of traffic lights [10]. As East-West through traffic takes place, cars on the North and South legs planning on a left-turn receive a traffic signal to cross over the oncoming traffic lane onto a separate lane on the other side [10]. This does not incur much of an efficiency loss because no traffic should be using the oncoming lane at that point in time anyway. In the second phase, North-South through traffic is released to go, and because the traffic intending to turn left already crossed over the lane of traffic that would have blocked it during the first phase, it is also free to go at the same time instead of requiring its own individual traffic signal [10]. So essentially, the method boils down to getting left-turning cars - that will need to cross oncoming traffic at some point - to do so at an earlier point in time when there is little opportunity cost, before they actually reach the intersection properly; allowing them to safely share signals for through-traffic instead of requiring their own one. For this reason, these types of intersections can also be referred to as Displaced Left-Turn intersections [11].

Fixed infrastructure design, like the CFI example we explored, has been a core aspect of transportation system improvement from the beginning. But, while these types of improvements have always been an important part of efficiency advancement, there are much newer and more cutting-edge concepts, building on the information age of data generation and analytics, that stand to offer even more innovation and benefit. One of the greatest examples of these types of technologies is that of reversible lane systems. Reversible lane systems are centered on the ability of overhead electronic road signs to change their signal of whether a particular lane is open or not. In such a scenario, the computerized system will typically display a lane-open green arrow sign on electronic signs in one direction, while the signs from the other direction display a red cross to let drivers from the other direction know not to use that particular lane during that time [12]. This allows traffic from one direction to flow while stopping the opposing traffic.

The computer-controlled signs can subsequently be easily reversed for a very efficient lane-change. This advanced traffic control process is indisputably effective in improving congestions levels through a more efficient and dynamic allocation of resources – particularly in peak hour traffic [13–15]. The driving force behind this efficiency improvement is the ability to quickly and easily reallocate lanes in a minor flow direction to the major flow direction – thereby improving the efficient utilization of the road lanes and preventing the need to build further lane capacity [14]. One must still consider the wider system in which this technology is to be utilized, and how to integrate reversible lanes into the existing infrastructure environment, if one is to achieve maximum efficiency through their use [13], but they are undoubtedly a powerful infrastructure technology available to alleviate traffic concerns.

Reversible lanes are not without their challenges, however, the greatest of which is often safety concerns for many people. Because they are often used in the absence of any physical barriers blocking opposing traffic; with the lane-changing process being facilitated by light signals alone, there is potential for head-on collisions if drivers do not obey the signs or if the process is not designed well. In some situations, like temporary road works, however, temporary barriers may be used in conjunction with reversible lanes [15], but this is often not the case. Common applications of reversible lanes, apart from roadworks situations, include improving commuter journeys and managing peak-hour surges, and as a part of managing planned and special events [14]. Overall, electronic reversible lane technology has been around for some time – since at least the 1970's in fact [12]. During this time, reversible lanes have been able to prove themselves, refinements have been able to be made around their operation, and now they are considered highly safe as well as effective – posing little additional risks to motorists that they were not already exposed to [15].

Reversible lanes are one example of how information systems technologies are beginning to invade and disrupt areas of the transportation industry that no one would have imagined in only the recent past. Infrastructure may have once been deemed entirely separate and untouchable by the digital revolution, but even this long-held belief is now swiftly changing.

4   Fusion of Vehicle Technologies and Transportation Systems

There are two key areas of research that hold a lot of promise within the fusion technologies area – connected vehicles and autonomous vehicles. We will investigate the advantages, disadvantages and likely impacts of both. Connected vehicle technology is concerned with the use of information systems to connect and analyse information from vehicles with other vehicles or with infrastructure. This technology, which combines elements of both paradigms, can be used to improve traffic flows by greatly improving traffic light signalling changes for instance [16].

Promising advances have been made in these directions in recent years – notably advanced self-driving capabilities from Tesla [17] and on the OnStar system developed by General Motors, which provides car owners with a wealth of new features, interactions, and conveniences supported by vehicles with onboard wireless networking capabilities [18]. Some of the OnStar features include turn-by-turn navigation and location-recommendation abilities; automatic crash response, which can detect when a crash has occurred and automatically request help if the driver is unable to; vehicle security, including the ability to remotely block the car's ignition or maximum speed; an onboard WiFi hotspot, for entertainment purposes; and self-diagnostic abilities, which can inform the driver of the health of the vehicle's engine, brakes, transmission and more [18]. OnStar Features are also available remotely through a mobile application [18] which greatly increase their convenience, and it is an impressive development overall – especially considering that it has been commercially available for some time now. However, there is a glaring limitation of both of these examples as they currently stand – both Tesla's self-driving capabilities and General Motor's OnStar technology do not allow for connectivity and data-exchange with other vehicles or with transportation infra-structure. Just as human development has been spurred more by interaction and knowl-edge sharing between people - rather than the isolated genius of individuals who did not communicate their revelations to others – so it can be assumed in regard to connected vehicles; the greatest benefits of all are likely to come from widespread vehicle-to-vehicle and vehicle-to-infrastructure data-sharing. If such a vision was achieved, traffic lights would not have to wait until a car pulls up to them in order to change their phase - they would already know that the car was coming; self-driving cars would not require as much reliance on their advanced sensors to react to the movements of other cars - they would already have notification of every cars' intensions before they even take place. Such a concept has the potential to increase safety and efficiency in the transpor-tation world in ways that non-connected methods simply cannot – and it is precisely this vision that is still in its infancy and that we will be referring to when we speak about the emergent 'connected vehicle' literature.

Simulation results from recent research, however, indicates that improvements in traffic signal timing, as a result of connected vehicle data, could result in up to 21.6% less delay and 13.9% fewer stops when compared with the current system [16]. The huge amounts of information and analytics that could be produced by this technology also have many other potential benefits to transportation systems – such as being able to improve fuel econo-mies and consequently reduce emissions through the coordination of vehicles speeds so that they are optimised for the conditions [19]. Driving naturally involves many instances of speed variations; accelerations, braking, cruising and idling [19]. Fuel efficiency varies as the speed and driving pattern of a vehicle changes - but until now this has been of little use as humans cannot completely avoid inefficient driving behaviours.

Connected vehicle technology, however, offers the possibility of optimising the speed and flow of vehicles without human error to achieve these potential benefits. Cutting-edge research conducted by [19] illustrates how infrastructure-to-vehicle (I2 V) communication combined with a modified A-star algorithm and dynamic programming optimization can greatly increase fuel efficiencies. Their model details how an efficient algorithm can be created based on the A-star algorithm, a very common and popular path-finding algorithm in computer science circles, and combined with signalling data from the infrastructure-to-vehicle communication in order to predict vehicle's paths and the constraints that will be put onto them [19]. This information is then formulated into a moving-horizon dynamic programming model which is rapidly solved; providing the optimal solution for vehicle speed and flow which is then communicated back to indi-vidual vehicles through the same I2 V channel [19]. The authors refined and tested this model using 30 popular vehicles in the United States; demonstrating that fuel efficiency gains of 5–30% can be achieved in the vicinity of signalized intersections [19]. Lever-aging greater data capture and analysis through the incorporation of communications technologies in the transportation sector, and utilizing connected vehicle technology, can, therefore, lead to very significant benefits in both shorter travel times and less fuel consumption and pollution.

Autonomous vehicle technology is another fusion technology which builds on the base of connected vehicle technology to allow for large amounts of information gath-ering and analysis so that vehicles are able to drive themselves to their passenger's desired destination with greater efficiency and less potential for human error. By reducing human decision making - which is sub-optimal in the current context - there is huge potential for improving vehicle flow efficiencies through the use of autonomous vehicles, although there are still many strengths and weakness of this emerging technology [20]. There have already been significant multi-disciplinary efforts in the literature directed towards improving and maturing self-driving and autonomous vehicle technologies; typically focussing on one of the greatest concerns in the field - safety [21]. With 1.24 million road traffic deaths worldwide every year, it is no wonder why safety is such a focus concern for new technologies that are still new and relatively unproven [21]. However, despite a few technical challenges and lingering doubts, the attitude of many is that self-driving cars present too many potential benefits to ignore. Proponents of self-driving cars advocate that widespread use of self-driving cars could lead to reduced traffic and parking costs, reduced roadway costs, less congestion and more efficient travel, reduced vehicle emissions, greater mobility for those who cannot drive, a more convenient and effective solution for public transport and even, in the end, fewer accidents and greater safety [22].

Many of these potential benefits are direct results of the greater efficiency with which autonomous vehicles could drive, leading to better traffic flow control, faster journeys with less fuel consumption and emissions, and less wear and tear on road infrastructure. Despite all of the fears around the technology, it could also be a significant aid in reducing the frequency and severity of crashes, as automated vehicles could be programmed to never take the risks that a human driver might do in a moment of emotionality and rashness. Speed management alone is a huge factor in this regard, with a 5% reduction in average speed resulting in a 30% reduction in the number of fatal crashes [21].

Autonomous vehicles could arguably bring an immense benefit to safety by adhering to speed restrictions far more stringently than humans alone – even when other factors of human frailty are not considered. Autonomous vehicle technology, however, is technically not a discrete phenomenon, but a spectrum of degrees of automation. This spectrum ranges from function specific technologies, such as cruise control and lane guidance, to fully autonomous systems that can make an entire trip without any sort of intervention and can even do so without a human occupant present if necessary [22]. Within these extremes, there are also limited-self-driving modes where vehicles are able to monitor external conditions and have full autonomous functionality until the situation changes in a way in which the driver's manual intervention becomes necessary again [22]. It is, therefore, important to note that autonomous vehicle technology is already present and a part of society to some extent, although we may not have been completely observant of its initial entrance and growing development. By far the greatest excitement and debate revolves around fully autonomous capabilities.

Perhaps one of the most well-known examples of a fully autonomous car is the Google self-driving car. Initially quite a secret affair, Google's self-driving Toyota Prius cars have now been exposed for the world to see for some time, with Google beginning work on the project in 2009 and more than 1.5 million self-driven miles now logged [23]. At a high level of conceptualization, the hardware and software in the Google cars that make self-driving capabilities possible are designed to answer the four implicit questions that all drivers face when piloting a vehicle: where am I? What is around me? What will happen next? And, what should I do? [23]. Advanced sensors of multiple technologies are required to gather information along different dimensions to help answer these questions. A sufficiently powerful computer system capable of instantly processing and combining this information is also required in the logical layer, and finally, these information systems must be connected to the physical car parts and motors that will begin moving the vehicle in accordance with the decisions of the computer system. One of the biggest factors is, therefore, the sensing capabilities of the vehicle, as it must be able to detect a wide range of classes of objects with very different physical characteristics. This is of utmost primary importance as you cannot react to anything you have not first detected. The Google car uses a combination of lasers, radars and cameras to detect objects in all directions along multiple dimensions [23]. Urmson, the technology lead for the Google self-driving car project, has stated that the heart of the car's sensing abilities is through the laser range-finder mounted on the roof of the car [24]. This laser has 64 beams that generates a detailed 3-D map of the car's immediate environment which is then combined with data from high-resolution street maps [24]. The result is that the car knows what street it is on, which lane it is in, and the objects and potential hazards that are surrounding this environment [23].

Aside from these primary sensor technologies, the Google self-driving car is equipped with four radar systems mounted on the front and rear bumpers which enable longer range detection of vehicles in order to enable travel on fast-moving motorways [24]. The camera system near the rear view mirror facilitates detection of traffic lights, and a GPS system and wheel encoders help the vehicle understand its position relative to its environment and keep track of its movements [24].

Google first started experimenting with self-driving cars in 2009 using the Toyota Prius on motorways in California [23]. In 2012 they began testing autonomous driving technology on Lexus RX450 h vehicles which are larger than the Toyota Prius and began testing on urban city streets rather than motorways – a much more complicated situation [23]. Finally, in 2014 Google unveiled its own prototype self-driving vehicle designed and built from the ground up to have self-driving capabilities [23]. Although the technology is still in its infancy, autonomous driving capabilities are fast becoming an ever more present reality, and greater discussion is needed around their acceptability and possible impacts on society before they emerge onto the marketplace.

5   Conclusion

Overall transportation efficiency is a complicated research area with many contributing and interrelated factors. From our literature review, we broke down the problem of transportation efficiency into two main areas, vehicle technology and transportation system technology. In recent years, we have also witnessed the rise of a third combined mechanism on transportation efficiency making use of information and communications technologies and data analytics to blur the boundaries between vehicles and the infrastructure systems they make use of. There are many different facets that we may want to focus on when it comes to improving the efficiency of transportation. Of immediate concern in many situations are congestion levels and ease of transit from one destination to another. However, we are also seeing a greater recognition of climate change and the growing threat of global warming issues.

We have seen that vehicle technology is the most important factor driving transportation efficiency in terms of environmental impact, as the most critical factor is the fuel source being used. Electric vehicles, whether fully electric or some form of hybrid, and hydrogen fuel cell vehicles are the two technologies capable of zero-emission impacts and are currently vying for the dominant place as the fuel of choice in the future. Of these options, however, electric vehicles are the better choice, and have the more significant advantage, as they have less safety and infrastructure problems to overcome, and also a much greater head start in the market and gaining consumer adoption. With increased competition within the electric car market, and many new and innovative companies, coupled with great advances in battery and other key technologies, our hopes for environmentally friendly transportation and the aversion of a global warming disaster are best placed in electric vehicles.

Transportation infrastructure efficiency has seen less widespread disruption than the automobile industry perhaps, and certainly less of the glamour, but it is equally important if not more so to overall transportation efficiency. Not only does the efficient design of infrastructure and rule systems improve transit times and the day-to-day experience of road users, this inherent efficiency in movement and shorter delay times also leads to economic benefits as well as less fuel consumption and thereby pollutants as well. This area has not seen as many significant advancements compared to the vehicle technology sector, however - except in the case of a few innovative new systems which have, disappointingly, not yet seen significant adoption. The nascent hybrid vehicle and infrastructure mechanism, with technologies such as automated and connected vehicles, however, has great potential to improve this situation and bring much needed disruptive change and movement efficiency improvements. These mechanisms will be highly reliant on information systems and communications technologies in order to function and will generate unprecedented amounts of data requiring analysis. If these data generation, transmission, and analysis challenges can be surmounted, these technologies could be the single biggest development in modern transportation and yield the largest potential benefits. Much will depend on whether data capture and analytics methods are ready for this challenge; and with the technology beginning to mature and already showing the first signs of emerging into the market, this is a challenge that deserves much greater research efforts and will soon be put to the test.

References

1. Chan, C.C.: An overview of electric vehicle technology. Proc. IEEE **81**(9), 1202–1213 (1993)
2. Tate, E.D., Harpster, M.O., Savagian, P.J.: The electrification of the automobile: from conventional hybrid, to plug-in hybrids, to extended-range electric vehicles. Citeseer (2008)
3. Emadi, A., Rajashekara, K., Williamson, S.S., Lukic, S.M.: Topological overview of hybrid electric and fuel cell vehicular power system architectures and configurations. IEEE Trans. Veh. Technol. **54**(3), 763–770 (2005)

4. Chan, C.C.: The state of the art of electric, hybrid, and fuel cell vehicles. Proc. IEEE **95**(4), 704–718 (2007)
5. Pilkington, A., Dyerson, R., Tissier, O.: The electric vehicle: Patent data as indicators of technological development. World Pat. Inf. **24**(1), 5–12 (2002)
6. Burke, A.F.: Batteries and ultracapacitors for electric, hybrid, and fuel cell vehicles. Proc. IEEE **95**(4), 806–820 (2007)
7. Bhagat, S.L., Khedkar, S.V., Thorat, P.V.: Fuel Cell Technology for Vehicles (2013)
8. Shinnar, R.: The hydrogen economy, fuel cells, and electric cars. Technol. Soc. **25**(4), 455–476 (2003)
9. Sun, W., Wu, X., Wang, Y., Yu, G.: A continuous-flow-intersection-lite design and traffic control for oversaturated bottleneck intersections. Transp. Res. Part C Emerg. Technol. **56**, 18–33 (2015)
10. The CFI - A low cost solution to congestion. Continuous Flow Intersections. http://www.continuousflowintersections.org/. Accessed 11 Oct 2016
11. Zhao, J., Ma, W., Head, K.L., Yang, X.: Optimal operation of displaced left-turn intersections: a lane-based approach. Transp. Res. Part C Emerg. Technol. **61**, 29–48 (2015)
12. Reversible Lane Control Systems.pdf', ISL Engineering and Lane services (2011)
13. Zhao, J., Ma, W., Liu, Y., Yang, X.: Integrated design and operation of urban arterials with reversible lanes. Transp. B Transp. Dyn. **2**(2), 130–150 (2014)
14. Li, X., Chen, J., Wang, H.: Study on flow direction changing method of reversible lanes on urban arterial roadways in China. Procedia Soc. Behav. Sci. **96**, 807–816 (2013)
15. Waleczek, H., Geistefeldt, J., Cindric-Middendorf, D., Riegelhuth, G.: Traffic flow at a freeway work zone with reversible median lane. Transp. Res. Procedia **15**, 257–266 (2016)
16. Hu, Y.: Improving Coordinated Traffic Signal Timing Through Connected Vehicle Technology. Swanson School of Engineering (2016)
17. Tesla. Autopilot. https://www.tesla.com/autopilot. Accessed 22 Jun 2017
18. General Motors, 'OnStar'. https://www.onstar.com/us/en/home.html. Accessed 22 Jun 2017
19. Kamalanathsharma, R.K., Rakha, H.A.: Leveraging connected vehicle technology and telematics to enhance vehicle fuel efficiency in the vicinity of signalized intersections. J. Intell. Transp. Syst. **20**(1), 33–44 (2016)
20. Roncoli, C., Papageorgiou, M., Papamichail, I.: Traffic flow optimisation in presence of vehicle automation and communication systems – Part I: a first-order multi-lane model for motorway traffic. Transp. Res. Part C Emerg. Technol. **57**, 241–259 (2015)
21. Diakaki, C., Papageorgiou, M., Papamichail, I., Nikolos, I.: Overview and analysis of Vehicle Automation and Communication Systems from a motorway traffic management perspective. Transp. Res. Part Policy Pract. **75**, 147–165 (2015)
22. Litman, T.: Autonomous vehicle implementation predictions. Vic. Transp. Policy Inst. **28** (2014)
23. Google Self-Driving Car Project. Google Self-Driving Car Project. http://www.google.com/selfdrivingcar. Accessed 16 Oct 2016
24. Guizzo, E.: How google's self-driving car works. IEEE Spectrum Online, 18 October 2011

Competing in a Rapidly Changing World: Elements and Models of an Adaptive Chinese Organization

Li Song, Gabrielle Peko[✉], and David Sundaram

Department of Information Systems and Operations Management, University of Auckland,
Auckland, New Zealand
lson795@aucklanduni.ac.nz, {g.peko,d.sundaram}@auckland.ac.nz

Abstract. China is attracting increasing attention because of its rapidly emerging economy. With development becoming increasingly sophisticated, the business environment in China is going through a transformational stage. Organizations in China have to be able to adjust to social, economic, cultural and technical changes by being adaptive. Adaptive organizations have been studied for some time, with investigations stemming from research on organizational change, organizational learning and complex adaptive systems. According to the literature, adaptive organizations maintain competitive advantage by adjusting their strategies, organizational structures, business processes and information systems. This paper focuses on a textile manufacturer in China. A case study approach is used to address how a manufacturing organization adapts in the Chinese business environment and to determine the key elements of adaptive organizations. Company strategy, leadership, networks, capability, communication and external environment were found to be the six key elements that enable the manufacturer to be adaptive. Interestingly, the evidence from the case study indicated that agility was not critically important to an adaptive manufacturer in the Chinese textile industry. It was found that the external environment significantly hinders adaptive behaviors, and that government policies play an important role in this. Interdependent relationships among the six key elements are illustrated using a series of structural and behavioral models.

Keywords: Adaptive organisation · Chinese manufacturer · Textile manufacturer · Key elements · Behavioral models · Structural models · Transformation

1 Introduction

The manufacturing industry in China is going through big changes, which bring many opportunities as well as many challenges. After more than three decades' of rapid economic growth, China has entered a slower stage in its economic development. Gross Domestic Product (GDP) growth has slowed in recent years, as shown in the Purchasing Manager's Indices (PMI) for both the manufacturing sector and the service industry [1, 2]. According to statistics reported by [3], the value of Chinese manufacturing dropped from about 33% of GDP in 2002 to 30.57% of GDP in 2012. The shrinkage of the manufacturing industry means that Chinese production should no longer rely heavily on low-cost, low-value-added

© Springer International Publishing AG 2017
R. Doss et al. (Eds.): FNSS 2017, CCIS 759, pp. 139–153, 2017.
DOI: 10.1007/978-3-319-65548-2_11

products with high energy consumption. The change in the economic development model has an impact on almost every manufacturer in China. Manufacturing organizations have to figure out ways to survive through being adaptive to their rapidly changing environments. Over the past decade, relative to other developing countries, China's competitive advantage of low production costs has been decreasing [4]. The low cost of Chinese products was mainly based on low wages, low cost of raw materials and long working hours, which prevailed for many years. However, with the launching of the new labor laws, policies related to wages and working hours became more explicit and powerful. In 2010, the minimum wage standards were improved in more than 10 provinces in China. On average, the cost of manpower in the textile industry, for example, increased by more than 10%. In some well-developed areas of China, such as the Yangtze River delta area and the Pearl River delta area, labor costs increased by 20%–40%. Low cost competition now comes from some South-East Asian countries, such as Thailand and Indonesia [4]. Driven by the low cost, many manufacturers now choose to open factories in, or to move their factories to, these countries. For instance, about 46% of the labor-intensive industries that had been located in Guangdong moved from China to Vietnam in the second half of 2005, according to [5]. After the economic crisis in 2007, advanced economies such as the United States and UK, became more aware of the importance of the manufacturing sector. It was realized that relying more on the real economy (e.g. manufacturing) than the virtual economy can keep economies more stable and sustainable. Governments began making efforts to encourage local companies to move their manufacturing back onshore. Apple, for example, is well known for its city-sized factories in China. It has recently decided to construct an assembly line for Mac computers in the US [6]. The manufacturing investment in China from advanced economies is being gradually pulled back.

2   The Case Study

2.1   The Chinese Textile Industry

Overall China's textile industry is commonly known as a traditional advantage industry [7]. The nature of this industry is labor-intensive. China is the world's largest producer and exporter of textiles and clothing. Although Chinese textiles are traditionally competitive, the business environment has been and is still going through some major changes. Before the 1980s, it was a closed market environment, but once China carried out its "Open Door policy," its manufacturing industry, including the textile industry, was exposed to a relatively open environment. The openness can be seen in many aspects, including the tariff rate. From 1982 to 2002, the tariff rate dropped by about 40% [8], showing that government protection for industries was weakening. Increased openness on one hand offered Chinese textile manufacturers more chance to collaborate with other textile and apparel makers in the world, but on the other hand it put pressure on the Chinese textile and apparel industry to be more competitive. In recent years, with the market becoming increasingly saturated, the textile industry has needed to develop and upgrade. The government launched laws and regulations regarding the upgrading of the textile industry, and many textile companies and factories shut down as a consequence of not being able to adapt to the new environment. In 1998, the industry contributed around 12 percent of China's GDP [9].

However, in 2011 the output value of the textile industry accounted for only 7.11% of China's GDP [10]. The textile industry and its markets are undergoing a period of transformation and transition. Therefore, it is interesting to look at China's manufacturing enterprises, taking the textile industry as an example.

This paper explores a successful textile company and seeks answers to the research questions "How do organizations adapt in the Chinese business environment?" and "what are the key elements of an adaptive Chinese organization?" It is anticipated that the company's experience may provide both academics and practitioners with some insights into potential ways of being adaptive. The first objective of this paper is to identify the critical elements of an adaptive organization (AO) in the Chinese context. The focus is on critical elements emerging from the case study and thematic analysis, based on existing theories and frameworks. The elements are identified in the form of themes. The second objective is to develop models of an AO. These models will represent the relationships among the identified elements of an AO.

It is essential for manufacturers in China to be adaptive in order to meet the demands of an increasingly dynamic and competitive business environment. These elements and models may provide a way to progress the understanding of AO's in the Chinese context. In the following section, the history and the development of a Chinese textiles company XYZ is described from both an employee's and employer's perspective.

2.2 The XYZ Textile Company

XYZ Textile Co. (XYZ) primarily produces denim fabric. It was established in 2000 in ABC province in China. The predecessor of XYZ was an ordinary dyeing factory. The business was not profitable and the factory split into two parts. One part continued with the dyeing business, while the other focused on denim production. The CEO and owner of the company, chose to take on the denim fabric business. After 13 years of development, it now has total assets of 200 million Yuan, and 800 employees. The annual output is 24 million meters of denim, 10,000 tons of cotton yarn and 2 million items of clothing. The main research and development (R&D) and production focus is on high and medium grade denim and denim clothes. In recent years, XYZ has constantly developed innovative and stylish series with new materials and technologies, which attracts many large and influential customers.

When The CEO first decided to separate the denim fabric business from the dyeing factory, his decision was based on market prospects in the denim sector. The CEO noticed the big potential of denim clothes in the near future, which would require the creative use of available denim fabric. Since the denim fabrics in China all appeared similar, XYZ had a lot of space to play with. After the new company was established, XYZ began working on developing new products, which indeed differentiated it from its competitors' fabrics. The timing of privatization gave small private companies, like XYZ, the opportunity to expand. At that time, China had just implemented the "restructuring, downsizing and efficiency" policy, which reduced the number of employees in the country's textile and clothing industry from 12.43 million in 1995 to 5.07 million in 2001 [11].

In 2001, China became a new delegate to the World Trade Organization (WTO). This opened the gate to a huge market for China, and led to the prospering of the Chinese textile industry. The general manager (GM) noted, "At that time Chinese textile products were really competitive in the global market, because we had cheap prices. Competitors in the same industry were keen on reducing their costs. If one textile producer sold a product at 10 Yuan, others definitely tried to sell the product at 9 Yuan, or even 8 Yuan. This price war still exists now."

When asked about the market circumstances back around 2000 to 2004, the GM recalled, "In the first several years, we positioned to produce cheap products selling in wholesale markets. The primary markets were domestic or overseas wholesale markets. They were all small-scale businesses. It was a hard time. At that time, many customers had almost no idea about how to tell the quality of jeans products. In the textile industry, one supplier followed another. The products on the market all appeared similarly cheap, and there was no creativity at all." But now the business model has become completely customer-oriented, "We only produce the fabric that can meet customers' requirements related to the end products."

The business model changed not only because of the end markets, but also due to raw material markets and political factors. For example, a significant factor that still impacts on XYZ's purchasing model and inventory structure is the cotton import quota. "With regard to cotton, the government comprehensively assesses export performance, size of business and other factors to divide the quotas. The total number of quotas is fixed. Large companies normally can get more than half of the total cotton import quotas, while smaller companies like us can only get a little," the supply manager said.

However, although top management did not state a vision explicitly, all the management levels knew that making cheap products was just a very temporary plan. To develop and thrive against its competitors, XYZ had to get rid of the restrictions resulting from inferior equipment. The manager of the equipment department noted that "At the beginning, all of our equipment were domestically produced and had low capacity. In 2000, we got equipment import autonomy from the government, and we purchased equipment several times afterwards. When we imported equipment, we chose the most advanced in the world for improving product quality." Each purchase was undertaken based on an analysis of customer demand. Through the continuous improvement of equipment, XYZ focused on a high quality strategy. Apart from the machines, human resources in the factory are another important determinant of business growth. Over more than a decade's development, the number of employees at XYZ decreased from 1,100 to 800. In the same period, its sales increased. Given its dramatic growth in order-delivery ability, XYZ shows its high efficiency in terms of using human resources.

Efficiency, however, is not just restricted to the shop floor. It also extends to the functional departments. Direct observation of the company showed that XYZ Textile has a unique company culture. The company culture means dealing with concrete matters related to work, rather than wasting time on formalism. Rather than spending money on flashy marketing materials, the CEO invests in improvements to product design and production. A worker commented that "The GM who is in charge of production comes to the production line every day. Sometimes, he even comes here twice a day." "The CEO asks all the employees in functional departments to make an inspection tour every day. Everyone is supposed to know what is going on in the factory," said the manager of the personnel department, face-to-face conversations help workers and management to build personal relationships beyond work. This personal relationship breaks down the old hierarchical organizational structures. It binds the organization in a more chaotic way on the surface, but in fact information is shared in an open way. The team spirit appears to be stronger, because people have a stronger awareness of taking care of each other.

When clients have new requirements, XYZ tries its best to meet those requirements. Since 2005, XYZ has started to work hard on energy conservation and environmental protection. Its point of departure was that both the government and its clients asked for more social responsibility. The production of denim fabric has many processes that can pollute the environment, especially the dyeing process. Before the regulation changes and clients' requests, the convention of the industry was to discharge waste water to the river. The toxic substances were not degraded or removed. Rather than being recycled in the system, water was treated as disposable. This approach can cause severe environmental contamination and huge waste.

As can be seen XYZ has many challenges and a need to adapt to continue to survive and thrive. In the following sections we first explore the elements and models of an AO and then follow it up by looking in detail at the structural and behavioral models of an AO.

3   Elements of an Adaptive Organization

In the literature, AO are often described as being composed of five elements: strategy, IT, people, capability and leadership [12, 13]. Although the management of human resources is emphasized in the AO literature, in this case it appears to belong under the concept of company capability. The characteristics of AOs, are often summarized as agility, leanness and flexibility. These are also part of the definition of AO capability [14–18]. Therefore, in essence, the elements of an AO are strategy, IT, people, capability and leadership. Through the stories of XYZ, it can be seen that strategy, technology, capability and leadership are all critical to the company's adaptation. At present, there is not enough explicit evidence to indicate that IT and agility are significant elements of an adaptive Chinese organization. However, a few other constructive elements seem to be stressed in the company's stories, such as networks, communication and interaction with the external environment which implies that IT through its support of these activities is an important element.

In terms of the data analysis, the interview data generated from the case study was synthesized using thematic analysis techniques. Mind mapping was used as the analysis tool to identify important themes. These themes, together with those from the AO literature became the basis for the re-examination of the thematic data in order to clarify, refine and confirm the important elements of an AO. The mind maps also serves the purpose of presentation as shown in Fig. 1. However, in Fig. 1 only the higher level themes and sub-themes are depicted for illustrative purposes with the theme 'Leanness' showing some of the supporting case study quotes.

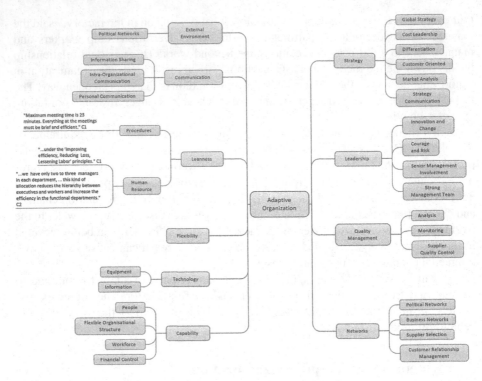

Fig. 1. Elements of an adaptive organization

In Fig. 1 'Adaptive Organization', as the core concept, is divided into 10 different sub-themes, including strategy, leadership, quality management, networks, capability, technology (which includes IT), flexibility, leanness, communication, and external environment. These themes are the findings, from the interview data, which were regarded as important for AO. Quotations were used to support the analysis.

In this section we briefly introduced the findings obtained from the thematic analysis. It indicates that political networks, communication, leadership, political environment and flexibility are important to the adaptability of an organization. However, the roles of IT and agility seem to be minor or even negligible in the context of a Chinese manufacturer. In the following sections a series of structural and behavioral models are proposed. They illustrate high-level relationships among the elements, which emerged from the synthesis of the literature, case study and analysis, from both static and dynamic perspectives.

4   Models of an Adaptive Organization

The research objective was to generate models that can enable organizations to be adaptive in their environment. Theory building involves a higher-level understanding of the interview data in the case study. [19] state explicitly the significance of model building from case studies, "it is a research strategy that involves using one or more cases to create theoretical constructs, propositions and/or midrange theory from case-based, empirical evidence." Since the important elements in AO were identified, it is necessary to work out the relationships among them. The model building process extracts the essence from the case study, producing graphical representations of the relationships between the identified elements in AO (mind map themes). The models in the following sections aim at representing the structural and behavioral relationships among the AO elements rather than showing the degree of interrelation. The models in Figs. 2, 3, 4, 5, 6 and 7 present the structural relationships from a static perspective while the models in Figs. 8, 9, 10 and 11 portray the AO elements from a dynamic, behavioral perspective.

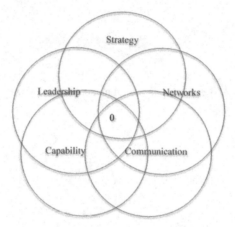

Fig. 2. Model of an adaptive organisation

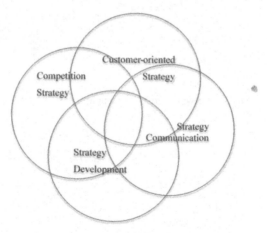

Fig. 3. Strategy model of an adaptive organisation

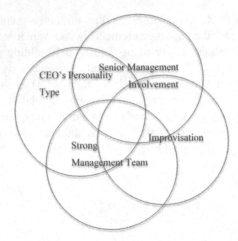

Fig. 4. Leadership model of an adaptive organization

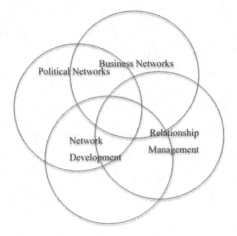

Fig. 5. Network model of an adaptive organization

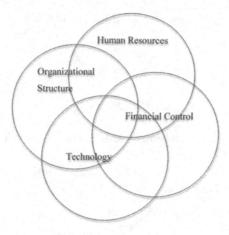

Fig. 6. Capability model of an adaptive organization

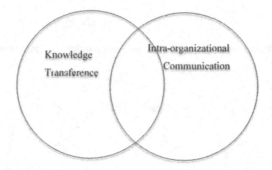

Fig. 7. Communication model of an adaptive organization

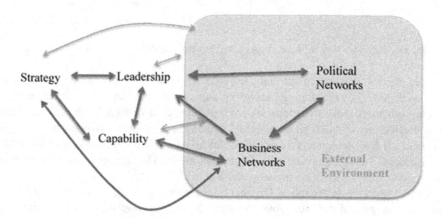

Fig. 8. Behavioral model of an adaptive organization

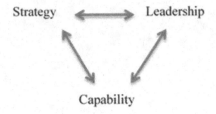

Fig. 9. Relationships between strategy, capability and leadership

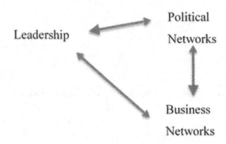

Fig. 10. Relationships between leadership and political and business networks

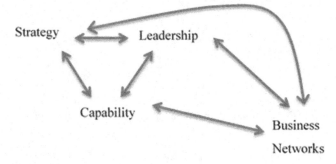

Fig. 11. Relationships between strategy, leadership, capability and business networks

From the mind maps in the data analysis, five themes emerged as the primary elements in AO. They are strategy, networks, capability, communication and leadership. In an organization, these five elements are interdependent with each other, as shown in Fig. 2. Reflecting on this high level model, the elements intersect with each other. The overlap of all five elements is a critical part of an AO. Although IT was also identified as an element, it does not appear in the high level model. IT is presented at a lower level, and appears later in a detailed model (refer Fig. 6).

In the Model of an Adaptive Organization (refer Fig. 2), interdependencies exist between strategy and the other four elements. Strategies have more intersection with leadership and networks, but less with capability and communication. It makes sense that leadership and networking are at strategic and tactical levels, which are more directly interpreted from the strategies. In comparison, capability and communication are more at the operational level, which are guided by the organizational strategy. In order to make their strategies work, organizations have to have certain levels of deployment of capability and supporting communication networks. Similarly, communication is interrelated with the other four elements. It has more intersection with capability and network, and less overlap with leadership and strategy. Leadership and strategy in organizational activities act as guidelines that highlight the principles of communication, but actual communication happens more often at the operational level and at the network level (both internal and external).

5   Structural Models of an Adaptive Organization

The following are the detailed models for each of the five main elements in the Model of an Adaptive Organization (refer Fig. 2).

5.1   Strategy Model of an Adaptive Organization

When the strategies of the case study company was examined closely, they were found to be composed of four parts or sub-elements (see Fig. 3). The interview data showed that the participants stressed each of them equally. Competition strategy needs to operate in combination with customer-oriented strategy, which is developed based on sound market analysis. In order for the strategy being effectively implemented, it needs to be delivered throughout the organization. To achieve that, strategy development and strategy communication provide mutual support. Similarly, the four sub-elements are therefore closely interrelated with each other.

5.2   Leadership Model of an Adaptive Organization

Within the leadership element, the CEO's personality type, senior management involvement, strong management team and improvisation are the four sub-elements (see Fig. 4). As the case study showed, the CEO's personality type significantly impacts an organization in terms of organizational culture, staffing, and management philosophy. The CEO's personality type is inter-related with senior management, strong management and improvisation. Senior management primarily consists of a strong management team which, to some extent, determines the use of improvisation in handling problems. The senior management team supervises the operating style at the operational level of the organization. Whether to improvise or not depends on guidelines from senior management. Thus, in the model, senior management involvement, improvisation and strong management team are closely connected and interdependent.

5.3   Network Model of an Adaptive Organization

Breaking down the primary element of networks, the interviews revealed four sub-elements: political networks, business networks, network development and relationship management (see Fig. 5).

The primary effect from political networks can also directly influence the organization's network development and relationship management. The expansion of the business network requires network development, while the maintenance of the business network needs relationship management. The four network sub-elements are heavily inter-related.

5.4 Capability Model of an Adaptive Organization

The sub-elements of organization capability were found to be organizational structure, human resources, financial control, and technology (see Fig. 6). Essentially, equipment improvement is part of manufacturing technology, which can also be combined with IT. Together, the new sub-element can be called technology. Therefore, organizational capability consists of organizational structure, human resources, financial control and technology as its four sub-elements.

5.5 Communication Model of an Organization

Examining communication in more detail revealed two sub-elements (see Fig. 7). One represents communication beyond organizational boundaries, called "knowledge transference"; while the other represents communication within organizational boundaries, also called "intra-organizational communication". Communication naturally occurs without boundaries, and information in the organization is shared among employees, customers, suppliers and business partners. Notably, the circles representing knowledge transference and intra-organizational communication overlap significantly in the model.

This section provided discussion of the findings obtained from the case study and thematic analysis. It indicates that political networks, communication, leadership, political environment and flexibility are important to the adaptability of an organization. However, the roles of IT and agility seem to be minor in the context of an adaptive Chinese organization. In the next section several behavioral models are proposed, which are based on the higher-level structural elements depicted in Fig. 2.

6   Behavioral Models of an Adaptive Organization

The series of models in this section illustrate the behavioral relationships among the elements that emerged from the case study and data analysis. As suggested, leadership, strategy, capability, network, communication and external environment have interdependence. In order to specify these interdependence, it is beneficial to use a dynamic behavioral model (see Fig. 8). The behavior between each pair of elements is two-way. The arrows in this model represent feedback and influence. Since communication happens between each of the elements, communication is not presented as an element but rather it is intrinsic to each of the model components. The external elements of political networks and business networks appear to exhibit slightly different behaviors, therefore, they are depicted as separate elements in the model.

Within an organization, the leaders have the determining impact on an organization's strategy and capability, while feedback from strategy implementation and capability affects the leaders' decisions. In addition, guidance from an organization's strategy decides what the organization's competencies are. This is illustrated in the inter-relationships signified by the arrows in Fig. 9.

Judging from the situation of the case study organization, the strength of influence of political factors and business networks appears to be different. Consequently, when discussing the dynamic influences among elements, they are discussed as two separate elements (see Fig. 10).

Political factors have strong impacts on an organization, and the effects will be noticed primarily by the leaders of those organizations. Since the organizational structure of the case study company is hierarchical, any impact on the leadership will be transferred to and manifested in the strategy, capabilities and business networks. For example, say the government launches a policy on energy saving and emissions reduction. The organization's leaders have to understand all the items in the policy and set their strategy correspondingly. The capability of the organization may have to be adjusted in order to meet certain requirements of the new policy; if some suppliers cannot meet the new requirements in terms of energy saving and emissions reduction, they are most likely to be dropped from future collaborations. On the other hand, an organization's leader can influence government policies to some extent. Since several of the leaders in the case study company XYZ also had political sway, they were able to express opinions and potentially influence policy outcomes. Similarly, business networks can also affect policies relating to the industry. For example, the cotton harvest available from cotton suppliers may affect related policy in that year. However, compared with the impact from the political factor, the impact on the political factor from and organization's leader is generally smaller. In summary, a bidirectional influence exists between political factors and leadership; it also exists between political networks and business networks. The impact of political factors on leadership is generally stronger than that of business leaders on political factors.

Business networks have an impact on strategy, leadership and capability, and vice versa (see Fig. 11). This is because regardless of the ideas of the leaders, or the strategy focus of the organization, all are heavily intertwined with the business environment. Changes related to suppliers or customers are all closely linked to the organization's ability to function. Leaders must keep an eye on industry dynamics and formulate their strategies accordingly. The implementation of strategies requires aligned deployment of the organization's capability. The organization's leadership, strategies and capabilities will also affect the behavior of the organization's business partners. For example, if the leader decides to produce for global customers, then the global strategy requires the organization to have suppliers who can meet global standards. A corresponding change will occur in the structure of the supply chain. Therefore, the influence between business networks and each of the other three themes (i.e. strategy, leadership and capability) is bidirectional.

The external environment has a direct impact on strategy, leadership and capability, and vice versa (see Fig. 12). Any changes, such as natural disasters, can change the approach of the leaders and their strategy. The external environment also includes some intangible factors, such as the educational level of the population. If the educational level increases on average, the expectations of average pay rates will increase correspondingly. This will put pressure on recruiting, which belongs to the human resource field. From another perspective, the organization's strategy, the ideas of the leader and the organization's capability may have chain reactions on other companies in the business network. As shown in the model, business networks belong to the external environment and are impacted by the external environment. A similar relationship holds between political networks and the external environment.

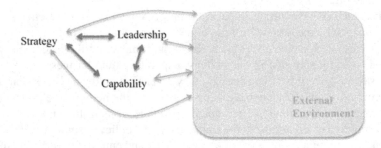

Fig. 12. Relationships between strategy, leadership, capability and the external environment

In this section several behavioral models were proposed that illustrated the high-level elements of an AO and the interrelationships among those elements from a dynamic perspectives. These interrelationships were also discussed including the significant influence the external environment has on AO behaviors.

7   Conclusion

The paper discusses AO and fills a knowledge gap about AO based on an analysis of the literature and a case study investigation of a successful textile manufacturer in China. Interviews were conducted with the owners and staff of the XYZ Textile Co. This case study approach indicated that a successful AO is driven by leadership, strategy, networks, capability and communication. In order to be adaptive in a dynamic business environment, an AO also needs to be lean and flexible and be aware of the external environment. These findings provide insight and achieves the first research objective of identifying the critical elements of AO in the Chinese context by highlighting significant elements. It was found that political networks are extremely important to organizational adaptation in China. Leadership style, technology, communication, external environment, and flexibility are also critical for adaptation in China while agility appears to be less so. The second objective was to develop models of an AO. These models represent the relationships among the identified elements of an AO. Strategy, leadership, networks, capability and communication were identified as the five basic elements. These elements intertwine with each other. Drilling down to examine the details of each of the elements, the relationships among the sub-elements of AO are also explained. After illustrating the relationships from a structural perspective, a model representing the dynamic behavioral relationships among these elements is provided. Strategy, leadership and capability all have influences on the external environment, including business networks and political networks, and vice versa. In the dynamic behavioral model, all influences are bi-directional, and the impact from political networks is highlighted.

References

1. PMI results highlight a slow recovery of Chinese Manufacturing. European Institute for Asian Studies.   http://www.eias.org/asian-news-outlook/pmi-results-highlight-slow-recovery-chinese-manufacturing. Accessed 26 Aug 2016
2. China: Official PMI Steadies. Global Economic Intersection. http://econintersect.com/b2evolution/blog1.php/2014/04/01/china-official-pmi-steadies. Accessed 15 Oct 2016
3. China- GDP growth data. Quandl. http://www.quandl.com/china/china-gdp-growth. Accessed 11 Nov 2016
4. Megatrends Q & Asia: A handful of Asian conundrums the world's boardrooms should chew over'. Bamboo Innovator. http://bambooinnovator.com/2014/06/10/megatrends-q-asia-a-handful-of-asian-conundrums-the-worlds-boardrooms-should-chew-over/. Accessed 1 Sep 2016
5. Harney, A.: The China Price: The True Cost of Chinese Competitive Advantage. Penguin, New York (2008)
6. 'How Made in USA' is making a comeback. Time Business & Money. http://business.time.com/2013/04/11/how-made-in-the-usa-is-making-a-comeback/. Accessed 25 Aug 2016
7. Alon, I.: Chinese Culture, Organizational Behaviour, and International Business Management. Greenwood Publishing Group, Westport (2003)
8. Zhang, K.H.: Is China the world factory? In: Zhang, K.H. (ed.) China as the World Factory, pp. 257–273. Routledge, Taylor & Francis Group plc., London (2006)
9. Zhao, J.: The Chinese Fashion Industry: An Ethnographic Approach. A&C Black, London (2013)
10. Research report on China's textile industry. Market Research.com (2012). http://www.marketresearch.com/China-Research-and-Intelligence-Co-Ltd-v3627/Research-China-Textile-7058589/. Accessed 13 Sep 2016
11. Yeung, G., Mok, V.: Does WTO accession matter for the Chinese textile and clothing industry? Camb. J. Econ. **28**(6), 937–954 (2004)
12. Scott Morton, M.S.: The Corporation of the 1990s. Oxford University Press, New York (1991)
13. Scott, W.R., Davis, G.F.: Organizations and Organizing: Rational, Nand Open Systems Perspectives. Routledge, Taylor & Francis Group, New York (2015)
14. Collis, D.J.: Research note: how valuable are organizational capabilities? Strateg. Manag. J. **15**, 143–152 (1994)
15. Grant, R.M.: Prospering in dynamically-competitive environments: organizational capability as knowledge integration. Organ. Sci. **7**(4), 375–387 (1996)
16. Winter, S.G.: Understanding dynamic capabilities. Strateg. Manag. J. **24**(10), 991–995 (2003)
17. Berkhout, F., Hertin, J., Gann, D.M.: Learning to adapt: organisational adaptation to climate change impacts. Clim. Change **78**(1), 135–156 (2006)
18. Danneels, E.: Trying to become a different type of company: dynamic capability at smith corona. Strateg. Manag. J. **32**(1), 1–31 (2011)
19. Eisenhardt, K.M., Graebner, M.E.: Theory building from cases: opportunities and challenges. Acad. Manag. J. **50**(1), 25–32 (2007)

Persuasive Educational Platform Design for Underprivileged Children

Yidi Wendy Wang[✉], Asfahaan Mirza, Michael Lawry,
and David Sundaram

Department of Information Systems and Operations Management,
University of Auckland, Auckland, New Zealand
{ywan916,mlaw405}@aucklanduni.ac.nz,
{a.mirza,d.sundaram}@auckland.ac.nz

Abstract. Education is a powerful key for children to unlock the world and achieve a higher quality of life. However, in today's world, there are millions of underprivileged children who do not have access to education. Research has long shown the benefits of technology-facilitated education – including higher achievement and improved attitudes towards learning. Despite these trends, technology-facilitated education remains restricted to the conventional education-system model and classroom setting; more of a tack-on than a truly disruptive force. We see great potential for quality, curriculum-approved education to soon be delivered via a software platform to even the most marginalized communities. Connecting key groups such as teachers, parents, and preschoolers, and bringing disruption in a similar way to how social media has revolutionized our cultural norms around interpersonal interaction. In this paper, we introduce the current trends and weaknesses of foundational areas in the literature: underprivileged preschool education, technology, and persuasive system design. Secondly, we outline the key gaps in the literature and explore the future research direction to create a persuasive educational platform for underprivileged children. Finally, we present and analyze a new integrated platform focused on enabling underprivileged children to have access to proper education. The platform we present is an integrated, persuasive, vocabulary learning system which connects configurers, parents, teachers, and preschoolers together. The functionalities of the system can be customized according to the current issues facing underprivileged children, although our system would suit normal children's learning requirements at the same time.

Keywords: Children · Education · Underprivileged · System design · Persuasive learning

1 Introduction

Nelson Mandela said that "Education is one of the most powerful weapons that you can use to change the world" [1]. In early 1948, the General Assembly of the UN declared that every single individual in this world has the right to education. It specifically stated that early-age education is important, and should be free and compulsory for everyone [2].

© Springer International Publishing AG 2017
R. Doss et al. (Eds.): FNSS 2017, CCIS 759, pp. 154–166, 2017.
DOI: 10.1007/978-3-319-65548-2_12

Most of us would agree that education is vital for every human being. However, many of us have neglected the fact that many people are living in underprivileged conditions and do not have access to education - especially young children. By the year 2014, there were 263 million young children and youth who did not have access to early education [3]. The reasons for this could include the countries' historical backgrounds, racial and gender inequality, family poverty, and the large gap between the rich and the poor, as well as many other reasons [4]. Human beings start learning at a very young age - ever since they are born in fact. Therefore, the rapid learning ability of children has a huge impact on their cognitive, social and emotional development, which in turn supports their growth, learning, and survival in the future [5]. Furthermore, research over the past 40 years has shown that equitable access to quality education can help a country increase their GDP per capita by up to 23% [6]. Education can not only improve an individuals' quality of life but also impact the future development of their country and the opportunities afforded to the next generation. As a result, there is an urgent need to look into specific needs of underprivileged children, and bring out effective solutions for their education.

In this paper, we look at the current literature surrounding underprivileged children, their current educational challenges, and the state of current educational systems tasked with supporting them. In particular, we focus our analysis on Vocabulary Learning Systems. We then analyze the requirements and opportunities that could potentially be leveraged to address the problems, issues, and research lacuna. Finally, we discuss our solution: the configuration and extension of Save Lingo application, and then eventually the creation of a Persuasive Educational Platform (PEP) for underprivileged children.

2 Systems to Support Underprivileged Children Education

Our research is mainly focused on underprivileged children, their education, and systems to support them. We first look into the current problems and issues that underprivileged children are facing. We endeavor to discover the current development of technology and how it can be applied to our problem. Our research gap is the overlap denoted in Fig. 1. We look into each area and propose a solution to address this gap.

2.1 Underprivileged Children

We cannot easily ignore the existence of underprivileged children. Many of them are forced to face lots of trials at the early stages of their lives. They are neglected, vulnerable, uneducated, and even abandoned. Childhood education has the greatest impact on children's cognitive learning. However, this particular group of children is missing out the best opportunity to know the world in this precious period of their life. The existence of underprivileged children will cause a ripple effect, not only to themselves as individuals, but also to wider society in the future.

Underprivileged children are mainly those who do not have the right to basic health care and living conditions due to poverty. Too many children who live in the rural areas are denied such essentials as water, food, electricity, and health care. Many of them are forced to carry responsibilities for their families in various household activities and even to go out to work at early ages [7]. In developing countries, the number of children who are employed full-time between the age of 5 to 14 could reach up to 120 million [4]. Moreover, due to the huge gap between the rich and the poor [8], the hardship of these children is often concealed by society; resulting in poor decision-making and resource allocation. Based on the principles of equality, human dignity and the worth of each child, the existence of underprivileged children could be seen as the denial of a human right [4].

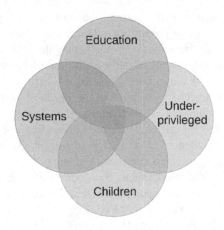

Fig. 1. Systems for the education of underprivileged children

The impact of uneducated children is tremendous. On an individual level, these children have a higher possibility of facing physical and mental health issues, as well as the impact on their personal development. Also, countries and society will suffer from higher crime rates [9], reductions in skill and productivity levels, a lower standard of health and educational achievement, as well as an increasing possibility of unemployment and dependence on welfare [5]. Therefore, to help underprivileged children come out of their current situation, providing them proper education would be the most basic but effective way.

2.2 Underprivileged Children Education

Children are born innovators. They are the hope and the future of the world. Children's cognitive learning starts way before they go to school [5]. It is a proven fact that early childhood education has persistent impacts on their future achievement and success [10]. The main reasons some children do not have proper access to education are: (1) they are forced to carry responsibilities for the family, (2) they have limited access to education, especially those who live in rural areas, and (3) their parents have less awareness of the importance of sending them to school.

While children are of a young age, their daily growth is mainly affected by family members. As they grow, their participation starts to expand to the community, school, public policy decisions, and, lastly, to wider society [11]. As a result, for those families who cannot afford the cost of sending their children to pre-school or educational institutions, it is important for them to be able to teach their children at home, or at any public libraries that are nearby.

One of the most effective ways to improve children's cognitive learning is through active learning [12]. Active learning is where children use traditional tools such as pencils, markers, or paintbrushes to draw and paint. Through active learning, children can increase their control over these tools and steadily present more accurate representations of their thinking [12]. Active learning highly improves children's cognitive learning and eye-hand coordination. Furthermore, it also allows teachers and parents to follow their development progress. Therefore, active learning is widely used in today's kindergartens, pre-schools, and primary schools.

Unfortunately, most of the active learning methods are done in pre-school and kindergarten. Active learning is barely applied to homeless children or those who live in rural areas. For this group of kids, their parents are too busy surviving to take an active role in guiding the education of their children. It is harder for such children to have a proper parental education or any learning materials at home - not to mention going to educational institutions.

As a result, there is an urgent need for discovering and providing a platform where underprivileged children can also access quality education, no matter where they are. It is necessary to provide an effective learning platform where these children can engage in the learning process and learn effectively by using exponential technologies, and smart devices within a short period of time. In this case, the exponential technologies refer to the latest technologies that have been making large disruptive impacts on society, such as Cloud Computing, Artificial Intelligence (AI), Sensor & Networks, etc. [13].

2.3   Systems to Support Underprivileged Children's Education

Young children nowadays are increasingly exposed to technology at very early ages – especially to tablets, e-readers, and smartphones [14]. Young children have the ability to analyze basic data and interpret and predict the most likely outcomes [15]. It indicates that using modern technology is not a critical problem for children. In fact, children are willing to explore and learn how to use modern technology since it provides visual and situational cases which allow them to think, interact, create, and learn actively [16].

Although children nowadays mainly use smart devices to play games [17], it is known that they are also keen to learn from interactive content that could help them with cognitive development [18]. There is evidence showing that children can effectively improve their vocabulary and literacy skill by using apps [17]. Compared to children who do not use technology in learning, those who use technology have shown improvement in cognitive learning, problem-solving, and language skills [17]. As mentioned earlier, active learning could quickly enhance children's development, especially in alphabet knowledge and vocabulary [19]. Since drawing on a tablet requires different fine-motor skills compared to freehand drawing [12], children could present more detailed drawings when presenting on a tablet. Since children see the tablet as a more interesting tool, they are more willing to engage and maintain their attention longer. Furthermore, using tablets also requires them to get familiar with the new movements and instructions. Therefore, it also enables children to express their thinking in another medium [12].

Many African countries have nearly the same cell phone coverage as the US (89%), and nearly 35% of Africans had a smartphone by the year 2014 [20]. The gap of smartphone ownership between developing and developed countries is closing rapidly [20]. Furthermore, since the underprivileged could potentially lower costs by sharing accessibility to smart devices, such devices can help improve learning equity and the task of reaching children from finically disadvantaged communities [17]. Research also shows that children who live in lower-income families are more likely to have more frequent technology usage as a part of education compared to higher-income children [21]. This could indicate that underprivileged children are already more familiar with learning from digital devices.

With respect to current systems, most of the educational apps on app stores are unregulated and untested in nature; a fact which does not align with known best practices for learning and development outcomes [22]. The development of effective and engaging educational apps is still a task that needs to be addressed [21]. Instead of looking at all educational apps for children we decided to focus on vocabulary learning apps. We evaluated some of the popular English vocabulary-learning apps and identified the system gaps that are most critical but are currently neglected, for persuasive learning (Table 1). The majority of current apps lack understanding of active learning, meaningful learning, social interaction, and engagement in the learning process in general, such as speaking, reading, matching, sketching and role playing. These elements are essential in the learning process.

3   Requirements and Opportunities

To address the gap in Fig. 1 and the gap in existing systems in Table 1, we identify three learning requirements. Furthermore, we identify opportunities that could be taken advantage of to address these three requirements.

The first requirement is the need to focus on underprivileged children's education specifically. Although general childhood education remains important, we need to help the group that is most vulnerable and neglected. In this case, we need to address the specific issues that underprivileged children face. Two key sub-dimensions of this are (a) access to education and (b) cost of education. Access to education is needed in remote areas, as well as access in inhospitable environments such as housing developments, homeless shelters, and emergency accommodation. The cost of education is also multi-faceted, and the cost of materials alone includes many variables of arguably differing value, such as books, writing instruments, and devices.

The second requirement relates to children needing to learn languages using multiple modalities to increase effectiveness. From the senses perspective, we need to enable children to write, speak, and read while learning words. From the language perspective, we need to categorize the learning process in words, phrases, and sentences. Furthermore, the system should also include images, audio, and videos; enabling children to learn in a fun and engaging way, but also to learn efficiently and effectively.

Table 1. Evaluation of vocabulary learning systems

Current Vocabulary Learning Systems	Learning	Speaking	Sketching	Reading	Matching	Role Playing	Memorizing	Repeating	Goal Setting	Rewards	Community Interaction	Chance to Self-correct	Accessibility Offline	In-depth Explanations of Words	Number of Languages Available	Quality of Content	Entertaining Level	Journey Metaphor	IOS /Android	Customer background checking
Hanging With Friends	0	0	0	0	0	7	8	0	0	8	8	9	0	0	1	7	9	3	10	1
Duolingo	9	0	0	5	8	2	7	7	6	7	5	0	0	4	7	9	8	7	10	2
7 Little Words	0	0	0	0	0	0	8	0	6	0	0	0	0	2	1	4	7	3	10	0
Anagram Twist	0	0	0	0	0	0	8	1	0	2	0	9	0	0	1	5	7	3	10	0
Word to Word Association	0	0	0	0	7	0	3	1	0	0	0	9	0	0	1	5	5	4	10	0
Textropolis	0	0	0	0	0	0	8	1	0	2	6	9	0	2	1	5	7	6	5	0
Vocabylary.com	9	0	0	7	0	0	5	0	0	6	0	0	0	9	1	9	4	5	10	2
Dictionary.com	9	0	0	6	8	0	5	0	6	0	4	7	0	9	9	9	4	3	10	2
Memrise	9	7	0	6	0	0	8	10	6	4	7	7	0	4	9	7	5	5	10	2
The Free Dictionary	9	0	0	7	8	0	5	0	6	0	4	0	0	9	7	9	5	5	10	2
Vocabulary Builder	7	0	0	5	7	0	5	1	0	2	4	0	0	5	1	7	4	5	10	8

Learning Pillars categories: Functionality, Engagement, Persuasion, Gamification

The third requirement is actually a set of requirements driven by the ten principles of future learning outlined by Davidson and Goldberg [23]. Here, we adopt and adapt some of them to fit our context. From an end users' point of view, we need to include *Self-learning* and *De-Centered Pedagogy*. From a teachers and parents' point of view, we need to include *Collective Credibility*. And overall, the system needs to have the features of *Networked Learning*, *Open Source Education*, *Learning as Connectivity* and *Interactivity*.

Some of the key opportunities that we see to address these requirements are (a) *social* media and *ubiquitous* technologies that could support easy cheap/free access to education, de-centered pedagogy, networked learning, collective credibility, and learning as connectivity (b) *persuasive* personalized and media rich systems that have the potential to engage with children using multiple modalities and help make learning fun and (c) *knowledge* systems that will help manage the content, people, and processes involved. In the following section, we explore our solution that is built on a system that exhibits these four vital elements namely social, persuasive, ubiquitous, and knowledge based.

4 Persuasive Educational Platform for Underprivileged Children

Based on the identified requirements and potential opportunities, we had to ensure that the proposed solution is social, persuasive and accessible anywhere anytime. In this section, we first describe the approach of configuring and extending an existing system namely *Save Lingo*, which helps address some of the requirements. We will then discuss the creation of a Persuasisve Educational Platform (PEP) for Underprivileged Children including its framework, architecture, and workflows.

4.1 Configuration, Extension and Creation

In order to design and implement our solution, we will take an incremental approach as illustrated in Fig. 2 to create the Persuasive Educational Platform (PEP). We will first configure Save Lingo to evaluate how we can leverage from features within Save Lingo to create PEP.

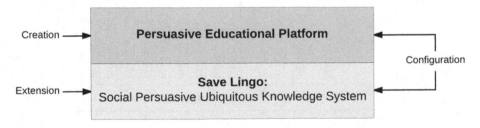

Fig. 2. Configuration, extension and creation of PEP

Save Lingo is a social, persuasive, and ubiquitous knowledge management system, which extends upon fundamental concepts from social media, knowledge & content management [24, 25], language revitalization, persuasion & gamification, and ubiquitous systems and devices [26–28]. Save Lingo is a highly interactive platform through which individuals and communities share, co-create, modify and learn user-generated content. The key Save Lingo features include: (1) creating content in multiple formats including text, image, and video; (2) curate content by accepting, rejecting or refining the captured data; (3) discover/browse content from the repository; (4) share content via social media integrations; (5) gamification mechanisms such as points, badges, and leader board rankings; and (6) bookmarking records for easy access [26–28].

Save Lingo was designed and developed in a modular and configurable manner. Moreover, it is built on a Service Oriented Architecture (SOA), which makes it extendible, flexible and compatible with other 3rd party systems. Therefore, we will use the Save Lingo platform's foundational architecture and configure its modules to suit our requirements to develop an interactive vocabulary learning app for underprivileged preschoolers. We will use the existing functionalities such as – capture, curate, discover, share, bookmark and gamification techniques as all of them fulfill the basic requirements of vocabulary learning pedagogy.

Secondly, we will be using Save Lingo as the main base and extend its functionalities by developing our own set of modules to meet our specific requirements for educating underprivileged children. Thirdly, based on the configuration and extension, and the lessons learned through the design science process, we will create a Persuasive Educational Platform which can be configured to meet the dynamic requirements of educating underprivileged children and beyond. In the next section, we will describe the creation of PEP in greater detail.

4.2 Creation of Persuasive Educational Platform

Persuasive Educational Platform (PEP) will be created to engage and persuade children, teachers and parents. Persuasive systems affect human attitudes and behavior and help people achieve particular goals [29]. It has also been shown that persuasive systems are particularly helpful in vocabulary learning [30]. Therefore, the persuasive and engagement learning elements cannot be ignored during the creation process.

There are many key elements that could help people with learning, especially regarding vocabulary learning. We have identified the key vocabulary learning pillars based on the literature (Table 1). Based on the system gaps that have been identified earlier, we intend to develop modules to facilitate "Speaking," "Sketching," and "Role Playing" as the new features of the app.

Most apps currently let children see and hear the word, but don't provide feedback on user input which could highly affect user' learning efficiency and effectiveness [22]. As a result, we are creating a feature where children could record their pronunciation of each word. The system would analyze the pronunciations by comparing to the standard audios that are contributed by teachers and parents and display a percentage that represents the similarity with the standard pronunciation.

Children will also be allowed to write down the letters by using their hands or pen from the tablet. By doing this, children can improve their writing and spelling ability. It will also give feedback about children's learning progress and their existing state of knowledge [31].

We will adopt "Role Playing" and the "Journey Metaphor" as our gamification and persuasive learning elements. These would help children engage in learning for a longer time and also improve their social interaction and independence [32].

Lastly, we are also in the process of adapting and configuring this new system to suit the particular requirements for underprivileged children. Since many underprivileged children do not have direct access to smart devices, we would also take this constraint into consideration while implementing PEP. For example, making most of the functionalities available at the end-user interface and supporting offline access (Table 1) will be critical. Furthermore, implementing and evaluating the system on the shared tablets using appropriate roles, rules, workflow and personalization mechanisms. We will now describe the framework and workflow that underpin the PEP.

4.3   Persuasive Educational Platform Framework and Workflow

Persuasive Educational Platform facilitates collaboration and interaction between parents, teachers, and children within one platform. The framework of PEP shown in Fig. 3. illustrates the various stakeholders/roles and key functions and processes each of them undertakes. The workflow begins with Teachers and Parents creating content

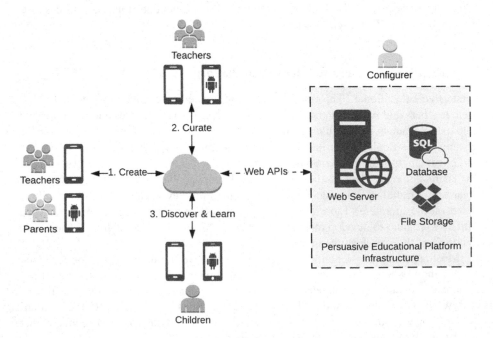

Fig. 3. PEP framework

as they are familiar with the current pre-school teaching curriculum. Once the content is created, it is curated by Teachers to ensure the created content is accurate. Lastly, children will be able to discover and learn the curated content such as vocabulary from their end-user interface.

All roles will use the appropriate system to interact with the platform. The data driven applications will communicate via Web APIs that securely allow users to retrieve and store content into the PEP back-end infrastructure. The PEP infrastructure consists of a Web Server to host the back-end code and Web APIs, Database – Microsoft SQL, and File Storage – Dropbox to store multimedia files. The configurer will be in charge of configuring the platform to suit the requirements and update the system based on feedback received from teachers and parents.

Since our platform is highly integrated among teachers, parents, and children, it allows each role to communicate with each other to share anything as shown in Fig. 4. Users could form their communities; enabling children to record audio messages to their teachers and parents within the learning platform, and for teachers and parents to also check on their children's learning achievements. Furthermore, teachers and parents are also able to provide feedback to the app configures so that they would improve the system on a regular basis. Having described the workflow and stakeholders of PEP, we now look at the architecture of PEP.

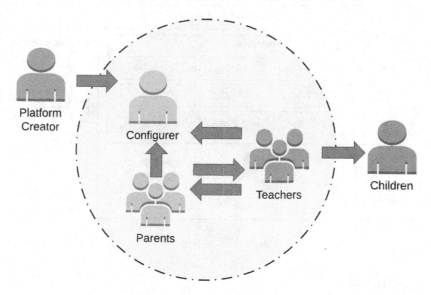

Fig. 4. PEP roles and workflows

4.4   Persuasive Educational Platform Architecture

The PEP architecture is illustrated in Fig. 5. The PEP web server consists of key modules, configuration components, database and file storage. The PEP's web server and its functionalities can be accessed through secure Web APIs. These allow developers to build specific independent apps for mobile, web, and/or wearable devices that leverage from the platform functionalities/modules. The applications can be used by various stakeholders such as children, teachers, parents, and the configurer.

The key modules layer consists of various modules that can be used by different users based on their roles. Each color of the module represents the user who will be using that particular module of the system. The children will be using modules such as Learn, Speak, Sketch, Read, Match, Scenario, Play, Repeat, Lessons and Assess. Parents will be primarily focused on creating the content using Create module. Teachers will be creating and curating content and developing lessons and assessments that are used by children. Therefore, they will be using Create, Curate, Lessons and Assess modules. Moreover, teachers will also be creating various lessons and assessments that will be used by the children.

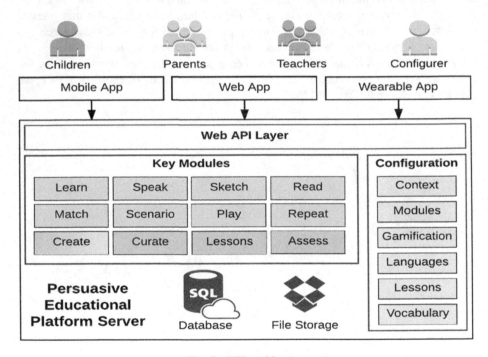

Fig. 5. PEP architecture

5   Conclusion

Overall, this research aims to design and develop a persuasive educational platform that could greatly benefit underprivileged children in gaining access to basic education. We initially configured and adapted necessary functionalities of the Save Lingo platform. We are in the process of extending and creating the Persuasive Educational Platform (PEP) based on Save Lingo to cater to the needs of underprivileged children.

The contributions of this research could be significant. Since it is an integrated platform which focuses on knowledge sharing and persuasive learning, it is more likely to have a broader market later on, not only for underprivileged children but children overall. Even though we are starting with the development of a vocabulary application, the PEP can be applied to many other learning aspects. PEP would engage and persuade children to increase their vocabulary efficiently and effectively.

However, due to the target audience of underprivileged children, the implementation and evaluation of the system may be challenging. Most underprivileged families lack the awareness of the importance of sending their children to school. Getting them to adopt a new way of learning could potentially be a challenge.

References

1. Doroshin, B.A., Doroshina, I.G.: Problems of modern education. In: VI International Scientific Conference (2015)
2. United Nations. Universal Declaration of Human Rights (2015)
3. UNESCO UIS. Leaving no one behind-how far on the way to universal primary and secondary education (2016)
4. UNICEF, et al.: Poverty reduction begins with children (2000)
5. UNICEF (ed.): Children in an urban world. UNICEF, New York, NY (2012)
6. WE.org. Education (2017)
7. Bhatty, K.: Educational deprivation in india-a survey of field investigations. Econ. Polit. Wkly. 10 (1998)
8. Reardon, S.F.: The widening academic achievement gap between the rich and the poor: new evidence and possible explanations. In: Whither opportunity? pp. 91–116 (2011)
9. Lochner, L., Moretti, E.: The effect of education on crime: evidence from prison inmates, arrests, and self-reports. Am. Econ. Rev. **94**(1), 155–189 (2004)
10. Barnett, W.S.: Long-term cognitive and academic effects of early childhood education on children in poverty. Prevent. Med. **27**, 204–207 (1998)
11. UNICEF, The state of the world's children. 1998 (1994)
12. Couse, L.J., Chen, D.W.: A tablet computer for young children? Exploring its viability for early childhood education. J. Res. Technol. Educ. **43**(1), 75–96 (2010)
13. Diamand, P.: 1. Abundance 2. Understanding Exponentials 3. Exponential Technologies (2015)
14. Gutnick, A., Robb, M., Takeuchi, L., Kotler, J.: Always connected: the new digital media habits of young children. The Joan Ganz Cooney Center at Sesame Workshop, New York (2011)
15. Schlottmann, A.: Children's probability intuitions: understanding the expected value of complex gambles. Child Dev. **72**(1), 103–122 (2001)
16. Nikiforidou, Z., Pange, J.: Shoes and squares: a computer-based probabilistic game for preschoolers. Procedia Soc. Behav. Sci. **2**(2), 3150–3154 (2010)
17. Chiong, C., Shuler, C.: Learning: is there an app for that. In: Investigations of Young Children's Usage and Learning with Mobile Devices and Apps. The Joan Ganz Cooney Center at Sesame Workshop, New York (2010)
18. Child Now. The Effects of Interactive Media on Preschoolers' Learning (2007)

19. Copple, C., Bredekamp, S., National Association for the Education of Young Children (eds.): Developmentally Appropriate Practice in Early Childhood Programs Serving Children from Birth Through Age 8, 3rd ed. National Association for the Education of Young Children, Washington, D.C. (2009)

20. Poushter, J., Oates, R.: Pew Research Center (2015). Pew-Research-Center-Africa-Cell-Phone-Report-FINAL-April-15-2015.pdf

21. Rideout, V.: Learning at home: families' educational media use in America. Joan Ganz Cooney Center (2014)

22. Hirsh-Pasek, K., Zosh, J.M., Golinkoff, R.M., Gray, J.H., Robb, M.B., Kaufman, J.: Putting education in 'educational' apps: lessons from the science of learning. Psychol. Sci. Publ. Interest 16(1), 3–34 (2015)

23. Davidson, C.N., Goldberg, D.T.: The Future of Learning Institutions in a Digital Age. MIT Press, Cambridge (2009)

24. Alavi, M., Leidner, D.E.: Review: knowledge management and knowledge management systems: conceptual foundations and research issues. MIS Q. 25(1), 107 (2001)

25. Kaplan, A.M., Haenlein, M.: Users of the world, unite! The challenges and opportunities of Social Media. Bus. Horiz. 53(1), 59–68 (2010)

26. Mirza, A., Sundaram, D.: Design and implementation of socially driven knowledge management systems for revitalizing endangered languages. In: Helms, R., Cranefield, J., van Reijsen, J. (eds.) Social Knowledge Management in Action, vol. 3, pp. 147–167. Springer, Cham (2017). doi:10.1007/978-3-319-45133-6_8

27. Mirza, A., Sundaram, D.: Architecting crowd-sourced language revitalisation systems: generalisation and evaluation to Te Reo Māori and Vietnamese. In: Nguyen, H.T.T., Snasel, V. (eds.) CSoNet 2016. LNCS, vol. 9795, pp. 333–344. Springer, Cham (2016). doi:10.1007/978-3-319-42345-6_29

28. Mirza, A., Sundaram, D.: Harnessing collective intelligence to preserve and learn endangered languages. In: Vinh, P.C., Barolli, L. (eds.) ICTCC 2016. LNICSSITE, vol. 168, pp. 224–236. Springer, Cham (2016). doi:10.1007/978-3-319-46909-6_21

29. Oinas-Kukkonen, H., Harjumaa, M.: Towards deeper understanding of persuasion in software and information systems, pp. 200–205 (2008)

30. Huyen, N.T.T., Nga, K.T.T.: Learning vocabulary through games. Asian EFL J. 5(4), 90–105 (2003)

31. Roschelle, J., Tatar, D., Chaudhury, S.R., Patton, C., DiGiano, C.: Ink, improvisation, and interactive engagement-learning with tablets (2007)

32. Smyth, J.M.: Beyond self-selection in video game play: an experimental examination of the consequences of massively multiplayer online role-playing game play. Cyberpsychol. Behav. 10(5), 717–721 (2007)

Business Analytics Generated Data Brokerage: Law, Ethical and Social Issues

Peiqing Guan[1] and Wei Zhou[2(✉)]

[1] Department of Accounting, University of Florida, Gainesville, FL, USA
[2] Information & Operations Management, ESCP Europe, Paris, France
wzhou@escpeurope.eu

Abstract. Today's fast growing big data and business analytics are introducing changes for which laws and rules of acceptable conduct have not yet been developed. Increasing computing power, storage, and networking capabilities, including the Internet and the IoT, expand the reach of individual and organizational actions and magnify their impacts. The ease and anonymity with which information is now communicated, copied, and manipulated in the cyber environments pose new challenges to the protection of privacy and intellectual property. The main ethical, social, and political issues, raised by business analytics generated information brokers, center around information rights and obligations, property rights and obligations, accountability and control, system quality, and quality of life. In this research, we investigate the key elements and compare the E.U. and U.S. law framework for the emerging social problem of analytical information brokerage.

Keywords: Analytical information broker · Privacy · Property right · Business ethics

1 Introduction

Big data and business analytics are introducing changes for which laws and rules of acceptable conduct have not yet been developed. Increasing computing power, storage, and networking capabilities-including the Internet-expand the reach of individual and organizational actions [13] and magnify their impacts. The ease and anonymity with which information is now communicated, copied, and manipulated in online environments pose new challenges to the protection of privacy and intellectual property. The main ethical, social, and political issues raised by information systems center around information rights and obligations, property rights and obligations, accountability and control, system quality, and quality of life.

Data analytics can be a double-edged sword. It has become the driver of many business benefits but it can also create new opportunities for invading privacy [3,15], and enabling the reckless use of that information in a variety of unauthorized situations. Associated law, ethical and social issues are intimately related.

© Springer International Publishing AG 2017
R. Doss et al. (Eds.): FNSS 2017, CCIS 759, pp. 167–175, 2017.
DOI: 10.1007/978-3-319-65548-2_13

Authorities have learnt from past decades' failed ethical judgment by senior and middle managers regarding information systems. Therefore, in today's new legal environment, managers who violate the law and are convicted could most likely face significant fines or even spend time in prison. As an example, U.S. federal sentencing guidelines adopted in 1987 mandate that federal judges impose stiff sentences on business executives based on the monetary value of the crime, the presence of a conspiracy to prevent discovery of the crime, the use of structured financial transactions to hide the crime, and failure to cooperate with prosecutors (U.S. Sentencing Commission, 2004).

Ethics refers to the principles of right and wrong that individuals, acting as free moral agents, use to make choices to guide their behaviors. Information systems raise new ethical questions for both individuals and societies because they create opportunities for intense social change, and thus threaten existing distributions of power, money, rights, and obligations. Like other technologies, such as steam engines, electricity, the telephone, and the radio, information technology can be used to achieve social progress, but it can also be used to commit crimes and threaten cherished social values. The development of information technology will produce benefits for many and costs for others.

Ethical issues in business analytics have been given new urgency by the rise of the big data [1,6,7] and various powerful analytical tools. Enabled by data analytical technologies, today's "big data" makes it easier than ever to assemble, integrate, and distribute information, unleashing new concerns about the appropriate use of customer information, the protection of personal privacy, and the protection of intellectual property. Other pressing ethical issues raised by business analytics include establishing accountability for the consequences of information systems, setting standards to safeguard system quality that protects the safety of the individual and society, and preserving values and institutions considered essential to the quality of life in an information society.

Although most instances of failed ethical and legal judgment were not masterminded by the information systems departments, IS and business analytics were instrumental in many of these frauds. In many cases, the perpetrators of information crimes and unethical activities artfully used complex information systems to hide these activities from public scrutiny. With the fast development of information analytical technologies, we anticipate more and more social, ethical, and legal issues to emerge. We are thus motivated to study the underlying social/legal structure, important elements, and their differences and connections.

In this research, we review the key elements and compare the E.U. and U.S. law frameworks for the emerging social problems raised by the analytical information brokerage. The rest of this paper is organized as follows. In Sect. 2, we list key elements in law, ethics and society that relate to the problem of business analytics generated data brokerage. In Sect. 3, we compare the U.S. & E.U. Regulations by studying the case of privacy protection. We conclude our preliminary work in the last section.

2   Data Analytics Related Law, Ethics, and Social Issues

Law, ethics and society are closely linked. In consequence, the moral dilemma faced by managers when it comes to information systems is often reflected in public debates. Firms have set rules and standards, which are supported and have a reflection in laws passed by either the parliaments or other political institutions. The laws prescribe behavior and foresee sanctions for violations. Emerging information systems and analytical technologies have majorly disturbed the stability that has been established by existing organizational rules and regulations. Social or political institutions do not always respond quickly and on time to these new situations. For example, it may take years to outline and develop social responsibility, politically correct attitudes and approve new rules in line with the emerging social problems.

Political institutions, such as parliaments, need time before passing new regulations and require the demonstration of real harm before they act. They are usually one step behind and react late. In the meantime, managers might have to act, and are obligated to take decisions in a legal gray area. We aim to understand the links and the interrelation among emerging data analytical technologies, ethics, society and politics. The introduction of new information technology has a destabilizing effect, raising heretofore unseen ethical, social and political issues, which should be dealt at the individual, social and legal levels. In summary, these issues can be categorized in five moral dimensions: information rights and obligations, property rights and obligations, system quality, quality of life, and accountability and control.

- Information rights and obligations: What information rights do people and companies have regarding themselves? What can these rights protect? What are the obligations for individuals and organizations with respect to this information?
- Accountability and control: Who will be responsible for the harm done to individual and collective information and property rights?
- Property rights and obligations: How will we protect traditional intellectual property rights in a digital society?
- System quality: What should be the standards and etiquette of data information system quality demanded to protect individual rights and the safety of society?
- Quality of life: What values should be protected in an information and knowledge-based society like ours? What institutions should be protected from violation? What cultural values and practices are supported by the new information technology?

2.1   Analytical Information Brokers

Non-Obvious Relationship Awareness (NORA) empowers government and private sector concerning profiling capabilities. NORA gathers information about individual from different sources, such as employment applications, telephone records, customer listings, "wanted" lists, and correlate relationships to find obscure hidden connections. Like most other information technologies, NORA shows positive aspect when it is extremely helpful for homeland security. If we take a look at the other side, it has important privacy implications because it provides such a detailed picture of the activities and associations of a person. Most of today's popular websites allow advertising brokers such as DoubleClick (Google) to track the activities of their users in exchange for revenue from advertisements based on visitor information. The information broker analyzes the data gathered to profile each customer. Thus, the information broker holds a complex and detailed dossier of a list of customers' personal information that is traded to third parties for targeted marketing or something even worse. Another example is ChoicePoint, a firm that gathers data from police, criminal, and motor vehicle records; credit and employment histories; current and previous addresses; professional licenses; and insurance claims to create and maintain electronic dossiers about almost every adult in the United States. ChoicePoint trades this information, which is bought by companies and government agencies. The demand for all these personal information is so high that data brokers as ChoicePoint or DoubleClick are flourishing.

Privacy protected first-hand data, once processed, becomes an intellectual property which creates value and generates revenue for the information brokers [10]. Intellectual property is a term referring to a number of distinct types of creations of the mind for which property rights are recognized. Under intellectual property law, owners are granted certain exclusive rights to a variety of intangible assets, such as musical, literary, and artistic works; discoveries and inventions; and words, phrases, symbols, and designs. Common types of intellectual property include copyrights, trademarks, patents, industrial design rights and trade secrets in some jurisdictions [3].

The developments in the information systems field has rippled old laws and social practices that protect private intellectual property. Currently it is difficult to protect intellectual property due to computerized information that can be easily copied or distributed on networks. The vast majority of developed nations have passed different copyright and patent regulations and have signed several international conventions and bilateral agreements, and these tools are used by nations to coordinate and enforce their own laws. Mechanisms have been developed to trade and distribute intellectual property legally on the Internet, for example: in the U.S., the Digital Millennium Copyright Act (DMCA) of 1998 provides copyright protection. The DMCA implemented a World Intellectual Property Organization Treaty that makes it illegal to circumvent technology-based protections of copyrighted materials. Internet service providers (ISPs) are required to take down sites of copyright infringers that they are hosting once they are notified of the problem. Media and content providers are represented by the Software and Information Industry Association (SIIA), which lobbies for new laws and enforcement of existing laws to protect intellectual property around the world. The SIIA runs an antipiracy hotline for individuals to report piracy activities, offers educational programs to help organizations combat software piracy, and has published guidelines for employee use of software.

2.2   Responsibility, Accountability, and Liability

Ethics is an obligation of human beings who have the freedom of choice. Ethical decisions are choices made by individuals who are responsible for the consequences of their actions. Freedom, from an existential perspective, cannot be separated from **responsibility**, since with freedom comes responsibility. Responsibility is a core element of ethical action; it means that the individuals accept the potential costs and duties derived from the decisions made. **Accountability** is characteristic of social institutions and it means that mechanisms are in place to determine who took responsible action, therefore who is responsible. **Liability** extends the concept of responsibility further to the field of laws and regulations. **Law** has a double feature, first of all it sets the framework and the rules in which individuals and corporations act in society, and secondly the body of laws and regulations permit individuals to recover the damages done to them by other actors, systems or organizations. **Due process** is a concept that belongs to societies governed by the rule of law. It is a process in which laws and regulations are known and understood and there is an ability to appeal to higher authorities to ensure that the laws are applied correctly.

All above-mentioned concepts are critically important to maintain a business analytical system when social issues are concerned. Professional groups and associations often publish "Professional Codes of Conduct". These organizations promulgate sets of "best practices", entrance qualifications and competence, taking responsibility for the partial regulation of their professions. By doing this they regulate themselves in the general interest of society, for example avoiding harm to others, respecting property rights and privacy among other moral imperatives. Examples of these Codes of Conduct are the ones promulgated by the American Medical Association (AMA), the American Bar Association (ABA), the Association of Information Technology Professionals (AITP), and the Association for Computing Machinery (ACM).

3   U.S. and E.U. Regulation Differences: Case of Privacy Protection

Privacy is the ability of an individual or group to seclude themselves or information about themselves and thereby reveal themselves selectively. The boundaries and content of what is considered private differ among cultures and individuals, but share basic common themes. Privacy is sometimes related to anonymity, the wish to remain unnoticed or unidentified in the public realm. When something is private to a person, it usually means there is something within them that is considered inherently special or personally sensitive.

Information technology and systems threaten individual claims to privacy by making the invasion of privacy cheap, profitable, and effective. Generally, the increased ability to gather and send information has had negative implications for retaining privacy [14,15]. As large scale information systems become more common, there is so much information stored in many databases worldwide that an individual has no way of knowing or controlling all of the information about themselves that others may have access to. Such information could potentially be sold to others for profit and/or be used for purposes not known to the individual of which the information is about. The concept of information privacy has become more significant as more systems that control more information appear. Also the consequences of violation of privacy can be more severe. Privacy law in many countries has had to adapt to changes in technology in order to address these issues and maintain people's rights to privacy as they see fit. But the existing global privacy rights framework has also been criticized as incoherent and inefficient. Proposals such as the APEC Privacy Framework have emerged which set out to provide the first comprehensive legal framework on the issue of global data privacy.

3.1   The U.S. Privacy Regulation

The claim to privacy is protected in the U.S. and the European countries' constitutions in a variety of different ways. In the United States, the claim to privacy protected primarily by the First Amendment guarantees freedom of speech and association, the Fourth Amendment protections against unreasonable search and seizure of one's personal documents or home, and the guarantee of due process. The Privacy Act of 1974 has been the most important of the federal statutes regarding privacy, regulating the federal government's collection, use, and disclosure of information. At present, most U.S. federal privacy laws apply only to the federal government and regulate very few areas of the private sector.

Most American and European privacy law is based on a regime called Fair Information Practices (FIP) first set forth in a report written in 1973 by a federal government advisory committee (U.S. Department of Health, Education, and Welfare, 1973). FIP is a set of principles governing the collection and use of information about individuals. FIP principles are based on the notion of a mutuality of interest between the record holder and the individual. The individual has an interest in engaging in a transaction, and the record keeper-usually a business or government agency-requires information about the individual to support the transaction. Once information is gathered, the individual maintains an interest in the record, and the record may not be used to support other activities without the individual's consent. In 1998, the FTC restated and extended the original FIP to provide guidelines for protecting online privacy. FTC's Fair Information Practice Principles include:

- Notice/awareness: Practitioners must disclose their information practices before collecting data, including identification of collector, uses of data, other recipients of data, nature of collection(active/inactive), voluntary or required status, consequences of refusal, and steps taken to protect confidentiality, integrity, and quality of the data.

- Choice/consent: There must be a choice regime in place allowing consumers to choose how their information will be used for secondary purposes other than supporting the transaction, including internal use and transfer to third parties.
- Access/participation: Consumers should be able to review the context and accuracy and completeness of data collected about them in a timely and inexpensive process.
- Security: Data collectors must take responsible steps to assure that consumer information is accurate and secure from unauthorized use.
- Enforcement: There must be in place a mechanism to enforce FIP principles. This can involve self-regulation, legislation giving consumers legal remedies for violations, or federal statutes and regulations.

The FTC's FIP are leading the way to achieve changes in privacy legislation. And it served as guideline for the Children's Online Privacy Protection Act (COPPA), approved by the U.S. Congress in 1998. This regulation obligates websites to get parental permission before collecting information about children under 13. FTC is constantly pursuing expanding legislation to cover online consumer privacy in advertising networks that collect data on consumer online activity in order to build detailed profiles, which are used afterwards by other companies to target online advertisement, as we analyzed before with the data brokers.

3.2   The European Privacy Regulation

For Europe, Article 8 of the European Convention on Human Rights guarantees the right to respect for private and family life, one's home and correspondence. The European Court of Human Rights in Strasbourg has developed a large body of jurisprudence defining this fundamental right to privacy. The European Union requires all member states to legislate to ensure that citizens have a right to privacy, through directives such as the 1995 Directive 95/46/EC on the protection of personal data.

Privacy is more protected in Europe than in the U.S. Unlike United States, European Union member States do not allow businesses to use personally identifiable information without consumers' prior consent. The European Commission approved the remarkable Directive on Data Protection on October 25, 1998. This legal instrument requires companies to inform clients when they collect information about them and disclose how it will be stored and used. People have to give their consent before any company can legally use data about them, and they have the right to access that information, correct it, and request that no further data be collected.

An important point is the informed consent that customer must provide before companies use their private data. This consent must be given with knowledge of all the facts needed to make a rational decision. As all directives, the European Union requires member states to achieve a particular result without dictating the means of achieving that result, nevertheless the directive firmly forbids the transfer of personal data to countries such as the United States, that do not have similar privacy protection regulations.

Working with the European Commission, the U.S. Department of Commerce developed a safe harbor framework for U.S. firms. A safe harbour is a private, self-regulating policy and enforcement mechanism that meets the objectives of government regulators and legislation but does not involve government regulation or enforcement. U.S. businesses would be allowed to use personal data from EU countries if they develop privacy protection policies that meet EU standards. Enforcement would occur in the United States using self-policing, regulation, and government enforcement of fair trade statutes.

4   Conclusion

Today's fast growing big data and business analytics are introducing changes for which laws and rules of acceptable conduct have not yet been developed. Increasing computing power, storage, and networking capabilities, including the Internet and the IoT, expand the reach of individual and organizational actions and magnify their impacts. The ease and anonymity with which information is now communicated, copied, and manipulated in the cyber environments pose new challenges to the protection of privacy and intellectual property. The main ethical, social, and political issues, raised by business analytics generated information brokers, center around information rights and obligations, property rights and obligations, accountability and control, system quality, and quality of life. In this research, we investigate the key elements and compare the E.U. and U.S. law framework for the emerging social problem of analytical information brokerage.

While analyzing the issues regarding the lawfulness and the ethical questions regarding the firms when it comes to handling big data and data analytics in the right spirit, we realized that a complex instrument such as law cannot be expected to fight the giant such as a fast moving wave of information and knowledge and thus we require a force inspired by ethical standards to come into place and announce itself as a self-regulatory mechanism. In other words, we suggest a common ethical footprint for all the big companies in the world who can join hands and chalk out a code of conduct when it comes to handling the various social, ethical, and legal issues with the analytical systems. Online companies that occupy a massive amount of consumer information from the Internet have to put a tab on their usability of this information as most of it is not extracted with user's explicit consent. There has to be line drawn by companies such as those beyond which they would not go into revealing information about their visitors for their own profit or for selling it to third parties. We suggest an association funded by these global giants that will have the task of defining the regulations by which these giants would be jointly bound. The issues can be solved by arbitration and one of the parties would always be in this association. The association would keep a check on the latest happenings in the information world and would self-govern regulations that would help consumers transaction to be more secured and protected, for example, while shopping or blogging online.

The need for such an organization arises because the laws are not similar throughout the world. We have countries following common law systems such as India, UK, China and Australia but on the other hand we have European countries like France, Germany, Spain, Italy and American subcontinent driven by civil law which is based upon written rules and regulations. This heterogeneity in the legal frameworks make it impossible to have a common regulation working in all these countries as there would be serious questions arising on jurisdiction and place of crime. As Internet has no barriers, we need regulations having no barriers. These association would have all the power to initiate action against the firm not abiding by the rules set by them. This resources collected would go to the development of security for the consumers and also for running the organization.

References

1. Arcondara, J., Himmi, K., Guan, P., Zhou, W.: Value oriented big data strategy: analysis & case study. In: Proceedings of the 50th Hawaii International Conference on System Sciences (2017)
2. Benbasat, I., Zmud, R.W.: The identity crisis within the IS discipline: defining and communicating the discipline's core properties. MIS Q. **27**(2), 183–194 (2003)
3. Chessell, M.: Ethics for Big Data and Analytics. IBM Corporation, Somers (2014)
4. Chen, H., Chiang, R.H., Storey, V.C.: Business intelligence and analytics: from big data to big impact. MIS Q. **36**(4), 1165–1188 (2012)
5. Nunan, D., Di Domenico, M.: Market research & the ethics of big data. Int. J. Mark. Res. **55**(4), 505–520 (2013)
6. Fairfield, J., Shtein, H.: Big data, big problems: emerging issues in the ethics of data science and journalism. J. Mass Media Ethics **29**(1), 38–51 (2014)
7. Kitchin, R.: Big Data, Open Data, Data Infrastructures and Their Consequences. Sage, London (2014)
8. Mittelstadt, B.D., Floridi, L.: The ethics of big data: current and foreseeable issues in biomedical contexts. Sci. Eng. Ethics **22**(2), 303–341 (2016)
9. Schroeder, R., Cowls, J.: Big data, ethics, and the social implications of knowledge production. In: Data Ethics Workshop, Bloomberg, vol. 24 (2014)
10. Shaver, D.: Toward an analytical structure for evaluating the ethical content of decisions by advertising professionals. J. Bus. Ethics **48**(3), 291–300 (2003)
11. Tene, O., Polonetsky, J.: Privacy and user control in the age of analytics. Nw. J. Tech. Intell. Prop. **11**, xxvii (2012)
12. Vayena, E., Salathé, M., Madoff, L.C., Brownstein, J.S.: Ethical challenges of big data in public health. PLoS Comput. Biol. **11**(2), e1003904 (2015)
13. Zhou, W., Alexandre-Bailly, F., Piramuthu, S.: Dynamic organizational learning with IoT and retail social network data. In: 2016 49th Hawaii International Conference on System Sciences (HICSS), pp. 3822–3828. IEEE, January 2016
14. Zhou, W., Piramuthu, S.: Technology regulation policy for business ethics: an example of RFID in supply chain management. J. Bus. Ethics **116**(2), 327–340 (2013)
15. Zhou, W., Piramuthu, S.: Information relevance model of customized privacy for IoT. J. Bus. Ethics **131**(1), 19–30 (2015)

Android Application Collusion Demystified

Fauzia Idrees Abro[1]($\boxtimes$), Muttukrishnan Rajarajan[1], Thomas M. Chen[1],
and Yogachandran Rahulamathavan[2]

[1] City University London, London, UK
Fauzia.Idrees.1@city.ac.uk
[2] Loughborough University London, London, UK

Abstract. Application collusion is an emerging threat to Android based devices. In app collusion, two or more apps collude in some manner to perform a malicious action that they are unable to do independently. Detection of colluding apps is a challenging task. Existing commercial malware detection systems analyse each app separately, hence fail to detect any joint malicious action performed by multiple apps through collusion. In this paper, we discuss the current state of research on app collusion and open challenges to the detection of colluding apps. We compare existing approaches and present an integrated approach to effectively detect app collusion.

1 Introduction

Android being the most popular platform for mobile devices is under proliferated malicious attacks. A recent threat is from app collusion; in which two or more apps collaborate to perform stealthy malicious operations by elevating their permission landscape using legitimate communication channels. Each app requests for a limited set of permissions which do not seem dangerous to users. However, when combined, these permissions have potentials to inflict a number of malicious attacks. Mobile users are generally unaware of this type of permission augmentation, they consider each app separately. Hence, their decision to install apps is thus limited in perspective due to unawareness of permission augmentation [1]. The main contributor of the app collusion is Android's Inter-Process Communication (IPC) mechanism. It supports the useful collaboration among apps for the purpose of resource sharing, however, it also introduces the risk of app collusion when the app collaboration is done with malicious intention.

Android implements sandbox and permission based access control to protect resources and sensitive data, however, being open source and developer-friendly architecture, it facilitates sharing of functionalities across multiple apps. It supports useful collaboration among apps for the purpose of resource sharing, however, cyber criminals exploit this to launch distributed malicious attack through app collusion [2].

Application collusion is possible with *Inter Process Communication (IPC)*, *covert channels* or system vulnerabilities. Malicious colluding apps are explicitly designed by cyber criminals by exploiting different methods such as developing

© Springer International Publishing AG 2017
R. Doss et al. (Eds.): FNSS 2017, CCIS 759, pp. 176–187, 2017.
DOI: 10.1007/978-3-319-65548-2_14

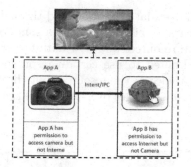

Fig. 1. Application collusion scenario

app with same User ID. Such apps have more chances for a successful collusion attack. In some cases, mis-configured apps also participate in the collusion attack with a complete obliviousness of colluding app [3]. One of the collusion scenarios is illustrated in Fig. 1: App 'A' has no permission to access the Internet, however it has permissions for camera. Similarly, App 'B' has no permission for the camera but can access the Internet. Assuming that the components of both apps are not protected by any access permission, they could collude to capture the pictures and upload on a remote server through the Internet.

Until recently, a small scale research is done on app collusion due to non availability of known samples of colluding apps for analysis [4]. Most of the existing works focus on identification of covert channels and development of experimental colluding apps. As a result of this innovative approach, the research on collusion gained momentum and there are now a few app collusion detection approaches available each with a limited scope. Despite the growing research interest, detection of malicious colluding apps has been a challenging task [5].

In this article, we give an overview of app collusion, potential risks and detection challenges. Aim of this article is to give an overview on the stealthy threat of app collusion and to repudiate the misconception about app isolation.

2   Android Primer

In Android, all applications are treated as potentially malicious. They are isolated from each other and do not have access to each others' private data. Each app runs in its own process and by default, can only access own files. This isolation is enforced with the sandbox, in which each app is assigned with a unique user identifier (UID) and own Virtual Machine (VM). App developers are required to sign the apps with a self-certified key. Apps signed with same key share User IDs and can use same sandbox [6].

Android app comes as .apk file, which contains the byte code, data, resources, libraries and a manifest file. Manifest file declares the permissions, intents, features and components of an app. The components that can be handled by an app are declared with intent filters.

System resources and user data are protected through permissions. Figure 2 illustrates the communication between apps in a sandbox environment. App 1 can use only those system resources and user data for which it has permissions. Similarly, app 2 is also limited to use certain resources. Although both apps have limited permissions to access the resources but through IPC, they are able to augment their permissions and get over-privileged access to system resources and user data.

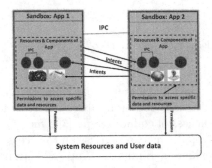

Fig. 2. Inter process communication

In this section, we provide an overview of IPC, which is a main facilitator of app collusion.

2.1   Android Security Architecture

Permission Mechanism. Permissions are used to restrict the access of system resources and user data on the device. Permissions are organized into permission groups so that they can be identified clearly with their capabilities and what resources or data they can use on the device [2]. Prior to installation, user are presented with a list of permissions. It is mandatory for the users to approve all the requested permissions as there is no option for the selection. Once granted, permissions remain valid unless the app is un-installed or updated [6].

There are four protection levels assigned to the permissions depending on the capabilities and possible security risks. These groups are: *Normal, Dangerous, Signature* and *Signature or system*. Android has a control system to certify if the app should be granted the permission governed by certain protection level [5].

Shared User ID. Android assigns a unique user ID to each app to ensure that it runs in its own process and can only access the allocated system resources. Android enforces app isolation by assigned user IDs, however, it also permits apps to share user IDs if they are developed with the same signature or certificate [3]. Apps with shared User IDs (shared Userid) can access each other's data and can run in same process, thereby limiting the effectiveness of isolation provided with user ID.

Components. Components are the basic modules that are run by apps or the system. There are four types of components: *Activities, Services, Content Providers* and *Broadcast Receivers. Activities* provide the user interface, each screen shown to a user is represented by a single activity. *Services* implement functionality of background processes which do not need user interface [4]. *Content Providers* provide database for sharing data among applications. Broadcast Receivers receive the notifications from system and other apps. It also sends messages to other components (activities or services).

Intents. Intents are messages used to communicate between the components of apps. These messages are used to request actions or services from other application components. Intents declare the intention to perform an operation [3]. It could be launching of an Activity, broadcasting Intent to any interested Broadcast Receivers or starting a background Service like music etc.

An intent contains mainly two parts: action and data. Action is the operation to be performed such as BOOT_COMPLETED, ACTION_CALL, SMS_RECEIVE, ACTION_BATTERY_LOW and NEW_OUTGOING_CALL etc. The data is a piece of information to operate on, such as a phone number, email address, web link etc.

Intents are of two types: *Explicit* and *Implicit. Explicit intent* specifies the component exclusively by class name. Explicit intents are mostly used by apps to start their components. *Implicit intent* does not specify a particular component by name. Apps with implicit intent only specify the required action without specifying particular apps or component [7]. System itself selects the app from device which can perform the requisite task. Implicit intents are vulnerable to exploits as they can combine operations of various applications, if they are not handled properly.

Sandboxing. Sandboxing isolates an app from other apps and system resources. Each app has a unique identifier and has access to the allocated System files and resources against the unique identifier. An app can also access files of the apps that are declared as readable/writeable/executable for others.

Access Control Mechanism. In Android, the access control mechanism of Linux prevails. It controls access to files by process ownership. Each running process is assigned a UserID and for each file, access rules are specified. File access rules are defined for a user, group and everyone, thus granting permissions to read, write and execute on file.

Application Signing. Cryptographic signatures are used for verification of app source and for establishing trust among apps. Developers are required to sign the app to enable signature based permissions, and to allow apps from the same developer to share the UserID. A self-signed certificate of the signing key is enclosed into the app installation package for validation at installation time.

2.2 Covert Communication Channels

A covert channel is a stealthy mechanism to exchange information between apps in a manner that it cannot be detected [8]. There are two types of covert channels:

Timing and *Storage.* Timing channels modulate the time spent on execution of some task or using some resource. Storage channels relate to modifying the data item such as configuration changes etc. Example of covert channel is sending user data to a remote server by encoding it as network delays over the normal network traffic [9]. Figure 3 depicts a covert channel, where a file of 20 bytes containing some data is sent through a normal communication channel. The file size is a covert information. This information might not be of any importance to the receiver but significantly valuable for the malicious party.

Covert channel typically exploit the shared resources to read, store and modify data as a medium for communication between two malicious entities. This type of information exchange is different from IPC based resource sharing. App collusion through covert channels is investigated by implementing high throughput covert channels in [2].

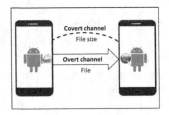

Fig. 3. Overt and covert channel

3   IPC Related Attacks

Android security builds upon sandbox, application signing and permission mechanism. However, these protections fail if the resource and task sharing procedures provided through IPC are used with malicious intentions. In this section, we discuss the IPC related attacks on Android devices.

3.1   Application Collusion Attack

In application collusion attack, two or more apps collude to perform a malicious operation which is broken into small actions [2]. Each of the participating apps communicate using legitimate communication channels to perform the part assigned to them. Apps do not need to break any security framework or exploit the system vulnerabilities for carrying out a collaborative operation [5]. App collusion helps in malware evasion as the current anti-malware solutions are not capable of simultaneously analyzing multiple apps.

3.2   Privilege Escalation Attack

In privilege escalation attack, an application with few permissions accesses components of more privileged application [10]. This attack is prevalent in misconfigured apps mainly from the third party market. The default device applications of phone, clock and settings were also vulnerable to this attack [11]. Confused deputy attack is a type of privilege escalation attack. A compromised deputy may potentially transmit the sensitive data to the destination specified in the spoofed intent. Consider an app which is processing some sensitive information like bank details at the time of receipt of spoofed intent. It is likely that such an information may be passed on to the url or phone number defined in the malicious intent.

3.3   Intents Related Attacks

Explicit and implicit intents may potentially assist in colluding attacks. Although, explicit intents guarantee the success of collusion between apps, implicit intents can also be intercepted by the malicious apps with matching intent filters. We discuss some of the known intents related attacks.

Broadcast Theft. A *public broadcast* sent by application is vulnerable to interception. As shown in Fig. 4, a malicious app 'M' can passively listen to the public broadcasts while the actual recipient is also listening. If a malicious receiver registers itself as a high priority receiver in *ordered broadcasts* and receives the broadcast first, it could stop further broadcasting to other legitimate recipients. The *ordered broadcasts* are serially delivered messages to the recipients that follow an order according to the priority of receivers. Public and ordered broadcasts may cause eavesdropping and Denial of Service (DoS) attacks [4].

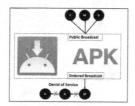

Fig. 4. Broadcast theft attack

Activity Hijacking. If a malicious app registers to receive the implicit intent, it may launch activity hijacking attack on successful interception of intent. With activity hijacking, a malicious activity can illegally read the data of the intent before relaying it to the recipient [2]. It can also launch some malicious activity instead of the actual one. Consider a scenario, in which an activity is required to notify the user for the completion of certain action. The malicious user can falsely notify the user for the completion of uncompleted activity like *un-installation of app* or *transaction completed.*

Service Hijacking. If an exported service is not protected with permissions, it can be intercepted by an illegitimate service, which may connect the requesting app with a malicious service instead of the actual one [5]. In this attack, the malicious user hijacks the implicit intent which contains the details of service and start the malicious service in place of the expected one.

Implicit intents are not guaranteed to be received by the desired recipient because it does not exclusively specify the recipient. A malicious app can intercept an un-protected intent and access its data by declaring a matching intent filter [6]. This type of attack may be used for Phishing, Denial of Service (DoS) and component hijacking attacks are possible with unauthorized intent receipt.

Intent Spoofing. In Intent spoofing attack, the malicious app controls the unprotected public component of a vulnerable app. It starts performing as the deputy of the controlling app and carries out the malicious activity on behalf of the controlling app [3]. This type of attack is also known as *Confused deputy attack* as the deputies (victim apps) are unaware of their participation in the malicious activities. Figure 5 illustrates the confused deputy attack.

A malicious broadcast injection is also possible with spoofed intent when a broadcast receiver that is registered to receive the system broadcasts trusts an incoming malicious broadcast as a legitimate one and performs those actions which need system triggers.

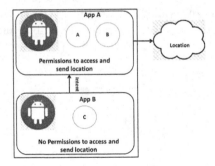

Fig. 5. Attack scenario: confused deputy attack

4   Detection of Colluding Apps: Open Challenges and Potential Measures

Detection of app collusion is a very complex proposition. There are a number of challenges in designing a solution to detect the malicious colluding apps and there remain big question marks over efficacy of such solutions. This is the prime reason that we don't have a lot of reliable choices available for such detections.

4.1   Challenges

First challenge in detection is classification of IPC into benign and malicious groups. Android is an open source platform, which encourages resource sharing among apps by re-using the components. IPC is mainly used by apps to interact with different inter and intra components. The main problem is to distinguish between the benign collaboration and malicious collusion. Such a distinction is likely to come up with a cost of very high false positives. Keeping the false positive rate to lowest, is another problem.

Secondly, considering the substantial number of apps available in the Android market (more than 2 Million apps by Feb 2016), there is a difficulty of analyzing pairs of apps. It is computationally challenging and cost exorbitant to analyze all possible pairs of apps to detect the malicious collusion between sets of apps given the search space. Analysis of all possible app pairs of total of N apps would require N^2 pairs. Similarly, to analyze sets of three colluding apps, it would require to analyze N^3 apps. An effective collusion detection tool must be capable of isolating potential sets of apps and carrying out further investigations.

Another glaring challenge is the presence of a number of covert channels in the system. Detection of covert channels is an NP-hard problem as it would require monitoring of all the possible communication channels [12]. Covert channels are difficult to detect because they use overt channels for conveying stealthy information.

Lastly, known malicious colluding apps are not available for analysis. The non-availability of known samples of colluding apps, makes it difficult to validate the experiment results. Analysis and validation of collusion detection is a quandary, we need known samples of colluding apps to validate the detection method, but to find the samples, a reliable detection method is mandatory, which itself is not available in an authenticated form.

An effective collusion detection system must overcome the aforementioned challenges and encompasses an integrated solution. The detection of IPC based collusion have been recently proposed in a few research papers [12–15]. The proposed approaches have a number of limitations and the accuracy and efficiency of these methods is questionable due to non-availability of universally accepted dataset of malware colluding apps.

The solution proposed in [12] is to re-design the security model of Android system to mitigate the risk of collusion. However, this would involve a big cost and complexity in re-writing the OS components and ensuring their compatibility and smooth functioning in conjunction with already available millions of apps in the Android market.

Another approach [13] is limited to the detection of collusion based on intents only. It analyzes the interaction of components through intent filters only and analyzes only two apps at a time. Currently, this approach suffers with a high false positive rate. It is a memory consuming approach which may not be feasible for mobile phones keeping in view the limited memory of phones. The extensive memory consumption may deteriorate the performance of device.

Similarly, [14] is also mainly based on intent messages. This approach faces the challenges of conventional rule based methods that are prone to evasion with obfuscation and reflection. Scalability is a major drawback of their approach.

Malware collusion detection tool [15] supports the latest API versions only, hence analysis of apps developed under earlier versions is not possible. Technical details of the tool are not available for performance verifications and evaluations. It generates a high number of false alarms mainly due to its reliance over information flows.

The detection of covert channels is still an under explored research area. [11,16] investigate the identification of covert channels. [11] has a limited scope of detecting covert channels related to shared resources only such as *reading of the voice volume, change of the screen state* and *change of vibration settings* etc. Similarly, [16] handles data flows only. However, it is possible to exploit these approaches for identification of other unknown covert channels.

4.2   Potential Measures

The complexity and challenges of collusion detection merit a hybrid framework. As a result of our analysis, we recommend an integrated approach for detection of app collusion. We also suggest that a covert channel may not be detected in isolation, but its existence may be realized whilst analyzing the IPC related security breaches. We argue that any mobile user downloads a limited number of apps as opposed to available millions of apps. A user cannot install millions of apps on a single device, hence, there is no need to analyze the millions of app pairs or triplets for possible collusion. On the average, a mobile user installs 20 to 30 apps. A system capable of analyzing 50^2 or 50^3 apps is sufficient for a common mobile user. This solution may also be augmented with a cloud based analysis engine if the number of concurrently analyzed apps is increased to 4, 5 or more. Cloud based analysis is an efficient and cost effective approach for high computational operations. We believe that adopting such an approach is essentially required to facilitate the identification of sets of colluding apps from a dataset of millions of apps.

Since permissions and intents facilitate inter and intra-app communication, analysis of these features has potentials to detect app collusion. Adding shared user IDs and publicly declared intents is also recommended as the collaborating apps may use same User IDs to make sure that the attack is successful.

The proposed system is shown in Fig. 6. In first stage, apps are analyzed to identify those which share user IDs as they have more potentials to collude successfully. In second stage, permissions and intents are extracted and analysed for *source permission, source intent, sink permission* and *sink intent*. A pairwise communication mapping of apps is generated from the source and sink permissions and intents. The identified communicating pairs of apps are further analysed to check if their communication is limited to each other or more apps. The classifier stage is used to classify the app into colluding or non-colluding ones and users are notified for possible collusion. In the proposed approach, permissions and intents are grouped into four categories: *source permissions, source intents, sink permissions* and *sink intents*. *Source* permissions or intents are those that initiate some operation, whereas the *sink* permissions and intents are those which act upon to complete the required operation [1].

With additional policy refinements, the identified colluding apps can be classified into benign and malicious apps. This approach may be integrated with the methodologies proposed in [11,16] to monitor the data flow sources and sinks of IPC and tracking of shared resources. Information flow system proposed in [16] to monitor the data flow sources and sinks in IPC is a good trade-off in detecting the covert channels however, it lacks the tracking of shared resources. Mapping structure of [11] helps in tracking the shared resources used by two interacting apps.

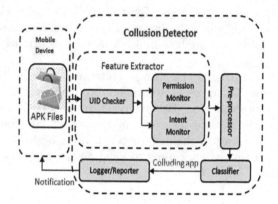

Fig. 6. Collusion detection model

Effective detection of app collusion requires monitoring of IPC and all possible covert communication channels: *shared resources* and *data flow sources and sinks*. The proposed framework integrated with Taintdroid [16] would be a good starter towards a comprehensive detection system.

5   Related Work

IPC and intents have not been explored the way permissions have been investigated. Most of the existing IPC based studies focus on finding the IPC related vulnerabilities. [17] investigated the IPC framework and interaction of system components. [3] detects the IPC related vulnerabilities. [18] suggested improvement in ComDroid by segregating the communication messages into inter and intra-applications groups so that the risk of inter-application attacks may be reduced. [19] characterized Android components and their interaction. They investigated risks associated with misconfigured intents. [20] examined vulnerable public component interfaces of apps. [21] generated test scenarios to demonstrate the ICC vulnerabilities. [22] performs information flow analysis to investigate the communication exploits. [23] investigated intents related vulnerabilities and demonstrated how they may be exploited to insert the malicious data. Their experiments found 29 out of a total of 64 investigated apps as vulnerable to intent related attacks. All of these works focus on finding communication vulnerabilities, and none of them used IPC and intents for malware detection.

6   Conclusions

The concept of colluding apps has emerged recently. App collusion can cause irrevocable damage to mobile users. Detection of colluding apps is quite a challenging task. Some of the challenges are: distinction between the benign and malicious collaboration, false positive rate, presence of covert channels and concurrent analysis of millions of apps. Existing malware detection system are designed to analyse each app in isolation. There is no commercially available detection system which can analyse multiple apps concurrently to detect the collusion.

In this paper, we discussed the current state and open challenges to detection of colluding apps. To address the problem, we have proposed an integrated approach to detect app collusion. However, the complexity of problem merits a collaborative large scale investigations to mitigate a very large number of known and unknown communication channels between apps besides known IPC and covert channels. Our future work aims to validate the proposed framework on real colluding apps.

References

1. Elish, K.O., Yao, D., Ryder, B.G.: On the need of precise inter-app: ICC classification for detecting android malware collusions. In: Proceedings of IEEE Mobile Security Technologies (2015)
2. Marforio, C., Ritzdorf, H., Francillon, A., Capkun, S: Analysis of the communication between colluding applications on modern smartphones. In: Proceedings of the 28th Annual Computer Security Applications Conference, pp. 51–60 (2012)
3. Chin, E., Felt, A.P., Greenwood, K., Wagner, D.: Analyzing inter-application communication in Android. In: Proceedings of the 9th ACM Conference on Mobile Systems, Applications and Services, pp. 239–252 (2011)
4. Bugiel, S., Davi, L., Dmitrienko, A., Fischer, T., Sadeghi, A.-R., Shastry, B.: Towards taming privilege-escalation attacks on android. In: NDSS (2012)
5. Idrees, F., Rajarajan, M.: Investigating the android intents and permissions for malware detection. In: Proceedings of IEEE Wireless and Mobile Computing, Networking and Communications, pp. 354–358 (2014)
6. Felt, A.P., Wang, H.J., Moshchuk, A., Hanna, S., Chin, E.: Attacks and defenses. In: USENIX Security Symposium (2011)
7. Idrees, F., Rajarajantitle, M., Conti, M., Chen, T.M., Yogachandran, R.: A novel Android malware detection system using ensemble learning methods. Comput. Secur. **68**, 36–46 (2017). Elsevier
8. Bagheri, H., Sadeghi, A., Garcia, J., Malek, S.: Covert: compositional analysis of android inter-app permission leakage. IEEE Trans. Softw. Eng. **9**, 866–886 (2015)

9. Gasior, W., Yang, L.: Network covert channels on the Android platform. In: Proceedings of the Seventh Annual ACM Workshop on Cyber Security and Information Intelligence Research, pp. 61–67 (2011)
10. Davi, L., Dmitrienko, A., Sadeghi, A.-R., Winandy, M.: Privilege escalation attacks on android. In: Burmester, M., Tsudik, G., Magliveras, S., Ilić, I. (eds.) ISC 2010. LNCS, vol. 6531, pp. 346–360. Springer, Heidelberg (2011). doi:10.1007/978-3-642-18178-8_30
11. Bugiel, S., Davi, L., Dmitrienko, A., Fischer, T., Sadeghi, A.-R.: Xmandroid: a new android evolution to mitigate privilege escalation attacks. Technische Universität Darmstadt, Technical report (2011)
12. Memon, A.M., Anwar, A.: Colluding apps: tomorrow's mobile malware threat. IEEE Secur. Priv. **6**, 77–81 (2015)
13. Bhandari, S., Laxmi, V., Zemmari, A., Gaur, M.S: Gaur Intersection automata based model for Android application collusion. In: Advanced Information Networking and Applications, pp. 901–908 (2016)
14. Asavoaeca, I., Jorge, B., Chen, T., Kumara, H., Muttik, I., Nguyen, H.N., Roggenbach, M., Shaikh, S.: Towards automated android app collusion detection (2016). arXiv preprint arXiv:1603.02308
15. Tristan, R., Rogan, C.E., Aaron, T., Adam, F., Trevor, E., Ledah, C.: Statically detecting android app. collusion. In: Proceedings of the 4th Program Protection and Reverse Engineering Workshop, p. 4 (2014)
16. Gilbert, W.P., Chun, B.-G., Cox, L.P., Jung, J., McDaniel, P., Sheth, A.N.: TaintDroid: an information flow tracking system for realtime privacy monitoring on smartphones. In: Proceedings of the 9th USENIX Conference on Operating Systems Design and Implementation (OSDI 2010), pp. 1–6 (2010)
17. Enck, W., Ongtang, M., McDaniel, P.: Understanding android security. IEEE Secur. Priv. **7**, 50–57 (2009)
18. Kantola, D., Chin, E., He, W., Wagner, D.: Reducing attack surfaces for intra-application communication in Android. In: Proceedings of Second ACM Workshop on Security and Privacy in Smartphones and Mobile Devices, pp. 69–80 (2012)
19. Maji, A., Arshad, F., Bagchi, S., Rellermeyer, J.: An empirical study of the robustness of inter-component communication in Android. In: International Conference on Dependable Systems and Networks, pp. 1–12 (2012)
20. Long, L., Li, Z., Zhenyu, W., Lee, W., Jiang, G.: Chex: statically vetting Android apps for component hijacking vulnerabilities. In: Proceedings of Conference on Computer and Communications Security, pp. 229–240 (2012)
21. Avancini, A., Ceccato, M.: Security testing of the communication among Android applications. In: Proceedings of 8th IEEE International Workshop on Automation of Software Test, pp. 57–63 (2013)
22. Gordon, M.I., Kim, D., Perkins, J.H., Gilham, L., Nguyen, N., Rinard, M.C.: Information flow analysis of android applications in DroidSafe. In: NDSS, pp. 1–16 (2015)
23. Gallingani, D., Gjomemo, R., Venkatakrishnan, V.N., Zanero, S.: Practical exploit generation for intent message vulnerabilities in Android. In: Proceedings of the 5th ACM Conference on Data and Application Security, pp. 155–157 (2015)

Acceptance of Technology-Driven Interventions for Improving Medication Adherence

Nawal Chanane[1(✉)], Farhaan Mirza[1(✉)], M. Asif Naeem[1], and Asfahaan Mirza[2]

[1] Department of Information Technology and Software Engineering,
Auckland University of Technology, Auckland, New Zealand
{nawal.chanane,farhaan.mirza,mnaeem}@aut.ac.nz
[2] Department of Information Systems and Operations Management, University of Auckland,
Auckland, New Zealand
a.mirza@auckland.ac.nz

Abstract. Medication Adherence (MA) plays an important role in managing patients with long term illness, enhance patient's health and wellness, and it reduces the economic cost and saves lives. The purpose of this research is to address the collaboration of technology with healthcare, in solving the challenge of medication adherence. A questionnaire of 25 questions was sent out through email to 200 people, to get their feedback about medication adherence, the reasons of non-adherent and their level of acceptance in using the mobile application technology as an interventional tool for medication adherence. Results showed a statistically significant correlation between age and medication adherence (P = 0.012). There is a statistical significant impact of forgetfulness on non-medication adherence (P-value = 0.0003). Additionally, majority of the participants identified their willingness to use the application to help in medication adherence (P = 0.001). The conclusion drawn from this study suggests that people are willing to increase awareness of medication adherence.

Keywords: Medication adherence · mHealth · Healthcare · Technology intervention in health · Collaboration · Technology feedback

1   Introduction

Technology contributed enormously in our world, specifically in the medical field. With the increased usage of mhealth technologies and tele-health services, health providers and patients both are experiencing the benefits of the new medical technologies. It is clear that technology is improving rapidly and new medications in the market exceeds expectations, even in difficult and long term health conditions. However, we still have patients continually visiting health providers seeking consultation. Dermatitis is one example of the cases being followed up [1]. When a simple question comes to mind: "is the patient taking medication as prescribed?", the thought directly points to medication adherence. Based on the researcher's conclusions in the domain, medication adherence is the main factor in the health equation. In addition, a wide intervention of technology is solving medication non-adherence issues.

© Springer International Publishing AG 2017
R. Doss et al. (Eds.): FNSS 2017, CCIS 759, pp. 188–198, 2017.
DOI: 10.1007/978-3-319-65548-2_15

The World Health Organization (WHO) defines adherence as "the extent to which a person's behavior taking medication, following a diet, and/or executing lifestyle changes, corresponds with agreed recommendations from a health care provider" [2]. It is commonly used when patients take their medications as per the health provider prescription, in the right dose at the right time, and as well to continue to take the prescribed medication [3].

It is well known that patients often fail to follow treatments or medical advice given by medical practitioners [4]. The study done by Wali & Grindrod [5] shows that patients with minimal literacy skills are 10–18 times less likely to adhere to or correctly identify their medication, in comparison to those who have adequate health literacy skills. Due to the poor understanding of medication information and making suitable health decisions, tailored medication counselling was required to match their basic needs [6].

A study done by New Zealand care chemist in 2009 revealed that 28% of patients forget to refill their prescriptions on time, and 52% suggested a pharmacy reminder for refill. However, 43% admitted forgetting to take their medication and 21% acknowledged careless adherence [7]. And in 2013, the news from Pharmacy Today in New Zealand, recorded that between 15% and 30% of patients don't have their medicine dispensed, based on the prescription issued by their health provider [8].

The purpose of this research is to (a) examine the impact of the demographic main variables on medication adherence (b) clarify some of the reasons for non-adherence to medication and (c) predict patient's willingness to use the technology as an interventional tool for medication adherence. This preliminary analysis is built upon a survey to gather patient's perspective.

2 Literature Review

Medication Adherence (MA) plays an important role in managing patients with long term illness, enhance patient's health and wellness, and it reduces the economic cost. There are several studies for intervention techniques in MA [9–14]. These studies apply techniques such as: reminder programs, raising awareness, and ongoing counselling for both individuals and caregivers; these efforts are positively associated with adherence. MA can have significant benefits in managing patients with long term illness, for example: heart failure, epilepsy disease, diabetes, obesity, cancer and Parkinson Disease [15–17].

2.1 Statistics Behind Medication Non-adherence

A shocking statistic published by the Center for Disease Control and Prevention in the USA [18] reports that 75% of adults are non-adherent to their medications in the USA. Moreover, 31% of the patients are medication non-adherents. As per statistic, the industry is expected to generate by 2018, 872 billion U.S. dollars in drug prescription internationally [19]. It causes a vast amount of economic wastage based on the non-adherent patients. Other records show that nearly 75% of adults in the USA are either not filling the prescriptions or not following the recommended dose [20]. On the other hand, 89% of patients acknowledge that the prescribed medication was essential for maintaining their health [11, 16].

Non-adherence can lead to severe consequences, including deaths. Also, it was expected that non-adherence to antihypertensive treatment causes 89,000 premature deaths in the USA annually [21]. Non-adherence causes approximately 30% to 50% of failures in treatment, 125,000 deaths annually and 10% to 40% risk of cardiovascular hospitalizations [22].

2.2 Technology Immersion in Healthcare System

One of the first projects concerned with patient's data collection to help clinician predict the long-term health status was introducing the mobile health monitoring presented in MobiHealth Project, a mobile phone health service platform as a base station to collect data through the wireless sensors worn on the body. The measurements get forwarded wirelessly through UMTS or GPRS to a service center. After the received data is collected and stored, it is then forwarded to a doctor or medical center. The data analyzed is sent as feedback to a specific destination using SMS [23].

The main goal of "Mobile phone messaging for preventive health care" was to evaluate the effects messaging through mobile phone as an interventional mode of delivery for preventive health care, on both health status and behavior outcomes. SMS or MMS as a mode of delivery for any type of preventive health care was included in their studies [21].

In 2010, the National Institute for Health Innovation (NIHI), a health information program for pregnant women and young children families, introduced a program to support healthy futures initiative to prevent childhood obesity. NIHI had the design with different versions for Maori, Pacific, Asian and South Asian families. In addition, they had a SMS4BG designed to support people with diabetes to self-manage between clinic visits. A pilot study across Waitemata DHB showed that the participants appreciated the program, which supported them to manage their condition better, and improved their control of diabetes. The NIHI received an award funding for its success.

New Zealand has also taken part in all these studies, where in 2013 a mobile health (mHealth) initiative was designed in the region of Otago and Southland. The people were set to benefit from TXT2Remind, a practice-patient messaging system to connect General Practice and their patients. The system lets (General Practice) GPs to send appointments, immunization reminders and health messages directly to the patient via text message and interactive mobile content delivery. It also helped targeting key areas such as cardio vascular risk assessments, smears, and influenza jabs. The management of reminders and recalls was more effective, which increased the acceptance of programs and enabled valuable information to be collected [8].

2.3 Assessment of Medication Adherence

There are several studies on MA intervention techniques and many methods for assessing patients' MA [9, 10, 12, 14, 30]. According to research, the most common methods used in adherence include; individual self-report of medication taking [24], real-time electronic monitoring, pharmacy refills, prescription claims databases, wearable sensors [13], and pill counts [25, 26]. However, there is no global or national standard for measuring MA [16, 27, 28] although some of these methods are considered to be robust, they still have limitations of adherence assessment [3]. Therefore, MA is still considered one of the biggest healthcare challenges [29, 31].

According to our literature review, several studies related to medication adherence were conducted; however, further investigation is required in this domain, especially in New Zealand, where technology is not yet included in the doctors' prescription as an intervention tool for MA. Researchers in New Zealand did not widely conduct studies in the field of MA, although, it's an important variable in the health equation, and, therefore, it is worthwhile addressing.

3   Research Design

3.1   Research Approach

This research follows a descriptive, quantitative approach with a cross-sectional questionnaire [32]. For this study, an online questionnaire was designed using Qualtrics Software [33], to collect information from patients or caregivers who went through difficulties and challenges of MA. We have used the online questionnaire, as an effective way due to the ease of accessibility. Participants lean towards answering questionnaires online at a convenient time, which is easier, as an alternative for paper and pen [32]. This allows the automatic processing method to collect data for analysis in an easy and quick way.

3.2   Data Collection

We collected data from people, who either went through challenges of MA or dealt with a family member or a friend who had difficulties to follow a prescribed medication. A questionnaire was used to gather feedback about medication adherence, the reasons of non-adherent and their level of acceptance in using the mobile application technology as an interventional tool for medication adherence. The reasons for non-adherence and their level of acceptance in using the mobile application technology as an interventional tool for medication adherence. The study was based in Auckland, New Zealand, during the month of October 2016.

A questionnaire was sent by email to a number of friends and colleagues, following the snowballing sampling technique. It is a multipurpose technique which was considered to be a suitable approach, for providing interpretations about social networks and relations in sensitive areas like health [34]. Through its use, it is possible to make interpretations about social networks and relations in areas in which sensitive, illegal, or deviant issues are involved. The email was sent to a total number of 200 people and only140 participated according to the responses through Qualtrics, and 5 submitted incomplete questionnaires.

The questionnaire contained 25 questions, each with a dichotomous scale (yes, no). The Questionnaire was divided into three Factors. Factor A captured information about the respondents, such as information regarding education, gender, age and health status of the participant. Factor B, questions inquired about their information on medication adherence level (follows prescription, careless to take medication every day, self-organized or prefers alternative therapies), which were adopted from the Morisky Medication Adherence Scale (MMAS-8). MMAS-8 is a validated, self-reported medication adherence measures [24]. Factor C tackled the level of acceptance for the technology-driven medication adherence (reliable app, health status on fingertips, experienced app and wellness of trying the app).

3.3   Scale Reliability and Validity

The self-reported measure of medication adherence was adapted from a validated 8-item scale and re- arranged with other items to address the current study [24]. The main theory behind MMAS-8, is that medication non-adherence accrues due to a number of reasons, for example, "do you sometimes forget to take your medication?", "When you feel worse following a medication, do you stop taking medication?". Such questions are phrased to avoid the "yes-answer" bias by reversing the wording. It is known that patients give their healthcare providers a positive response.

3.4   Research Questions

This research will be answering the following questions:

1. What is the impact of the demographic variables on medication non-adherence?
2. What are the reasons for medication non-adherence (ex: carelessness, forgetfulness, or lack of communication with the health provider) which affects the treatment outcomes as a consequence?
3. What is the rate of acceptance of technology as an interventional tool in improving MA?

3.5   Statistical Analysis

Descriptive statistics was used to analyze participant's demographic information in Factor A. While Fisher Exact Test or Maximum Likelihood Estimation (MLE), was used to generate the standardized parameter estimates, due to its robustness in dealing with data that diverge from multivariate normality [35]. Calculations were based on a 95% confidence interval $\alpha < 0.05$). Only fully answered questionnaires were considered, whereas incomplete ones were discarded. Based on Morisky scale by Morisky et al. [24], a sample size of at least 140 participants was needed for the study to get feasible results. Hypotheses were tested by examining the impact of age and forgetfulness on the acceptance of technology and an interventional tool for medication adherence. All statistical tests were performed using RStudio, Version 0.99.893 – © 2009-2016.

4   Findings

4.1   Results for Factor A: Demographics

From 200 people who were invited to do the questionnaire in this research, only 145 attempted to participate, however, 5 participants submitted incomplete questionnaire, therefore they have been eliminated. The total number of eligible questionnaires for analysis was 140. According to Table 1, out of 140 participants, 46.43% were male and 53.57% female. Among these, 46.4% of the participants aged from 18–24, and 35.71% ranged from 25–34, and 14.29% ranged from 35–44, and 3.57% ranged from 45–54, and no participant exceeded 55.

Table 1. Demographic characteristics of the participants (N = 140)

Socio-demographic characteristic	%
Gender	
Female	53.57
Male	46.43
Age	
18–24	46.4
25–34	35.71
35–44	14.29
45–54	3.57
>55	0
Marital status	
Married	38
Never Married	62
Ethnicity	35.71
New Zealander	
Maori	0
Asian	17.86
Indian	3.57
Middle-Eastern	35.71
Other	7.14
Qualification	
High school or less	25
Diploma	3.57
Bachelors	35.71
Masters or above	35.71
Health Status	
Never had medication to follow	58
I had before medication to follow	32
I am following a medication (short term)	4
I am following a medication (long term)	6

Regarding the level of education, 25% had a high school diploma or less, 3.57% holds a diploma, 35.71% with a bachelor degree and 35.71% has a master's degree or above. While, for the ethnicity, an equal 35.71 for New Zealander and Middle Eastern's, 17.86% Asian, 3.57% Indians, 7.14% falls under the category other ethnicity and there were no Maori participants. The impact of the demographic variables (gender, health status, ethnicity, marital status, qualifications) on medication adherence was statistically not significant except for age (P-value = 0.012).

4.2   Results for Factor B: The Reasons for Medication Non-adherence Which Affects the Treatment Outcomes as a Consequence

There is a statistical significant impact of forgetfulness on non-medication adherence (P-value = 0.0003 with 95% confidence interval and odds ratio 0.28). The forgetfulness percentage of taking medication is more likely to be higher in the age group 18–24 with 46.43% and 25–34 with 35.71%. While, 44.44% in both age groups of 18–24 and 25–34 prefer taking alternatives instead of prescribed medication. The majority of the respondents who admit lack of confidence of the health providers were males with 63.41%, and 52.94% females, while 47.06% females admit not taking their medication when they are on vacation. And a total of 82.14% don't use dose organizers when they are following a treatment (see Table 2).

Table 2. Technology as an Interventional tool for medication adherence

Item	% (yes)
The application will help in adhering to medication.	41
It will be reliable application.	90
The application will be useful in getting up to date health status.	94
I don't need to know my health status, if I'm sick I just go to the GP.	48
Patients with serious health conditions will be in need for it more than ordinary patients.	90
I would like to try using it then I can give my opinion.	94
Do you use any app for health and wellbeing information?	32
Since it keeps me in touch with my health provider, I will definitely use it.	80

4.3   Results Factor C: Mobile Application as a Technology-Driven Intervention

In the study of Martin and Upvall [36], participants constantly discussed the feeling of being cared of when using the mobile apps to monitor their medication adherence. Moreover, the study done by Wade et al. [37] evaluated Medisafe as one of the mobile apps for medication adherence, and the participants were significantly more persistent. The wide use of this technology could lead to better control of chronic diseases and their costs to the health care system.

The analysis conducted in this study showed that participants on medication did not use applications for medication management. However, the correlation between health status and acceptance of technology as an interventional tool was clearly shown in Table 3 that it is statistically significant (P-value = 0.004, with 95% confidence interval and odds ratio of 0.147).

Table 3. Odds Ratios of Factors of Medication non-Adherence

	Odds Ratio	95% Confidence Interval
Health Status	0.147	0.024-0.610*
Coping	1.015	0.246-3.762*
Confidence	0.745	0.268-1.950*

*Significant at P < 0.05

5   Discussion

Non-adherence to medication has become a social and an economic burden, consequently, research was prioritized to overcome barriers to medication adherence. Although the MMAS-8 verified increased adherence to medication, the intervention needs multiple resources, therefore, it couldn't be applied easily to various unlike settings. The findings of our study supported the results of the assessment done by Gupta et al. [8] on the impact of technology on medication adherence awareness, that the intervention will help in solving medication non-adherence when the health provider is involved. Moreover, supported the study by Choi et al. [38] on his review of the existing applications, and user's feedbacks, that users will be able to retrieve up-to-date health status.

This study focused on New Zealand, participants as a preparation for providing a mobile health related application, considering the variables and feedback provided. The 90% individuals, who are willing to use the mobile application as an interventional tool, were mostly between the ages of 18–34. This could be due to their access to technology more than older individuals, although their health status is more likely to be better than individuals in the age groups of >45. In addition, older individuals could be engaged in other commitments than the ones in age group 18–24 who are mostly students.

6   Future Work

Innovative strategies can be applied to support patients in medication adherence for health supervision. A potential strategy for this is to implement non-traditional modalities, which includes usage of mobile technology to help with patient MA. It will provide a substantial contribution to improve medication adherence, especially when the factors of patient's non-adherence, like experiencing side effects, costs, cognitive deficiency and/or treatment complexity [40] are put in consideration.

Although several studies covered the issue of medication adherence, still there is a missing circle to complete the chain of health and wellbeing. Most studies focus [41]

on reminding the patients to take their prescribed medication but not following up with the patient while under medication and getting their instant feedback, which supports the continuity of the treatment (Fig. 1). Therefore, we will be working on a Precise Medical Adherence Intervention (PMAI) model and obtaining feedback on whether the medication taken was effective or not (a step beyond the PMAI reminders). This feedback can be received via Precise Medical Adherence Feedback request (PMAF). This research can potentially enhance MA and transform healthcare delivery from an episodic to a non-episodic model (i.e., real time) of treatment and decreasing the economic burden. It will also have a great opportunity to commercialize its outcomes since the notion of obtaining feedback after a medication intervention is revolutionary.

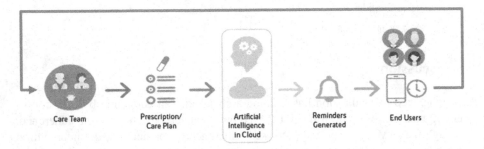

Fig. 1. High Level Overview of the PMAI workflow

The outcomes will provide beneficial outcomes in terms of cutting costs by delivering timely and precise patient support. The mobile application artifacts can be adapted as extensions to health software products. This research will provide the required Clinical Decision Support (CDS) to enhance and extend medicine products. Furthermore, the output from the statistical analysis and simulation model will help discover medication adherence levels using test Research and Development data.

References

1. Lawton, S.: Childhood atopic eczema: Adherence to treatment. Nurse Prescribing **12**, 226–231 (2014). doi:10.12968/npre.2014.12.5.226
2. Who: Adherence to long-term therapies. Who 1–194 (2003)
3. Ho, P.M., Bryson, C.L., Rumsfeld, J.S.: Medication adherence: its importance in cardiovascular outcomes. Circulation **119**, 3028–3035 (2009). doi:10.1161/CIRCULATIONAHA.108.768986
4. Cramer, J.A., Mattson, R.H., Prevey, M.L., et al: How often is medication taken as prescribed? A novel assessment technique. JAMA **261**, 3273–3277 (1989). doi:10.1016/0959-8049(93)92083-5
5. Wali, H., Grindrod, K.: Don't assume the patient understands: qualitative analysis of the challenges low health literate patients face in the pharmacy. Res. Soc. Adm. Pharm (2016). doi:10.1016/j.sapharm.2015.12.003
6. Ngoh, L.N.: Health literacy: a barrier to pharmacist-patient communication and medication adherence. J. Am. Pharm. Assoc. 49, e132-NaN-e149 (2003, 2009). doi:10.1331/JAPhA.2009.07075

7. Care Chemist Care chemist launches prescription reminder service to improve medication compliance in New Zealand. https://www.nzdoctor.co.nz/un-doctored/2010/november-2010/11/care-chemist-launches-prescription-reminder-service-to-improve-medication-compliance-in-new-zealand.aspx. Accessed 14 Jun 2017

8. Michelle, N.: Non-adherence costly for patient health and NZ health system - Pharmacy Today (2013). https://www.pharmacytoday.co.nz/news/2013/february-2013/28/non-adherence-costly-for-patient-health-and-nz-health-system.aspx. Accessed 14 Jun 2017

9. Atreja, A., Bellam, N., Levy, S.R.: Strategies to enhance patient adherence: making it simple. MedGenMed **7**, 4 (2005)

10. Chen, C., Kehtarnavaz, N., Jafari, R.: A medication adherence monitoring system for pill bottles based on a wearable inertial sensor. In: 2014 36th Annual International Conference IEEE Engineering in Medicine and Biology Society EMBC 2014, vol. 1, pp. 4983–4986 (2014). doi:10.1109/EMBC.2014.6944743

11. Horne, R., Weinman, J.: Patients' beliefs about prescribed medicines and their role in adherence to treatment in chronic physical illness. J. Psychosom. Res. **47**, 555–567 (1999). doi:10.1016/S0022-3999(99)00057-4

12. Kalantarian, H., Motamed, B., Alshurafa, N., Sarrafzadeh, M.: Evolving classification of intensive care patients from event data. Artif. Intell. Med. **69**, 43–52 (2016). doi:10.1016/j.artmed.2016.03.004

13. Kalantarian, H., Motamed, B., Alshurafa, N., Sarrafzadeh, M.: A wearable sensor system for medication adherence prediction. Artif. Intell. Med. **69**, 43–52 (2016). doi:10.1016/j.artmed.2016.03.004

14. Vervloet, M., Linn, A.J., van Weert, J.C., et al.: The effectiveness of interventions using electronic reminders to improve adherence to chronic medication: a systematic review of the literature. J. Am. Med. Inf. Assoc. **19**, 696–704 (2012). doi:10.1136/amiajnl-2011-000748

15. Shin, J.Y., Habermann, B., Pretzer-Aboff, I.: Challenges and strategies of medication adherence in Parkinson's disease: a qualitative study. Geriatr. Nurs. (Minneap) **36**, 1–5 (2015). doi:10.1016/j.gerinurse.2015.01.003

16. Lehmann, A., Aslani, P., Ahmed, R., et al.: Assessing medication adherence: Options to consider. Int. J. Clin. Pharm. **36**, 55–69 (2014). doi:10.1007/s11096-013-9865-x

17. Tang, F., Zhu, G., Jiao, Z., et al.: Self-reported adherence in patients with epilepsy who missed their medications and reasons for nonadherence in China. Epilepsy Behav. **27**, 85–89 (2013). doi:10.1016/j.yebeh.2012.12.022

18. Benneyan, J.C., Lloyd, R.C., Plsek, P.E.: Statistical process control as a tool for research and healthcare improvement. Q. Saf. Healcare **12**, 458–464 (2003). doi:10.1136/qhc.12.6.458

19. Statista: Total prescription drug revenue global projection 2016-2022 | Statistic (2016). https://www.statista.com/statistics/309387/global-total-prescription-drug-revenue-projection/. Accessed 27 Feb 2017

20. PhRMA: Improving Prescription Medicine Adherence. Pharma Adherence Br (2011). doi: 10.1177/1545109712437244

21. Engla, N.E.W.: Perspective. N. Engl. J. **363**, 1–3 (2010). doi:10.1056/NEJMp1002530

22. Prakash, A., Jayaprakash, S., Linus, T., et al.: A review on medication adherence in stroke patients **6**, 37–42 (2015)

23. Prince, M., Patel, V., Saxena, S., et al.: No health without mental health. Lancet **370**, 859–877 (2007). doi:10.1016/S0140-6736(07)61238-0

24. Morisky, D.E., Green, L.W., Levine, D.: Concurrent and predictive validity of a self-reported measure of medication adherence. [Morisky Medication Adherence Scales: MMAS]. Med Care 67–74 (1986). doi:10.1097/00005650-198601000-00007

25. Billingsley, L., Carruth, A.: Use of technology to promote effective medication adherence. J. Contin. Educ. Nurs. **46**, 340–342 (2015). doi:10.3928/00220124-20150721-12

26. Kalantarian, H., Alshurafa, N., Le, T., Sarrafzadeh, M.: Non-invasive detection of medication adherence using a digital smart necklace. In: 2015 IEEE International Conference on Pervasive Computing and Communications Work PerCom Work 2015, pp. 348–353 (2015). doi:10.1109/PERCOMW.2015.7134061

27. Buelow, J.M., Smith, M.C.: Medication management by the person with epilepsy: Perception versus reality. Epilepsy Behav. **5**, 401–406 (2004). doi:10.1016/j.yebeh.2004.02.002

28. Kathleen, F., Brenda, M.: Which measure is right for your program? J. Manag. Care Pharm. **6**, 499–501 (2000)

29. Martin, L.R., Williams, S.L., Haskard, K.B., Dimatteo, M.R.: The challenge of patient adherence. Ther. Clin. Risk Manag. **1**, 189–199 (2005)

30. Kalantarian, H., Alshurafa, N., Nemati, E., et al.: A smartwatch-based medication adherence system. In: 2015 IEEE 12th International Conference Wearable Implant Body Sensors Networks, BSN 2015, pp. 1–6 (2015). doi:10.1109/BSN.2015.7299348

31. Mcdaniel, M.A., Einstein, G.O.: Emerging IT for Medication Adherence, pp. 49–75 (2016)

32. Bryman, A., Bell, E.: Business Research Methods, 4th edn. Oxford University Press, Oxford (2015)

33. LLC Q (2017) Qualtrics LLC. https://www.qualtrics.com/lp/apac-ppc-demo-request/?utm_source=google&utm_medium=ppc&utm_campaign=Qualtrics_Brand_(S)_-_APAC&campaignid=790680124&utm_content=&adgroupid=42339957305&utm_keyword=%2Bqualtric&utm_term=%2Bqualtric&matchtype=b&device=c&placemen

34. Sadler, G.R., Lee, H.-C., Lim, R.S.-H., Fullerton, J.: Research Article: Recruitment of hard-to-reach population subgroups via adaptations of the snowball sampling strategy. Nurs. Health Sci. **12**, 369–374 (2010). doi:10.1111/j.1442-2018.2010.00541.x

35. Williams, G.C., Rodin, G.C., Ryan, R.M., et al.: Autonomous regulation and long-term medication adherence in adult outpatients. Health Psychol. **17**, 269–276 (1998). doi:10.1037/0278-6133.17.3.269

36. Martin, C.A., Upvall, M.J.: A mobile phone HIV medication adherence intervention: acceptability and feasibility study (2016). doi:10.1016/j.jana.2016.07.002

37. Wade, R., Clancey, B., Michaeli, J.: Improvement in antihypertensive and cholesterol-lowering medication persistence using a mobile technology application. Value Heal **19**, A306 (2016). doi:10.1016/j.jval.2016.03.658

38. Choi, A., Lovett, A.W., Kang, J., et al.: Mobile applications to improve medication adherence: existing apps, quality of life and future directions. Adv. Pharmacol. Pharm. **3**, 64–74 (2015). doi:10.13189/app.2015.030302

39. Gupta, V., Hincapie, A.L., Frausto, S., Bhutada, N.S.: Impact of a web-based intervention on the awareness of medication adherence. Res. Soc. Adm. Pharm. (2015). doi:10.1016/j.sapharm.2015.11.003

40. Choudhry, N.K., Isaac, T., Lauffenburger, J.C., et al.: Rationale and design of the Study of a Tele-pharmacy Intervention for Chronic diseases to Improve Treatment adherence (STIC2IT): a cluster randomized pragmatic trial. Am. Heart J. (2016). doi:10.1016/j.ahj.2016.07.017

41. T DJ, Atun, R., Car, J.: Mobile phone messaging for preventive health care (Review) (2012). doi:10.1002/14651858.CD007457. pub2.www.cochranelibrary.com

Author Index

Printed in the United States
By Bookmasters